Business Ethics and Sustainability

This book equips readers with the knowledge, insights and key capabilities to understand and practice business activities from ethical and sustainable vantage points.

In our interconnected global business environment, the impacts of business activities are under increased ethical scrutiny from a wide range of stakeholders. Written from an international perspective, this book introduces the theory and practice of ethical and sustainable business, focusing in particular on eco-environmental sustainability, intergenerational responsibilities, current disruptive technologies, and intercultural values of the business community and consumers. Written by an expert author who also brings to the fore non-Western concepts and themes, this book:

- features positive case studies, as well as transferrable and applicable key insights from such cases;
- highlights the importance of taking cultural differences into account;
- takes a transdisciplinary approach which considers findings from research fields including conceptual and empirical business ethics, behavioral economics, ecological economics, environmental ethics, and the philosophy of culture;
- weaves in pedagogical features throughout, including up-to-date case studies, study questions, thought experiments, links to popular movies, and key takeaways.

Written in an accessible and student-friendly manner, this book will be of great interest to students of business ethics, environmental ethics, applied ethics, and sustainable development, as well as business practitioners striving toward ethical, sustainable, and responsible business practice.

Roman Meinhold is an Associate Professor of Philosophy teaching Business Ethics and Sustainability at Mahidol University's International College, Thailand. He has taught Ethics and Philosophy courses at Assumption University of Thailand, the National University of Lesotho, and at the Weingarten University of Education, Germany. His publications deal with issues in Business Ethics, Sustainability, Environmental Thought, Well-Being, Cultural Critique, Art, and Aesthetics. His current research is focused on sustainability and organizations' environmental, intergenerational, transcultural, and technological responsibilities. Roman is a member of the Australasian Business Ethics Network (ABEN) and the editor of the *Asia Pacific Journal of Religions and Cultures* hosted by Mahachulalongkornrajavidyalaya University.

"In business as in life there is no ethics-free zone, and students will look for guidance in steering their course through the many challenges awaiting them. This book prepares them well by laying a solid foundation in ethical theory with only a minimum of technical terminology, but with numerous cases and thought experiments for ethical decision-making that stimulate students' moral imagination to develop their own pathways towards solutions they can ethically justify."
— **Gerhold K. Becker**, *Founding Director, Centre for Applied Ethics, Hong Kong Baptist University*

"Gandhi once pointed out that commerce without morality is a social sin. In this excellent book, Roman Meinhold has provided practical ethical guidelines not only for business students but also entrepreneurs and professionals. It is an invaluable asset for our future commercial society."
— **Warayuth Sriwarakuel**, *Vice President for Research, Assumption University of Thailand*

"*Business Ethics and Sustainability* is an incredibly valuable asset for any businessperson, young or experienced, to challenge old norms about business ethics and profitability working against each other, and hopefully it will allow more people to understand that these two concepts can in fact work harmoniously hand-in-hand."
— **Quincy Yu**, *Senior Vice President, Tycoon Music Co. Ltd.*

"The book is a highly recommended useful tool for current students and future global leaders."
— **Khothatso Tšooana**, *Principal Secretary Ministry of Health, Lesotho; former Commissioner of Police, Lesotho Mounted Police Service, Lesotho*

Business Ethics and Sustainability

Roman Meinhold

First published 2022
by Routledge
2 Park Square, Milton Park, Abingdon, Oxon OX14 4RN

and by Routledge
605 Third Avenue, New York, NY 10158

Routledge is an imprint of the Taylor & Francis Group, an informa business

© 2022 Roman Meinhold

The right of Roman Meinhold to be identified as author of this work has been asserted by him in accordance with sections 77 and 78 of the Copyright, Designs and Patents Act 1988.

All rights reserved. No part of this book may be reprinted or reproduced or utilised in any form or by any electronic, mechanical, or other means, now known or hereafter invented, including photocopying and recording, or in any information storage or retrieval system, without permission in writing from the publishers.

Trademark notice: Product or corporate names may be trademarks or registered trademarks, and are used only for identification and explanation without intent to infringe.

British Library Cataloguing-in-Publication Data
A catalogue record for this book is available from the British Library

Library of Congress Cataloging-in-Publication Data
Names: Meinhold, Roman, author.
Title: Business ethics and sustainability / Roman Meinhold.
Description: Abingdon, Oxon ; New York, NY : Routledge, 2022. | Includes bibliographical references and index.
Identifiers: LCCN 2021020307 (print) | LCCN 2021020308 (ebook)
Subjects: LCSH: Sustainability. | Business ethics. | Business—Environmental aspects.
Classification: LCC HC79.E5 M44155 2022 (print) | LCC HC79.E5 (ebook) | DDC 174/.4—dc23
LC record available at https://lccn.loc.gov/2021020307
LC ebook record available at https://lccn.loc.gov/2021020308

ISBN: 978-0-367-65058-2 (hbk)
ISBN: 978-0-367-65060-5 (pbk)
ISBN: 978-1-003-12765-9 (ebk)

DOI: 10.4324/9781003127659

Typeset in Bembo
by codeMantra

Research for this book was partly funded by Mahidol University International College (MUIC), Mahidol University, Salaya, Buddha Monthon, Nakhon Pathom, Thailand

To
Lyneo Theano Sophia
and
Einstein
^--^
(>'.'<)
in memoriam
HP Roland H. Meinhold
and
Univ. Prof. Dr. Karl Anton Sprengard
"To seek everywhere for usefulness is the least appropriate
for great souls or free spirits"
(Aristotle: *Politics*, 1338b)
"Humans cannot create matter. We can, however, create value"
(Tsunesaburo Makiguchi: *The Geography of Human Life*, 1903)

Contents

List of figures ix
List of case studies xi
Acknowledgements xiii
Preface xv

1 Business and ethics: contradiction and success story 1

2 Ethics and business: down the philosophical rabbit hole 13

3 Normative ethical foundations of business ethics: the big five 28

4 Sustainability and organizations' environmental responsibility: trash and treasures 74

5 Ethical stakeholder analysis and ethical SWOT analysis 104

6 Disruptive technologies and business ethics 122

7 Business ethics in media, marketing, advertising, and fashion 140

8 Intercultural business ethics and sustainability 156

9 Systemic issues 171

10 Conclusion 184

Index 191

Figures

1.1	Business as contradiction, marketing tool, business philosophy	3
1.2	T-shaped education and business ethics	5
1.3	Descriptive vs normative ethics	6
1.4	Sustainability compass	10
1.5	Taking business ethical actions	11
2.1	Law and ethics	17
2.2	Levels of ethics (meta, normative, applied)	18
2.3	Hypernorms vs microsocial norms	19
2.4	Meta-ethics: Motivations	20
2.5	"Big five" normative ethical theories	23
2.6	Business stakeholder relations	26
3.1	"Big five" normative ethical theories	30
3.2	Business ethical relevant theories	31
3.3	Instrumental vs intrinsic value	33
3.4	Value thought experiment	34
3.5	Indicators of well-being	37
3.6	Types of eudaimonia	41
3.7	Ethical vs intellectual virtues	42
3.8	Ethical virtues	42
3.9	Ikigai	44
3.10	Types of utilitarianism	58
3.11	Care, compassion, community	59
3.12	Supercar parking (only)	62
3.13	Forms of justice	63
3.14	Power and responsibility correlation	67
3.15	Overview: Ethical theories applied to business	70
4.1	Environmental ethics and CER	76
4.2	Stakeholders in the sustainability context	77
4.3	Environmental and health impacts	81
4.4	Up-, re-, and downcycling	83
4.5	Environmental issues and business	85
4.6	Intergenerational vs intra-generational justice	87
4.7	Triple bottom line	90

4.8	Integrated sustainability model	91
4.9	Discounting values	93
4.10	Instrumental vs intrinsic value	96
5.1	Business stakeholder relations	107
5.2	Alibaba's three important stakeholders	109
5.3	Primary stakeholders	110
5.4	Primary and secondary stakeholders	110
5.5	Ontological dependency: Nature, non-human species, future communities	111
5.6	Steps in stakeholder engagement	112
5.7	Stakeholders' forms of power	113
5.8	Stakeholder relevance	114
5.9	Stakeholder responsibility matrix	116
5.10	CSR pyramid	117
5.11	Stakeholders' potential for cooperation and threat	118
5.12	Ethical SWOT	119
6.1	Existential threats	124
6.2	Bio-tech & AI	125
6.3	Businesses' utilization of technology	126
6.4	Knowledge and information gap	134
6.5	Privacy, security, convenience tradeoff	137
7.1	Purposes of media	142
7.2	Fortification of humans in adverts	150
7.3	Deceptions in fashion marketing	150
7.4	Anthropological implications of fashion adverts	151
8.1	Intercultural business issues	160
8.2	Merging of horizons	165
8.3	Normative interculturality	167
9.1	Issues in business ethics studies	173

Case studies

1.1	Freitag	3
1.2	Boston Consulting Group: Total Societal Impact	8
1.3	Unethical businesses will go bankrupt	9
2.1	The Boeing 737 MAX scandal	26
2.2	The "philosopher-designer" Brunello Cucinelli and his humanistic capitalism	26
3.1	The Harvey Weinstein case	50
3.2	The Ford Pinto case	58
3.3	The Facebook–Cambridge Analytica scandal	70
4.1	Micro- and nanoplastic in water, animals, food, and humans	82
4.2	Rubber Killer	83
4.3	Patagonia	84
4.4	The 5G network: between pre-actionary and precautionary considerations	100
5.1	Volkswagen's Dieselgate scandal	119
5.2	Fjällräven's commitment to the environment and future communities	120
6.1	The social credit system in China	132
6.2	Trump vs Twitter	133
6.3	GDPR	136
6.4	UAVs (drones)	138
7.1	The Darknet	146
7.2	Malaysian girl commits suicide over Instagram poll	147
7.3	Meta-goods in advertising	152
7.4	Influencers	152
7.5	Controversial fashion marketing	154
8.1	Rammstein: Amerika	158
8.2	Monkey business	160
8.3	Programming ethics into algorithms	163
8.4	Hofstede's cultural dimensions theory	169
9.1	Facebook quasi-monopoly	176
9.2	Sikkim organic state	179
9.3	Circular economy	180
9.4	World Happiness Report	182

Acknowledgements

Business ethics is one of those important fields that do not only pertain to managers, scientists, and business and ethics students, but everyone who "does not live in a cave", and rather moves through the world with open eyes. This became even more apparent in the process of writing this book when so many people, whose well-informed perspectives I cherish, offered their help in reading and commenting on the manuscript. First and foremost, I am deeply indebted to my colleague and friend Dr. Christoph Wagner, Chair of Business Ethics, University Hohenheim, Germany, with whom I discussed the content of each chapter and who helped me, complementing the text with essential and additional passages which not only made the text more comprehendible and comprehensive, but also more practically relevant.

The initial idea for writing the book goes back to the year 2016 when I was searching, among the many good books in this field, for a business ethics book that takes encouraging and recommendable ethical examples concerning businesses, sustainability, environmental responsibility, disruptive technologies, and intercultural vantage points into account. The major encouragement to kickstart the process came from Asst. Prof. Dr. Alessandro Stasi, BBA Chair, Mahidol University International College (MUIC), Mahidol University, Thailand, who constructively commented on the pilot chapter on environmental responsibility. Prof. Dr. Gerhold K. Becker, Founding Director, Centre for Applied Ethics, Hong Kong Baptist University, constructively commented on the ethics sections. Setthawut Steven Fang (MUIC) proofread parts of the book in its preliminary form, and Jotaro Sera (MUIC) drafted chapter abstracts, chapter keyword lists, and key takeaways, and designed images and the raw layout. John Graham Wilson, MA, MSc, Guna Chakra Research Center Bangkok proofread the final draft. Annabelle Harris and Matthew Shobbrook at Routledge provided professional editorial guidance and support from proposal to print. Finally, I would like to thank the Research Promotion Management section at MUIC, in particular Asst. Prof. Dale Konstanz, Ms. Jeerawan Thongsakol, Ms. Sasithon Panyanak, and Mrs. Chanettee Poonthong for their encouragement and support.

Anyone who is reading this book and who discovers an issue, or a concept, topic or case that you think is worth including in future editions of this book, feel free to drop me a line: roman.mei@mahidol.edu.

Roman Meinhold, Sriracha

Preface

The Founding Director of the Centre for Applied Ethics at Hong Kong Baptist University, Prof. Dr. Gerhold K. Becker, stated that "there is no ethics-free zone", neither in business nor in any other domain of life. Ethics, one of the most important philosophical subdomains, is becoming increasingly important today. Business-ethical issues we are facing today, and in the future, are imminent, versatile, and multiple. Artificial intelligence and the algorithms on which it is based must be charged with (quasi-)ethical decision-making capabilities, but also the intensification and increasing volume of international business activities and transcultural interactions require cross-cultural ethical decision-making competencies and skills. If we do not manage climate emergencies and eco-environmental crises in an ethical way, that includes considerations for humans, future communities, non-human species, and natural ecosystems, we will need neither ethics nor business. Because "If we don't have a planet, we're not going to have a very good financial system", as James Gorman, Chairman and CEO of Morgan Stanley, once said, and because "Companies that don't adapt will go bankrupt without question" as Mark Carney, a former governor of the Banks of Canada and England stated.[1] Therefore, this book communicates sustainability and intergenerational responsibility throughout, and not only in a dedicated chapter.

Any major recent scandal in the business world is, in its deepest sense, an ethical scandal. The Facebook–Cambridge Analytica scandal, for example, revealed how our data were used in a successful attempt to manipulate the US presidential (and many other) elections. The Boeing 737 MAX crashes uncovered a deep-seated safety issue at Boeing, and the Harvey Weinstein sexual harassment scandal, via the #MeToo movement, shed light on the "instrumentalization" of actors, and not only women, in the film industry, not simply in Hollywood, but around the world. Moreover, the global financial crisis in 2008 was also triggered due to an ethical issue related to the lending of so-called "subprime" mortgages. The Volkswagen "Dieselgate" or "Emission Possible" scandal demonstrated that one of the largest and most reputable automotive companies (and not only those) had a serious issue with honesty that brought the company into a reputational crisis from which it is yet to recover completely. Engineers had invented a fraudulent device that helped the company to advertise its vehicle fleet as environmentally friendly.

To the best current knowledge of the author, this textbook, unlike any other on the market (as of April 2021), also exemplifies with dedication and in great detail how ethically guided and sustainability-oriented business is highly successful in many cases. Gradually, although very slowly, but successively, ethical and sustainability-oriented business is moving from a niche existence toward a more mainstream approach. The book, therefore, also features various "positive cases" such as Ecosia, the search engine that plants trees, environmental responsibility pioneer Patagonia, the "philosopher-designer" Brunello Cucinelli and his humanistic capitalism, the Freitag brothers, who think and conduct business in cyclic economic and ecological patterns, and Toms' caring capitalism, to name just a few.

Positive cases are usually a rare feature in business ethics books. Positive examples in mainstream business ethics books are mentioned here and there, but are almost never treated and analyzed in the same depth and with comparable dedication as "negative cases". Positive cases, in contrast, have the great advantage that the reader can easily understand why such positively perceived companies are ethically commendable and what can be learned from their sustainable or ethical approaches and transferred meaningfully into similar or other business contexts. Interestingly, no one would consider it appropriate or reasonable to analyze mainly unethical examples in order to communicate what is ethical, but in mainstream business ethics books, so far, this has been a standard didactical feature.

The book follows a transdisciplinary synthetic approach, taking into account research findings in the fields of behavioral economics, ecological economics, conceptual and empirical ethics and business ethics, applied ethics, in particular environmental thought, philosophical anthropology, social psychology, cultural studies, and philosophy of culture. Many mainstream business ethics books are often written by business scholars with limited background in ethics. In addition, most standard business ethics textbooks disregard cultural differences among their readership and of what is considered ethical in a business context from different cultural perspectives. At the same time, despite this diversity of perspectives, it is not overlooked that management in general is a multidimensional process and therefore every form of business ethics, at least if a pragmatic and practical approach is sought, not only has to take into account the ethical, but also the economic, legal, cultural, and eco-systemic dimensions.

The text of this book tries its best to be accessible and tangible even to non-native English speakers and attempts to take a more international (less Western-centered) perspective than its competitors. Despite the fact that I myself fall into the much feminist-criticized scheme of "white, Western, male", I have worked in the fashion industry (in Germany, Switzerland, Turkey, India, and Pakistan), studied, taught, and researched across the globe, in particular several years of teaching experience in Africa, Asia, and

Europe. Therefore, the book also refers to non-Western concepts (e.g. African "Ubuntu" ethics, Thai "sufficiency economy philosophy", Asian ideal of "saving face", and the Japanese concept of "Ikigai"), a feature that is largely neglected in standard or mainstream business ethics textbooks.

This book contains numerous didactically and pedagogically meaningful and well-explained diagrams, many tangible examples, up-to-date cases and thought experiments. Examples are very important in order to illustrate concepts, approaches, or theories that may not be easy to understand at first glance.

This first edition of the book contains nine main chapters, with Chapters 3 and 4 having triple or double the size of the other chapters. **Chapter 1** introduces the fact that business ethics is entirely unavoidable. Even those who prefer to ignore it have to deal with business ethics and sustainability. But the chapter also demonstrates the importance of business ethics for sustainability and well-being in a wider sense. Ethical business became a success story for a number of pioneering businesses within their industry, such as Ecosia, Toms, Patagonia, Freitag, and Brunello Cucinelli. **Chapter 2** situates business ethics in the wider academic, economic, and lifeworld context. Acting within the framework of the law does not automatically mean that an action is also contemporaneously ethical, while some actions, considered ethical, may actually be against the law. Some laws may be considered immoral. **Chapter 3** introduces the major ethical theories that are relevant for sustainable and ethical business. While the theories are presented in a nutshell in their relevance for application in the business world, they are accompanied by elucidating case studies and further supporting material for easier but thorough understanding. This chapter occupies three times the space of the previous chapters and thus can be subdivided, respectively, in terms of learning and teaching. **Chapter 4** deals with the wider range of corporate environmental responsibility, sustainability, and eco-environmental implications of business and economic activities. In the light of climate disasters, environmental emergencies, and the Fridays for Future movement, businesses can no longer ignore eco-environmental implications, Sustainable Development Goals and future generations' concerns, even if they neglect the fact that the existence of businesses ultimately depends on the eco-environment. This chapter occupies two times the space and time of the following chapters and thus can be subdivided respectively in terms of teaching and learning. **Chapter 5** covers ethical stakeholder and ethical SWOT analyses. It introduces three highly relevant stakeholders that can no longer be neglected in the light of the facts introduced in Chapter 4: future communities, non-human species, and natural ecosystems. **Chapter 6** is dedicated to disruptive technologies which are invented, marketed, sold, and maintained by businesses. Artificial intelligence, fully autonomous driving, and genetic engineering are technologies that need ethical influx more than any other technology has before due to their wide-spanning and potentially highly disruptive implications. Technology does not tell us what to do with it (it is not determinative), but technological development and implementation cannot be stopped (technological determinism). **Chapter 7** touches on the ethical and philosophical anthropological implications of media, marketing, and advertising, zooming in on the phenomenon of fashion, a quite popular topic with students. **Chapter 8** renders business ethics in the intercultural context, focusing on basic comprehension and strategies within transcultural settings, not only in the business world. **Chapter 9** situates ethics and sustainability in the systemic macro context of economic systems and introduces alternative systems that take sustainability concepts at the macro, meso, and also at the micro level of the concrete business world more seriously. **Chapter 10** sums up the book's key issues and concepts and concludes that there is a need for a wider business ethical perspective, including multidimensional perspectives on the concepts of stakeholders, value, and sustainability.

Note

1 Both quotations: Carrington, D. (2019, October 13). Firms ignoring climate crisis will go bankrupt, says Mark Carney. *The Guardian*. www.theguardian.com/environment/2019/oct/13/firms-ignoring-climate-crisis-bankrupt-mark-carney-bank-england-governor

1 Business and ethics
Contradiction and success story

Abstract

This chapter addresses the concept of the "unavoidability" of ethics in business. Almost any decision-making process involves ethical implications. Ignoring ethical concerns can lead to business consequences that can have a long-lasting negative effect. Decision-makers in organizations must understand basic theories of normative ethics and set up standards that will be carried throughout the organization. Business ethics has now been embedded in management through frameworks such as TSI (Total Societal Impact), illustrating the relationship between being ethically responsible and economically successful. Ethics can be systemically implemented through widespread awareness, reasoning, evaluating, and action. Ethics is not an exact science, like mathematics, chemistry, or physics, however, ethics cannot be evaluated void of a multidimensional understanding of value. Businesses must not only focus on increasing economic value, but need to be aware of other forms of value that are contributing positively to well-being, society, and nature. This chapter includes case studies, e.g. on Freitag and Total Societal Impact.

Chapter keywords

(1) Business ethics
(2) The unavoidability of ethics
(3) Total Societal Impact (TSI)
(4) B corporations
(5) Values
(6) Normative vs descriptive

Study objectives

After studying this chapter readers will be able to understand and explain the relevance of ethical issues in business contexts.

DOI: 10.4324/9781003127659-1

2 *Contradiction and success story*

Case studies

1.1 Freitag
1.2 Boston Consulting Group: Total Societal Impact
1.3 Unethical businesses will go bankrupt

Films

(1) *The Big Short*

Chapter 1 introduces the topics of business and ethics and clarifies why business and ethics have been viewed as contradictory concepts, but from today's consumers' and inventors' perspectives are rather seen as necessary and often as an essential fusion. This chapter explains why it is meaningful to study business ethics and why it is impossible to avoid ethical decision-making. It very briefly covers etymological and genealogical aspects of business ethics and a few preliminary ethical concepts such as descriptive vs normative, the concept of values, and business ethics as a highly complex decision-making process that demands managers combine ethical, economic, and legal requirements. Case studies illustrate the concepts dealt with. The cases cover predictions, such as that of the former Governor of the Bank of England, who suggested that unethical businesses, especially those with negative environmental impacts, are very likely to fail in the future. Environmentally responsible and sustainable businesses like the Swiss upcycling company Freitag successfully expand globally while the Boston Consulting Group provides empirical evidence suggesting that ethically responsible businesses in general usually have a brighter and more successful future than ethically unsustainable companies (BCG, 2019).

Not too many decades ago a course like "Business Ethics" did not exist at universities. The mainstream understanding at that time was that business and ethics are a contradiction in terms. It forms a useless combination of contradicting words – an oxymoron, a mission impossible. If anything, ethics is a purely private matter and has nothing to do with organizations and businesses. It used to be a common (mis)understanding that business is only concerned with maximizing profits, while ethics is only about helping others in a purely philanthropic sense.

Meanwhile, the mainstream understanding of business ethics has changed. Nowadays business ethics, or ethical business, is seen as an almost indispensable marketing tool that increases sales. All major companies, especially larger corporations, have one or more Corporate Social Responsibility (CSR) campaigns, which, from some critical perspectives, are seen as whitewashing or greenwashing campaigns. Whitewashing or greenwashing are actions by companies that are, or appear to be, ethical or environmentally friendly, but in fact rather try to cover up some unethical actions or an environmental problem or even a disaster caused by the company. However, one should be careful not to rashly dismiss the socio-ethical commitment of companies as

Figure 1.1 Business as contradiction, marketing tool, business philosophy

greenwashing and propaganda, especially since the internet and social media make it easier for critical consumers to expose greenwashing attempts by companies.

Only for a few companies is ethics an integral part of their business philosophy or part of their business DNA. But the number of businesses that take CSR, ethics, and sustainability very seriously is growing, be it through external pressure or – what is (virtue) ethically more desirable – through their own ethical insight. Prominent examples are Patagonia, Brunello Cucinelli, Freitag, Ben & Jerry's, Toms, Ecosia, and many other companies, some of which are listed as so-called "B corporations" (https://bcorporation.net/). B corporations are companies that take CSR and environmental responsibility seriously as part of their business identity. Many of these companies' customers would stop purchasing products and services from these businesses if the company deviated from its ethical agenda, bearing in mind that these customers are willing to pay a higher price for a fairly or organically produced item. In such a situation many socially responsible investors would prefer more ethical and responsible brands and corporations.

Case study 1.1: Freitag

Research Freitag's sustainable business.

(1) Explain and discuss the entrepreneurial and sustainable dimensions of Freitag.
(2) What is the difference between a Freitag bag and a mass-produced bag?
(3) Can two customers have exactly the same bag? Explain.
(4) What can we learn from Freitag's entrepreneurial and sustainable approach?

1.1 The aim of this book: Why studying business ethics?

There is a German saying narrated from the perspective of a child addressing its parents. This saying communicates the child's wish and reads: "when I am young you should give me roots, but when I get older you need to give me wings". This metaphor means that when we are younger, or when we are inexperienced beginners, we do need solid foundations, but when we are more advanced, we need the skills to be independent and we must be in a position to make crucial decisions with far-reaching consequences by ourselves. We also should be able to "think out of the box" and be able to "expand our horizons" (Gadamer, 2013). Likewise, according to the subsidiary principle, we should be able to help ourselves. The approach of considering unconventional ideas is an essential trait of unorthodox or open-minded philosophers, innovative engineers, and successful start-ups entrepreneurs alike.

Those who are responsible for educating us are required to have the ability to provide us with the necessary critical thinking and sound decision-making tools. This idea of this dual skill set can be easily transferred into the educational context, because once we begin to learn something novel and unfamiliar, we need to have a solid foundation on which we can build on, like the roots of a tree which need to carry and support the stem, the branches and the canopy of the tree, even in hurricane season. But once we are advanced and we need to apply the skills independently in real-world scenarios, we need to be able to navigate quickly, swiftly, and professionally like a bird flies with the help of its wings. In this regard this book, and a business ethics course for which this book is written, like any other course, should be able to accomplish both, namely to supply the learner with solid foundations but also with the tools that enable the learner to navigate swiftly, professionally, and independently in the real world of business transactions, which confronts us with a wide variety of ethical requirements and problems.

This idea of combining solid foundations and specific expertise is also expressed in the image of the ideal of "T-shaped education". The horizontal bar of the letter "T" represents the ability to collaborate across disciplines with experts in other areas and apply knowledge in areas of expertise other than one's own field of knowledge. The vertical bar represents the depth of one's expertise in a specialized field. Business ethics is situated at the junction between the horizontal and the vertical bars. We need to be aware of ethical issues in our field and beyond and tackle those ethical issues by synthesizing ethical theories with our expert knowledge.

From the Boston Consulting Group's research on Total Societal Impact (see below) we can easily deduce that unethical business activities quite often lead to business failures (BCG, 2017). Affected stakeholders can impact positively or negatively in various ways on a business and its activity. How stakeholders will react to certain company practices in the end is contingent upon various factors. Therefore, it is crucial in business decisions to take the well-being, an important holistic value, of all stakeholders into account.

Contradiction and success story 5

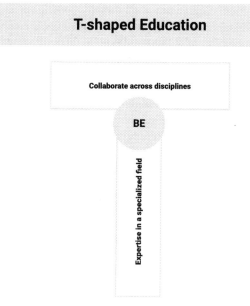

Figure 1.2 T-shaped education and business ethics

But another reason for studying business ethics is that it contributes to one's own personal intellectual, social, and psychological well-being due to fostering cross-disciplinary knowledge and peace of mind in decision-making processes. Business ethics should enable managers to make decisions that allow them to look in the mirror with a clear conscience.

1.2 Unavoidability of ethical decision-making

In business ethics, as elsewhere in ethics, especially in applied ethics, there exists a fact that can be called an "unavoidability of ethics" or, more precisely, an unavoidability of ethical decision-making. Even if we decided we wanted to ignore ethics, we still are making decisions that have ethical implications, for example by making choices of consumption, by purchasing particular food items or information and communication technology devices. Buying organic Fair Trade coffee is a more ethical choice than buying coffee that is contaminated with heavy metals, pesticides, and insecticides, having negative health impacts on farmers and consumers, produced with the help of poorly paid or forced child labor.

The unavoidability of ethics could be very clearly seen in the 2020/2021 Covid-19 crisis when medical personnel were faced with what has been called "triage" (Baker & Fink, 2020). In circumstances of limited time, personnel, and resources, especially ventilators, the medical personnel, in an emergency ethical decision-making process, have to distinguish and divide patients into three groups. 1) Those who do not need immediate help, 2) those whose recovery is very likely and promising, and 3) those whose recovery is very unlikely. The medical personnel in such situations cannot avoid making ethical decisions. Those who do not need immediate help will be sent home. Those whose recovery is highly unlikely will be left to die because the restrictions of medical personnel and equipment dictate that resources must rather be employed for the second group, whose recovery is very likely and promising. Comparable ethical considerations were required in 2021 when determining which groups of people should be vaccinated against Covid-19 first.

Similarly, although not with such immediate consequences, our everyday consumption choices do have ethical implications as indicated in the coffee example above. As the French philosopher Jean-Paul Sartre wrote, we are "condemned to be free" (Sartre, 2017), we must actively make choices and exercise our free will. We cannot assume, like a determinist, that everything is predetermined. Most of those choices have ethical implications. So even if we decided to ignore ethics, we cannot run away from it, therefore it is better to know more about ethical theory, its applications, and about the ethical consequences and implications of our choices.

1.3 Descriptive vs normative

One important distinction in ethics is the differentiation between descriptive and normative ethics or between descriptive and prescriptive ethics. Descriptive comes from the expression "to describe" and means that in the process of ethical decision-making we are simply describing or explaining circumstances or a case, without making an ethical judgment or without giving any ethical recommendation yet. However, purely describing and explaining what has happened is not of ethical significance (Velasquez, 2014).

Normative and prescriptive means that we are evaluating a situation, setting up standards, norms, and rules; in other words, we are judging and giving recommendations based on different normative ethical theories that

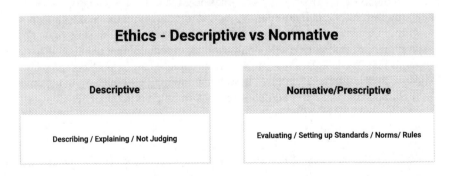

Figure 1.3 Descriptive vs normative ethics

appear appropriate depending on the case under consideration (Velasquez, 2014). It could be claimed that many universities, by including compulsory business ethics courses in their educational programs, are making a shift from a descriptive to a normative or prescriptive account by making an educational claim that an ethics course in the business educational context is something that is no longer optional or recommended but essential and compulsory.

1.4 Business and ethics etymologies

The word business is etymologically related to busy. The Old English word "bisig" means careful, anxious, busy, occupied, and diligent. The Old English word "busyness" means "state of being much occupied and engaged" (www.etymonline.com/).

The word "ethics" comes from "aethos" which is Greek and means habitual residence, custom, or character. A similar Greek word "ethos" means habit and custom. The words "morality" or "moral" come from the Latin word "custom". The etymological meaning of both words is that ethics or morality is something that is done traditionally in a particular cultural context and is considered to be "good", "acceptable", and "commendable" (www.etymonline.com/). In a nutshell, ethics is a theory of what is considered to be good, especially in terms of human conduct and behavior, in particular toward other people, but also toward oneself, animals, the environment, or entities like groups, peoples, states, and conglomerates of states, such as the UN (United Nations), the AU (African Union), the EU (European Union), or ASEAN (Association of South East Asian Countries).

We can define ethics as analysis, systematization, evaluation, and recommendation of correct, right, or good conduct. In line with this definition business ethics can be simply defined as analysis, systematization, evaluation, and recommendation of correct, right, good conduct in the business context, i.e. in the context of different operational as well as strategic corporate and management decisions. This procedure of analyzing, systematizing, evaluating, and recommending follows the approach we will utilize when looking at business ethics case studies.

1.5 The story of business ethics

The academic discipline of ethics in the Western context is more than 2000 years old, but in many cultures around the globe (today's Australia, Middle East, China, Indus Valley, and Central America), literature and other cultural manifestations with ethical implications go far further back in history. Business ethics is a relatively young academic sub-discipline that emerged in the 1970s, and corporate scandals in the early 2000s increased its popularity and importance. The 1970 essay "The social responsibility of business is to increase its profits" by Milton Friedman, which is probably the most cited essay on business ethics, also contributed to the awareness of business ethics – despite the fact that Friedman himself has vehemently spoken out against any business ethics or any ethical responsibility of companies that goes beyond normal business activities (Friedman, 1970).

Until recently the mainstream understanding questioned the existence of any overlapping domain of business and ethics, and considered the term "business ethics" as oxymoronic – business ethics, or ethical business would be a contradiction in terms. However, recent research from the Boston Consulting Group has revealed that businesses increase their Total Shareholder Return (TSR) if they seriously take the Total Societal Impact (TSI) into account (BCG, 2017).

Conversely, if businesses do not take the TSI into account, in many cases, that will have a negative impact on the TSR and may lead to a negative impact on the business in general and even to bankruptcy. Consumers more and more tend to purchase ethically acceptable products and services while investors increasingly switch to socially and environmentally responsible investment that can be characterized by greater stability in the long term (BCG, 2017).

Case study 1.2: Boston Consulting Group: Total Societal Impact

Research the Boston Consulting Group's pledge to businesses to focus more on TSI (BCG, 2017).

(1) Explain TSR and TSI in your own words.
(2) Why should companies focus more on TSI (there are several reasons)? What are the opportunities/benefits when applying the "TSI lens"?
(3) What obstacles hamper managers from focusing on TSI?
(4) Why is it sometimes not possible or very difficult to generate both positive societal impact and business benefits?
(5) Are there differences regarding the importance of TSR and TSI, especially Socially Responsible Investment (SRI) in different parts of the world? Which ones? How can they be explained? What do these differences mean for multinationals?
(6) Research and choose a company or a product of a company as an example and explain in which quadrant of the TSR and TSI matrix they are located. Why are they located there according to your understanding?

Case study 1.3: Unethical businesses will go bankrupt

Research statements by former Governor of the Bank of England Mark Carney claiming that unethical businesses will go bankrupt (Carrington, 2019): "Companies and industries that are not moving towards zero-carbon emissions will be punished by investors and go bankrupt, the governor of the Bank of England has warned" (Carrington, 2019). "CEO of Morgan Stanley, said the other day: 'If we don't have a planet, we're not going to have a very good financial system'. Ultimately, that is true" (Carrington, 2019).

(1) Imagine you were an entrepreneur planning a startup. How would you turn this "climate emergency" into a business opportunity, considering various stakeholders in your business approach?
(2) "20 fossil fuel companies have produced coal, oil, and gas linked to more than a third of all emissions in the modern era" (Carrington, 2019). What would it be ethically advisable to do if you were the CEO of one of those fossil fuel companies?

1.6 Values

Values are what guide us in our everyday decision-making, although it should be noted that there are very different types of values. In the economy or the business domain, we usually consider mostly economic values, monetary values, or money. If we talk about the success of companies we usually have their revenue in mind; revenue is a monetary value. But there are many other values, for example reputation, competence, or creativity, that can be viewed as performance values in the broader sense and also play an important role not only in the business domain but in life in general. Another interesting example would be aesthetic values.

If we, for example, buy a fan, the purpose of which is cooling the room including ourselves, we consider several values, such as the price, which is a monetary value, but also the functions. Further, we may consider, for example, if the fan swivels, if it has different speeds, a timer function, remote control, or other specific features and modes. But we are also interested in how the fan looks, its color, for example, and its shape. We can see that besides monetary and functional or technical values, aesthetic values also play an important role in choosing products and services. When buying the fan, legal values (such as legal security) are also important, even if we are not consciously aware of them during the payment process. Have you been attracted by the speed, friendliness, or the physical appearance of the cashier when deciding in which row to stand in line in the supermarket? Speed, service-mindedness, and aesthetic appearance are all highly important factors influencing values. Other important values include for example perfection and optimization. German cars, for example, are often chosen for their reliability, perfection, and optimization of technology, engineering work, and design. Ethical values, such as impartiality, integrity, justice, fairness, and cooperation are those values that are related to moral goodness, for example, "virtues" – we will explore virtues in detail in Chapter 3. There are also holistic values, for example, well-being, happiness, and flourishing. Such "umbrella" values or values to which other values lead, are, or seem to be, *ends in themselves*, something we try to achieve not because of something else.

Values also help when finding directions in life, like a compass. Some companies, for example Fjällraven, use the so-called "Sustainability Compass" developed by Alan AtKisson (cf. atkisson.com), in which North represents nature, East reflects the economic dimension (which no company can ignore in market competition), South stands for the society or the community, and West represents well-being. These are corporate values that Fjällraven considers particularly important for shaping the character of the company's corporate responsibility. AtKisson developed the compass from Herman "Daly's Pyramid" (Atkisson & Hatcher, 2001). We will explore this compass in more detail in Chapter 4.

Such values come into play when making complex decisions in the business context. As has become clear above all, business ethics is based on a multidimensional understanding of the term "value". Nevertheless, in the context of business ethics, economic and ethical values seem to be the most decisive. Economic problems cannot be solved with ethical values (morality) alone, but also require economic competence. Conversely, it is just as impossible to try to meet moral questions and problems solely with economic values. Business ethics is also concerned with decision-making in controversial or dilemma

Figure 1.4 Sustainability compass
Source: Redesigned from Alan AtKisson's "Sustainability Compass" (cf. atkisson.com)

Figure 1.5 Taking business ethical actions

situations, in other words, situations in which some form of undesirable outcome seems inevitable. This is why we often can see images of scales, crossroads, and signposts on the cover of business ethics books.

Learning about and teaching business ethics involves raising one's general awareness, increasing the ability for critical reasoning, being in a position to carefully evaluate a situation and its consequences, especially the impacts on stakeholders, but also the stakeholders' potential impacts on the company, and finally to act appropriately according to one's reasoning, evaluation, and imagination.

Business ethical challenges arise due to fierce competition, an already existing unethical business culture, and conflicts between values and preferences, for example personal preferences and values and those of a company.

> **Film case study 1.1:** *The Big Short*
>
> Watch the movie *The Big Short* (Paramount Pictures, 2015) and explain how the following factors are narrated as ethical challenges in the film:
>
> (1) Fierce competition.
> (2) An already existing unethical business culture.
> (3) Conflicts between values and preferences, for example, personal preferences and values and those of a company.

Key takeaways

(1) Business ethics is unavoidable and usually not a contradiction to long-term business goals.
(2) Responsible business will enhance success if understood and implemented well.
(3) Business ethics is the foundation of responsible decision-making.

(4) Ethics is not only about describing situations; it must be integrated into the business's norms and responsible persons' actions.
(5) Economic value is not the only value to be considered in everyday business life.

References

Atkisson, A., & Hatcher, R. (2001). The compass index of sustainability: Prototype for a comprehensive sustainability information system. *Journal of Environmental Assessment Policy and Management, 3*(4), 509–532. www.jstor.org/stable/enviassepolimana.3.4.509

Baker, M., & Fink, S. (2020, March 31). At the top of the Covid-19 curve, how do hospitals decide who gets treatment? *The New York Times.* www.nytimes.com/2020/03/31/us/coronavirus-covid-triage-rationing-ventilators.html

BCG. (2017). *Total Societal Impact: A New Lens for Strategy.* www.bcg.com/publications/2017/total-societal-impact-new-lens-strategy.aspx

BCG. (2019). *How Companies – And CEOs – Can Increase TSI and TSR.* www.bcg.com/publications/2017/corporate-development-finance-strategy-companies-ceos-increase-tsi-tsr.aspx

Carrington, D. (2019, October 13). Firms ignoring climate crisis will go bankrupt, says Mark Carney. *The Guardian.* www.theguardian.com/environment/2019/oct/13/firms-ignoring-climate-crisis-bankrupt-mark-carney-bank-england-governor

Friedman, M. (1970, September 12). The social responsibility of business is to increase its profits. *New York Magazine,* 122–126.

Gadamer, H.-G. (2013). *Truth and Method* (Reprint ed.). Bloomsbury Academic.

Paramount Pictures. (2015). *The Big Short Trailer (2015)* www.youtube.com/watch?v=vgqG3ITMv1Q

Sartre, J.-P. (2017). *Existentialism Is a Humanism.* CreateSpace Independent Publishing Platform.

Velasquez, M. (2014). *Business Ethics Concepts and Cases* (7th ed.). Pearson Education Limited.

2 Ethics and business
Down the philosophical rabbit hole

Abstract

Law is derived from ethical discourse yet acting lawfully does not automatically mean one is acting ethically. Ethical theory can be subdivided into meta-ethics, normative ethics, and applied ethics. Business ethical relevant meta-ethical dimensions include the integrated social contacts theory framework which identifies hyper-norms and microsocial norms and approaches ethical decision-making by considering these two layers of norms. Meta-ethics also views decision-making through the lens of human motivation. Normative ethics which acts as a general guideline that can be applied in various circumstances, and can be rendered through the "big five" ethical theories (virtue, deontological/duty, utilitarianism, care, environmental). Applied ethics includes business ethics, which highlights the importance of business stakeholder relationships including stakeholders beyond customers, employees, suppliers, and shareholders, such as the society as a whole, the environment, non-human species, and future generations. The chapter includes case studies on the Boeing 737 MAX scandal and Brunello Cucinelli's humanistic capitalism.

Chapter keywords

(1) Applied ethics
(2) Normative ethics
(3) Norms
(4) Law and ethics

Study objectives

After studying this chapter readers will be able to:

(1) Explain how ethics is situated in academic and business contexts.
(2) Appreciate the relativity of ethical rules in diverse business practices.
(3) Understand the basic difference between law and ethics.

DOI: 10.4324/9781003127659-2

Case studies

2.1 The Boeing 737 MAX scandal
2.2 The "philosopher-designer" Brunello Cucinelli and his humanistic capitalism

Films

(1) *The Corporation*

2.1 Situating ethics

This chapter situates ethics within the academic, every day, and business contexts. While there exist(ed) laws that are considered unethical from a hypernorm perspective, some actions considered morally sound can be against the law. The chapter briefly explains how ethical reasoning and acting is grounded in human nature and social contexts and how ethical thinking and decision-making can be culturally relative plus globally overarching, as *hypernorms*, at the same time. Business ethics, as one of many disciplines within applied ethics, makes use of the application of normative ethical theories, which themselves are deeply rooted in philosophical reasoning. Business ethics is heavily concerned with the responsibilities companies have toward their stakeholders, because businesses can impact on their stakeholders in multiple ways. However, what is too often neglected is the diversity of impacts that the stakeholders can have on business activities. The Boeing 737 MAX case illustrates how the reaction of several stakeholders to the two Boeing 737 MAX crashes finally halted the production of the most successful narrow-body jet airliner ever produced and, as a result, Boeing lost its reputation and its status as the market leader over Airbus. Studying the "philosopher-designer" Brunnello Cucinelli illustrates the concepts of value, responsibility, and the philosophical grounding of ethical business, and foreshadows a number of ethical theories discussed in the next chapter.

Ethics is a sub-discipline within the domain of philosophy, among many other philosophical sub-disciplines such as logic, aesthetics or philosophy of art, political philosophy, epistemology (the study of how to acquire knowledge), ontology (the enquiry into existence), metaphysics (the study into phenomena that go beyond physics, such as questions of whether humans have a soul or a mind, or if a god exists), and history of philosophy. Philosophical sub-disciplines can also be divided into historical traditions such as ancient Greek philosophy, medieval philosophy, philosophy of the Enlightenment, modern philosophy, post-modern philosophy, and contemporary philosophy. The division can also be cultural or geographical, such as Anglo-American or analytic philosophy, and Continental philosophy which mainly refers to traditions that have been launched in France and Germany. Non-Western traditions such as African philosophy, Chinese philosophy,

Indian philosophy, and Eastern philosophical traditions are becoming increasingly popular within mainstream philosophical curricula. In some passages of this text the reader will also be referred to non-Western traditions, which is a largely neglected feature in business ethics books, despite the fact that the majority of business transactions and activities take place outside the Western world, which is why China, or Asia, is sometimes referred to as the workbench of the world.

While details regarding the development and relations of these traditions and specific sub-disciplines belong to an introduction to philosophy or an introduction to the history of philosophy, what needs to be noted at this point is that ethics has become one of the most important sub-disciplines of philosophy. This is the case because rapidly developing technologies and the accelerated and compressed way we live together in societies demand a constant update of ethical reasoning that takes into consideration the challenges of today's societies, which are confronted with issues such as, for example, pandemics, nuclear disasters resulting from nuclear energy production or storage, and threats of nuclear attacks. Many of these challenges stem from technologies whose implementation and use are ethically ambivalent, meaning there are positive and negative implications at the same time. Some technologies disrupt our lives in such a way that it could even lead to the end of humanity, while the same technologies have the potential to improve humanity's quality of life in an unprecedented way, such as AI (Artificial Intelligence) and genetic engineering. Finally, there is the complex problem of climate change, global warming, and environmental destruction which could result in the extinction of humanity in a few decades, if we do not make an eco-ideological U-turn in terms of our production approaches and consumption patterns. This book features two chapters (4 and 6) which respectively deal with environmental problems on the one hand and with technological challenges on the other, tackling the ethical issues that businesses face in the light of these two challenges.

2.2 Ethics and law

Important neighboring domains of ethics are political science, psychology, sociology, and law, among many others. There is a triangular connection between law and ethics because usually, before a law is enacted, an ethical discourse takes place regarding what future laws should look like. An example would be an ethical discourse on the question of whether genetic engineering on fetuses should be allowed for eliminating terminal diseases only or if we allow the same technology to be used for aesthetic alterations, so that parents can decide, for example, the sex, potential height, and skin color of their children. Discussing these questions in diverse cultures and milieus may result in different outcomes. In traditional Chinese contexts male children may be preferred while in traditional Thai contexts female children may be preferable. In some African and southeast Asian cultures parents may opt for a fairer skin color. However, most parents would agree to eliminate terminal diseases if that were genetically possible.

Some laws are considered unethical such as certain former apartheid laws in South Africa, or former particular laws in Saudi Arabia disallowing women particular privileges, such as driving in public, or other laws in the Islamic context that prosecute homosexuals. These cultural differences in the understanding of laws and ethics are called *cultural relativity*, to which we will return in detail in Chapter 9 on intercultural business ethics.

There is another connection or disconnection between law and ethics which is related to the fact that sometimes and under certain circumstances it may be considered ethical to act against the law. In particular emergencies or situations of scarcity, for example, it could be considered ethical to steal food from a garden where nobody can be seen around who one could ask for permission to take the food. Stealing is against the law, but stealing food in order to nurture and rescue a person that is almost starved to death or cannot afford or access food at this point in time can be considered morally acceptable or ethically commendable. Edward Snowden, an American citizen and former NSA (National Security Agency) contractor, considered it ethical to disseminate classified information to the public in order to inform the worldwide public about the fact that the NSA in the US is basically spying on each and every citizen in the world who operates a mobile phone or a computer (Poitras, 2014). Co-founder of WikiLeaks Julian Assange published masses of classified information on the WikiLeaks website which he thought the public should be aware of (sunshinepress, 2010) because the citizens are the ones voting for politicians who then make decisions regarding security and privacy on behalf of the citizens within a nation-state. These acts of whistleblowing are considered to be unlawful, not only by US legislation, which is one of the reasons why only very few countries were ready to grant asylum to either Julian Assange or Edward Snowden. However, according to many citizens' opinions throughout the world, especially journalists, these acts of whistleblowing were considered ethically justifiable because many governments were "spying" on their citizens without consent or the citizens' knowledge. While many citizens are willing to trade in privacy for security, a fact that we can see in many countries where mobile phone applications are used to track Covid-19 infections, citizens want to know about, democratically discuss, and give informed consent to such acts of mass surveillance (Halpern, 2020). Consent is the prerequisite for being able to ascribe ethical legitimacy to the exchange of privacy for security.

What we have to keep in mind for the business ethical context is that acting lawfully does not always automatically mean acting ethically and acting ethically does not always mean acting within the framework of the law, although most of the time laws and ethics go hand-in-hand. But the ethical discourse is much wider than what finally becomes a law.

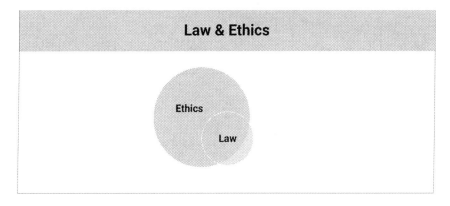

Figure 2.1 Law and ethics

2.2.1 Levels of ethics

Ethics can be subdivided into three levels (iep.utm.edu/ethics). The most obvious level is the one in which ethical theories are applied, therefore called "applied ethics". Business ethics is an applied ethical discipline. Applied ethics means that we are relating ethical theory to particular circumstances. But what are we applying? We are applying what is called "normative ethical theories". "Normative ethics" is what is usually understood by the term ethics. It is this part of ethics that comes up with suggestions, recommendations, as well as pro and con arguments which serve as general guidelines that can be applied to particular circumstances, such as the business context. The fundamental question is, in short, what is the right thing to do? But when we ask questions regarding what is ethical behavior, where does ethical behavior come from, why do we act unethically, and so forth, these are questions within the "meta-ethical" level. Meta-ethics is, so to speak, one level above normative ethics. It is less about the question of pros and cons, (as is the case with normative ethical theories), but rather about questioning the logic of ethical arguments; this is also the reason why meta-ethics sometimes appears a bit abstract, theoretical, or even rather strange. For example, it examines how the arguments of the agents involved run and how rational they are, what premises their arguments contain, what is taken for granted in their arguments, whether there are breaks or contradictions in the arguments, and so on.

2.3 Cultural relativity of values

The term "value" is multidimensional and has multiple meanings in common parlance, two of which are also at the center of business ethics: on the one hand, economic values (such as shareholder value), on the other hand, moral

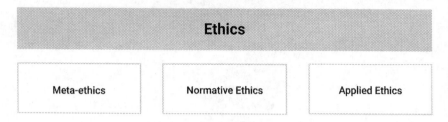

Figure 2.2 Levels of ethics (meta, normative, applied)

values (such as justice, transparency, solidarity, etc.). Even if there is no clear social ranking of values, values should provide a certain directional orientation. In a sense, they serve as vantage points for orientation. One of the meta-ethical issues is the question of whether all values are eternal, universal, and absolute or if values are rather human inventions and dependent on culture, time, and place, and are subject to particular circumstances, being culturally relative. Most people around the world would probably agree that in ordinary everyday circumstances, killing other people is something that is considered to be unethical. This value, which could also be referred to as a "meta-", "hyper-", or "global-" value, is largely consistent across cultures, time, and space. Killing people in specific war-like or imminent and life-threatening circumstances may be considered not acceptable by everyone, but by some, as we can see with the examples of extra juridical killings of terrorists or potential terrorists as initiated by US governments, which was condemned by many Western- and Islamic-oriented governments (Barnes, 2019).

Depending on the culture, there are differing views as to which values, rituals, norms or communication rules are viewed as right or wrong, which in turn can have far-reaching consequences for economic life. The objectively identical business situation can be perceived and thus evaluated and decided upon very differently by individuals depending on their cultural affiliation or background. Being straightforward and direct in a conversation, pointing out mistakes very clearly and giving recommendations on how this could be improved is a value that is considered constructive and helpful in many Western cultures. "Saving face", meaning being very diplomatic and careful when criticizing someone openly, for example in Thai culture, may not be appreciated by all members of a culture that rather appreciates a more straightforward approach. Here we have examples that demonstrate the fact that culturally relative values are not appreciated in the same way across the globe. This in turn also shows that culturally relative values represent an important factor for the formation and success of business transactions on an international level.

Integrated social contracts theory tries to reconcile values and norms that seem to be valid across geographical, cultural, and temporal boundaries with those norms or values that seem to differ and depend on cultural or historical contexts (Donaldson & Dunfee, 1995). Norms and values that are generally accepted by all societies, for example human rights, or at least some particular human rights, are considered to be "hypernorms". Specific cultural or religious norms that are only accepted by members of specific societies, cultures, or religions, for example the tradition of saving face in the Thai cultural context or respecting older people's advice as supreme in a traditional African context, are called "micro-social" norms.

In business contexts managers should follow micro-social norms of specific host cultures as long as they do not contradict or violate hyper-norms (Velasquez, 2014). An example would be that it is acceptable to save someone's face (e.g. not making public who made a (minor) mistake that resulted in a short disruption in the production line resulting only in minor consequences) as long as this act of saving face is not covering up a major ethical issue, such as criminal acts (e.g. embezzlement, fraud or balance sheet manipulation, corruption, sabotage, or spying and sharing trade secrets) that are considered to be against a hyper-norm.

Cultural relativism means that different cultural values may result in different cultural principles, laws, and political decisions. In a rather neoliberal-oriented economic system a citizen or employee has a very high responsibility for his or her own health, this is why we may not find comprehensive compulsory health insurances widely applied across the social spectrum (meaning for everyone) in neoliberal-oriented economies. But in a social-ecological market economy, such as in Germany, it is assumed that unforeseen and unpredictable circumstances may happen that cannot be financially covered by individuals and therefore it is better that people have compulsory health insurance, which in turn is part of a comprehensive social security system that also financially covers risks in old age, in the event of a need for care and unemployment. In the Covid-19 crisis we can see how different health care systems, which are based on different cultural values (such as high risk

Figure 2.3 Hypernorms vs microsocial norms

aversion and a strong desire for security), impact on the more or less widely accessible availability of medical equipment and personnel, and thus on the ability to combat a pandemic.

2.3.1 Meta-ethical considerations: "Why do(n't) you give something to the beggar?"

Another example of a meta-ethical consideration is the question of the motivations behind our ethical or unethical behavior patterns. Examples for types of ethical motivations are egoism, altruism, emotion, reason, nature, and social cultural contexts.

Imagine going home from a busy day at work and on your way home you pass by a beggar sitting on a pedestrian bridge who is asking you for some coins. Why do you give something or nothing to this or any other beggar? Do we act ethically out of egoistic reasons? For example, that we may simply not want to be bothered by bad conscience if we do not give the beggar some coins. Or that we want to appear as responsible and good people to others who may observe us in this moment. And thus, we hand out some coins for the egoistic reason of having peace of mind. Or is it a genuine altruism, i.e. a genuine moral interest which motivates us to give something to the beggar?

Is it that many humans really care about others, sometimes more than themselves? Can this explain the commitment of medical professionals in the Covid-19 crisis? Or is it a spontaneous emotion that motivates us at a certain moment to give something to a beggar? Is it that we feel good if we share or that we feel bad if you don't share? Or is it rather reason that motivates us to share something with a beggar? We can surely reason and understand that we most likely have more financial means than the beggar and if we give some coins to the beggar, then the beggar will have a slightly better life, and if

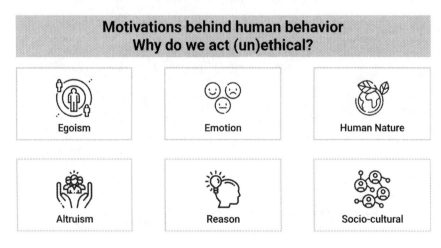

Figure 2.4 Meta-ethics: Motivations

other people also share some coins with the beggar, then this will improve the beggar's quality of life significantly. Is this kind of logical reasoning behind our motivation to act ethically? Or is it nature that motivates us to give something to the begging person? Meaning that we are good by nature and give something to the beggar because we humans are intrinsically good. Or are we evil by nature? Is this the reason that we do not give something to the beggar?

The Slovenian philosopher Slavoj Žižek (Taylor, 2005) once said "we are just pretending to be humans, in fact we are all demons". Or is it the sociocultural context that is responsible for our actions? If you grew up in the context in which sharing is an important value then you are more inclined to give something to the beggar, but if you grew up in a very individualistic context, where you are told and taught that "everyone has to take care of her or himself, and that people such as these beggars are lazy people living from freeriding in a society of hard working citizens", then you may be more inclined not to put yourself in the position of the beggar and also not to give them any coins.

Most likely the motivation behind our ethical or unethical behavior is a mix of these and probably many more motivations that play a role in the local context. But we cannot go more deeply into this area because this belongs to the domain of meta-ethics and we are more interested in applied ethics. Nevertheless, we will notice later that even when applying normative ethical theories to business contexts, meta-ethical questions, such as those we ask ourselves when facing the beggar, do come back to us frequently. It must also be added that most likely even if you asked a number of people passing by the beggar why they have given something or not given something to the beggar, these pedestrians' answers would not necessarily reveal the truth about their real motivations of sharing or not sharing. There are very different factors (such as effects of social desirability) that can influence their responses. Ultimately, however, we do not really know if these people would tell us the truth or if they are really aware of their own motivation or the mix of their motivations. This is a topic for behavioral economists, social psychologists, and sociologists, who epistemically have better vantage points and appropriate research tools to tackle such an issue. Social psychologists such as Philip Zimbardo would argue that the political, economic, social, religious, cultural, and historical contexts are responsible for making people who they become and how they act. This is what Zimbardo tried to validate with his infamous Stanford Prison Experiment (Zimbardo, 2007), which is considered one of the most famous empirical studies in psychology. In 1971, in the basement of Stanford University, a prison situation made up of inmates and guards (both groups comprised of students) was simulated to determine how people behave when they gain power over others. The experiment had to be stopped after a few days, as some prisoners showed strong signs of depression, whereas the guards developed a cruel and sadistic behavior towards the prisoners. What Zimbardo wanted to make clear above all is that ultimately all people can show such behavior depending on the nature of the social situation and context.

2.4 Normative ethics

As already indicated above, normative ethics aims to regulate moral attitudes and behavior by arriving at and suggesting or prescribing moral standards. In the business context this is relevant for "codes of ethics", which are more general, "codes of conduct", or more specific, Corporate Social Responsibility (CSR), and corporate environment responsibility. However normative ethics is relevant for its application value to any kind of business ethical situation.

There are at least five standalone normative ethical theories that we need to explore due to their business contextual relevance. Depending on the interpretation of what is a major ethical theory there may be more or less than these five standalone ethical theories. But for the purpose of applications into the business context it makes sense to differentiate between these five theories, which in fact have significant differences in their design and framework, their meta-ethical assumptions, and in outcome if they are applied in the business context. The application of two or three different theories to the same context may arrive at the same or a different result but the outcome also depends very much on the interpretation of the ethical theories. There is no such thing as the "perfect", "correct", or "overall most useful" ethical theory, but in some contexts certain ethical theories make more sense than others. In any case, not every normative ethical theory is suitable for every concrete application situation. Conversely, this means that in certain situations only certain theories appear suitable and helpful. For example, in many tragic (one could also say ethically dilemmatic) situations there is nothing left but to make utilitarian decisions (Wagner, 2019). An example of this is the above mentioned Covid-19 disaster situation. In such an emergency situation a triage practice needs to be applied (this means that a decision has to be made as to who can and cannot receive intensive medical care in the event of limited capacities in the hospital), which is based on the ethical theory of utilitarianism, by maximizing the usefulness for the majority of the citizens. Care ethics, which may consider the most vulnerable as a priority, in such disaster circumstances only makes sense from the perspective of a government that needs to cater for the majority of its citizens, when it is combined with emergency triage. We will discuss both theories – care and utilitarianism – in detail in the next chapter.

Michael Walzer, who has been called the "Dean of Just War Theory", once stated that in a war situation or in a disaster situation, when one is "back against the wall", one may have to be less ethical than in circumstances where one has the leeway not to make decisions under higher pressure. Michael Walzer called a situation in which a disaster is imminent and potentially annihilating for a group of people, for example a village, a city, or an entire state, a "supreme emergency". In that case, the ethical decision-making spectrum is much more limited or restricted by the circumstances than in normal ordinary day-to-day situations (Walzer, 2015).

Applying normative ethical theories to particular real-world circumstances is more like learning to play an instrument than applying mathematical formulas to particular mathematical problems. Although there is a lot of logic involved when applying ethical theory, like in mathematics, there is also the need to try things out, figure out how theories work as a result of an application. Practicing the application of ethical theories to particular business ethical circumstances is like trying certain notes or chords on an instrument and listening to how it sounds. Another parallel we may invoke is making use of tools in a toolbox. It is of course obvious that for driving screws into a wooden surface or block we had best use a screwdriver, but if we are in a hurry and if we need to attach a wooden board very fast with sharp short screws onto some wooden pillars, it may make sense to hammer the screws into the wood with a hammer for the sake of making speedy progress. In this tool example there's some process of trial and error involved and this is often true for applying normative ethics as well.

The best advice for applying ethical theories is probably to consider both strategies simultaneously, to apply logical reasoning as thoroughly as possible and at the same time develop a certain feeling of how ethical theories make sense in particular circumstances. While all these comparisons about playing instruments and using tools may sound quite fuzzy, nevertheless we can see that when we interpret certain business behavior from real world scenarios we can in fact detect ethical theories that are underlying the business behaviors. Many examples will follow in the coming chapters.

2.5 The "big five": Standalone normative ethical theories in a nutshell

The major five standalone normative ethical theories are the following. Virtue ethics, deontological ethics or duty theory, consequentialist (teleological) ethics including different forms of utilitarianism, care ethics, and environmental ethics.

Virtue ethics is based on the individual virtues and the moral actions of the actors involved. It is guided by the assumption that we should develop good habits and a good character by cultivating our virtues. If we work hard

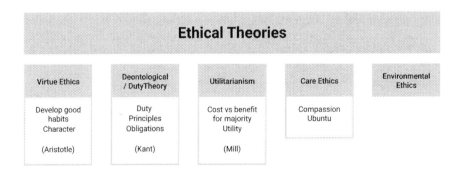

Figure 2.5 "Big five" normative ethical theories

on our virtue development, not only are we ourselves becoming persons that experience well-being, but we are also helping others to pursue the development of their own virtues and well-being. This theory and practice is based on the ancient Greek philosopher Aristotle's virtue theory, developed in his *Nicomachean Ethics* amongst many other lecture notes left by him (Aristotle, 2018). The Italian designer and entrepreneur Brunello Cucinelli's business approach can be interpreted in the line of this tradition. He himself calls his approach "humanistic capitalism" (Cucinelli, 2020). Humanism has a double meaning here. On the one hand, the humanistic tradition is the study of ancient culture and literature for the sake of proper character development, and on the other hand humanism is an essential humane component that is part of Cucinelli's understanding of how capitalism should look ethically. There are similar virtue ethical accounts in many other traditions, but the Aristotelian account is the most prominent, especially in the Western context.

The deontological theory of ethics, which can be understood as the most important counterpoint to the utilitarian ethics addressed below, is based on the idea that we need to come up with and follow duties, principles, obligations, and laws. If we do that, we can assume that the world will be a better place. But these duties, principles, obligations, and laws need to be developed on a rational foundation of what the German Enlightenment philosopher Immanuel Kant calls the *categorical imperative*, which is a specification of the Golden Rule found in many cultures, a universal law, a kind of hyper-norm. Many of the existing laws can be seen in the light of this tradition.

The British philosopher John Stuart Mill further developed utilitarian ethics first made prominent by his teacher and father's friend, Jeremy Bentham. Utilitarianism is a cost-benefit analysis having the majority of people in mind and their maximization of utility, usefulness, pleasure, and well-being. This is also the reason why utilitarianism represents the concept of ethics which is generally the most comprehensible and sympathetic for economists and corporate managers. While utilitarianism is geared towards the maximization of utility and benefits for the greatest number of people or sentient beings, care ethics can be somewhat biased toward a selected group of people. Care ethics takes into consideration that we can especially take care of people who are in close proximity or for whom we can make a clearly monitorable difference. Brunello Cucinelli is also a care ethicist because he is focusing on improving the life of a selected group of stakeholders for whom he can make a significant and by him monitorable difference.

Environmental ethics in contrast to the other four ethical theories takes into account that most of the preceding ethical theories have a clear focus on humans, somewhat neglecting the eco-environment and non-human sentient beings. Companies like Patagonia and Freitag are taking environmental ethical considerations seriously into account. Environmental ethics has become a prominent ethical theory in the recent decades. It can no longer be neglected. This can clearly be seen in the momentum the Fridays for Future movement has gained over the last years, criticizing our production methods and consumption patterns, most of which are totally unsustainable. Chapter 4 will be dedicated to environmental business ethics, corporate environmental responsibility, and sustainability.

While this is just an overview of the big five standalone ethical theories, we will delve more into the details of these theories in the next chapter and develop how exactly they are relevant in the business context.

2.6 Responsibility in business and applied ethics

There are a growing number of areas in applied ethics besides business ethics, for example the above-mentioned highly pertinent area of environmental ethics, biomedical ethics, which plays a major role in the Covid-19 crisis, the ethics of war and peace, intercultural ethics, media ethics, professional ethics such as police ethics, and counseling ethics, to name just a few. More recent academic ethical disciplines consider, for example, robotics, AI, outer space research and travel, genetic engineering, fully autonomous driving, ICT infrastructure, and cryptocurrencies.

Ethics, especially applied ethics, and in particular business ethics, is concerned with responsibility. We have many responsibilities in our life; in traditional cultures it is emphasized that we have responsibilities toward our family members. Many states and cultures emphasize that there must be responsibility shown towards the nation-state (e.g. traditional Chinese and African cultures). More individualistically minded cultures emphasize that we are most particularly responsible for ourselves, while religions emphasize the responsibility toward a god or a higher entity or toward the entire creation. Human rights activists emphasize the responsibility for humanity as a whole, and environmental activists point out the responsibility toward nature and the cosmos. Business ethics is especially concerned with the responsibility of companies or organizations toward all stakeholders.

CSR or corporate responsibility (CR) is sometimes also translated as corporate stakeholder responsibility (Freeman, 1984). Businesses have responsibilities toward their stakeholders, for example in matters of environmental protection. At the same time businesses create values for their stakeholders, for example through the creation of jobs or the development of innovative and sometimes even vital products (such as vaccines). Stakeholders are entities or persons that are affected by or can affect businesses or organizations. In a nutshell, businesses have responsibility toward stakeholders, they create values for their stakeholders, affect their stakeholders, and are affected by their stakeholders – both in a positive and negative way. If, for example with an environmental NGO, the situation is becoming a serious existential problem for the CEO of a major company, the business will no longer be able to ignore this NGO as a major stakeholder. Ignoring the NGO's demands could have far-reaching negative consequences for the success and even the very existence of the entire company. Not least because of this, practically all large companies today have set up a CSR department (Readfearn, 2020). We will deal with stakeholders in detail in Chapter 6.

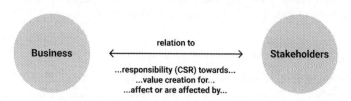

Figure 2.6 Business stakeholder relations

> **Film case study 2.1:** *The Corporation*
>
> Watch the classic documentary *The Corporation* and explain why the corporation as a "person" (by law) is considered an "irresponsible psychopath" in this documentary.

> **Case study 2.1: Boeing 737 MAX**
>
> The Boeing 737 MAX scandal.
>
> (1) Analyze important ethical implications of this case.
> (2) How can different stakeholders have an impact on Boeing in this particular case?
> (3) If you were the newly appointed Chief Engineer of Boeing, what would be the ethically advisable measures that you would take?
> (4) If you were the newly appointed CEO of Boeing, what would be the ethically advisable measures that you would take?

> **Case study 2.2: The "philosopher-designer" Brunello Cucinelli and his humanistic capitalism**
>
> Research how business is currently developing for the Italian designer and entrepreneur Brunello Cucinelli.
>
> (1) Explain how different stakeholders benefit from the Brunello Cucinelli company and how stakeholders may have an impact on the Brunello Cucinelli company.
> (2) Why is this form of business "humanistic"? What exactly is meant by this?
> (3) What can we learn from this case?

Key takeaways

1) Laws and ethics are connected and related, but not congruent.
(2) There are three levels of ethics: meta-ethics, normative ethics, and applied ethics.
(3) Normative ethical theories are frequently applied to business situations.
(4) Business ethics is applied ethics and focuses on business stakeholder relationships.

References

Aristotle. (2018). *Nicomachean Ethics*. The Internet Classics Archive. http://classics.mit.edu/Aristotle/nicomachaen.1.i.html

Barnes, J.E. (2019, December 29). US launches airstrikes on Iranian-backed forces in Iraq and Syria. *The New York Times*. www.nytimes.com/2019/12/29/world/middleeast/us-airstrikes-iran-iraq-syria.html

Cucinelli, B. (2020). *My Idea of Humanistic Capitalism*. www.brunellocucinelli.com/en/humanistic-capitalism.html

Donaldson, T., & Dunfee, T.W. (1995). Integrative social contracts theory: A communitarian conception of economic ethics. *Economics & Philosophy*, *11*(1), 85–112. https://doi.org/10.1017/S0266267100003230

Freeman, R. (1984). *Strategic Management: A Stakeholder Approach*. Pitman.

Halpern, S. (2020, March 27). Can we track Boeing 737 MAX and protect privacy at the same time? *The New Yorker*. www.newyorker.com/tech/annals-of-technology/can-we-track-Boeing737Max-and-protect-privacy-at-the-same-time

Poitras, L. (2014, October 31). *Citizenfour* [Documentary; Film]. Artificial Eye Film Co. Ltd.

Readfearn, G. (2020, February 4). Indigenous envoy challenges Siemens in Germany over Adani mine. *The Guardian*. www.theguardian.com/environment/2020/feb/04/indigenous-envoy-challenges-siemens-in-germany-over-adani-mine

sunshinepress. (2010, April 3). *Collateral Murder—Wikileaks—Iraq*. www.youtube.com/watch?time_continue=1&v=5rXPrfnU3G0&feature=emb_logo

Taylor, A. (2005, November 18). *Zizek!* [Documentary; Film]. Hidden Driver Productions.

Velasquez, M. (2014). *Business Ethics Concepts and Cases* (7th ed.). Pearson Education Limited.

Wagner, C. (2019). *Managementethik und Arbeitsplätze: Eine metaphysische und moralökonomische Analyse*. Springer-Verlag.

Walzer, M. (2015). *Just and Unjust Wars: A Moral Argument with Historical Illustrations*. Basic Books.

Zimbardo, P.G. (2007). *The Lucifer Effect: Understanding How Good People Turn Evil*. Random House.

3 Normative ethical foundations of business ethics

The big five

Abstract

This chapter elucidates five major normative ethical theories for the business context: virtue ethics, deontological ethics or duty theory, consequentialist (teleological) ethics or utilitarianism, care ethics, and environmental ethics, which will be covered in further depth in Chapter 4. Virtue ethics aims to develop human character and well-being, based on Aristotle's eudaimonia theory in the Nicomachean Ethics. Immanuel Kant's deontological ethics renders our actions ethically correct if they can be formulated according to a universal moral law, called the categorical imperative. Utilitarianism, popularized by Jeremy Bentham and John Stuart Mill, measures morality by the amount of happiness or benefits delivered to the greatest number of people. Care ethics which takes care, compassion, and interpersonal relationships as foundational derived it's origins from feminism. Lastly, environmental ethics focuses on our responsibility towards the eco-environment and future communities (covered in Chapter 4). Two further important theories will be discussed that are not considered "standalone ethical theories": John Rawls's theory of justice, which aims at fairness by removing biases through a thought experiment of the "veil of ignorance" in the "original position", and Amartya Sen's account of the positive correlation between power and responsibility. The chapter includes case studies, e.g. the Harvey Weinstein Company scandal and the Facebook–Cambridge Analytica case.

Chapter keywords

(1) Virtue ethics
(2) Well-being
(3) Duty ethics, deontological ethics
(4) Categorical imperative
(5) Consequentialism
(6) Utilitarianism
(7) Greatest benefit for the greatest number

DOI: 10.4324/9781003127659-3

(8) Care ethics
(9) Veil of ignorance
(10) Justice, fairness
(11) Power and responsibility

Study objectives

After studying this chapter readers will be able to:

(1) Understand the major normative ethical theories.
(2) Apply ethical concepts in business contexts.
(3) Understand relevant normative ethical theories and their importance for application in the business context.

Case studies

3.1 The Harvey Weinstein case
3.2 The Ford Pinto case
3.3 The Facebook–Cambridge Analytica scandal

Ethical theories

(1) Well-being and virtue ethics
(2) Duty theory
(3) Utilitarianism
(4) Care ethics
(5) Environmental ethics (Chapter 4)
(6) Fairness and impartiality
(7) Power and responsibility

3.1 Normative ethical theories in a nutshell

Chapter 3 introduces five standalone normative and a few supporting non-mainstream/non-Western ethical theories (e.g. African Ubuntu ethics and the Japanese concept of Ikigai) and links them to business examples. The chapter meaningfully compresses complex philosophical ethical theory into business ethically relevant tangible and applicable tools. The major five standalone normative ethical theories illustrated are virtue ethics, deontological ethics or duty theory, consequentialist (teleological) ethics or utilitarianism, care ethics, and then environmental ethics in Chapter 4.

Virtue ethics is based on the assumption that we should develop good habits and a good character by cultivating our virtues. If we work hard on our virtue development not only are we becoming persons that experience well-being but we also help others as well to pursue the development of their

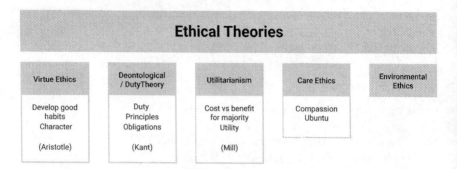

Figure 3.1 "Big five" normative ethical theories

character, virtues, and well-being. These theories and practices are based on the ancient Greek philosopher Aristotle's virtue ethics (Aristotle, 2018). The Italian designer and entrepreneur Brunello Cucinelli's business approach, "humanistic capitalism", can be interpreted in line with this tradition (Cucinelli, 2020). There are similar virtue ethical accounts in many other traditions, and therefore the understanding of what constitutes virtue and well-being has a culturally relative dimension that should not be omitted, but the Aristotelian account is the most prominent one, especially in the Western context. In contrast, the deontological theory is based on the idea that we need to come up with and follow duties, principles, obligations, and laws. If we do that, we can assume that the world will be a better place. But these duties, principles, obligations, and laws need to be developed on a rational foundation of what the German Enlightenment philosopher Immanuel Kant calls the categorical imperative (Kant, 1993), which stands for the endogenous (for the human intellect an inherent) moral point of view, and is a universal law. One could also view it as the most foundational hyper-norm one could think of. Many of the existing laws, which can be based on or which represent hyper-norms, can be seen in the light of the deontological tradition of thought. The British philosopher John Stuart Mill (Mill, 2017) further developed utilitarian ethics which was first made prominent by his teacher Jeremy Bentham (Bentham, 2009). Utilitarianism is a kind of cost-benefit analysis having the majority of people in mind and the maximization of their utility, usefulness, pleasure, and well-being. While utilitarianism is geared towards the maximization of utility and benefits for the greatest number of people or sentient beings (Mill, 2017), care ethics can be somewhat focused toward a selected group of people. Care ethics takes into consideration that we can especially take care of people who are in close or reachable proximity, or for whom we can make a monitorable difference. Brunello Cucinelli is also a care ethicist because he focuses on improving the life of a selected group of stakeholders for whom he can make a significant difference. Further theories discussed in this chapter are John Rawls's justice as fairness

(Rawls, 1999), which contrasts with care ethics due to its impartiality condition, and Amartya Sen's assumption that power positively implies responsibility (Sen, 2011). Environmental ethics expands the horizon of morality beyond mainly anthropocentric or human-centered perspectives. It is the ethical foundation for ecological economics and corporate environmental responsibility which will be dealt with in Chapter 4.

The classic Ford Pinto case (discussed further down) illustrates that especially a very economic interpretation of the maximization of utility is not always the best ethical choice (Lee, 1998), while a very strict interpretation of utilitarianism would encourage an Artificial Intelligence (AI) ruled governing body to get rid of, or at least paralyze, humanity as in the sci-fi classic "The Matrix" (Wachowski & Wachowski, 1999) in order to halt humanity's environmental destruction, because anthropogenic destruction could ultimately pose an existential threat for such an AI. Cases about Apple and Facebook, such as the Facebook–Cambridge Analytica scandal (Wong, 2019) make it evident that the largest existing corporations do not act responsibly enough in many ways. Applying Sen's normative demand that power should be in line with responsibility becomes even more crucial in the context of (quasi-)monopolistic power.

With many caveats and limitations, as indicated before, these ethical theories can be compared with a toolbox. To screw a Phillips screw into a wooden wall, we could use a normal screwdriver, or maybe even a hammer and just

Figure 3.2 Business ethical relevant theories

hammer the screw in, both methods somehow work. But the most fitting tool is the correct size Phillips screwdriver; no other tool solves the problem better. If we routinely apply ethical theories we will consider and choose a theory as we grab the appropriate tool for the job to be done. However, the application of ethical theories is more complex and more complicated, due to the many variables and complexities in real-life business situations.

3.2 Well-being, character, and virtues

3.2.1 Instrumental vs intrinsic value

An Ancient Greek theory that has experienced a significant revival during the past decades is the theory of well-being. The theory of well-being, or eudaimonistic ethical theory, is based on the assumption that we ultimately do everything to achieve well-being for ourselves, but also society. The underlying assumption is based on a teleological causality. The word teleological comes from the Greek notion "telos", meaning target or goal (www.etymonline.com). According to Aristotle, well-being or happiness is the most important and ultimate goal in human life (Aristotle, 2018). Everything we are doing in our life is subsumed under this overall target of a good life or should guide us to this overarching goal. Eating something, sleeping, learning, even studying business ethics, being ethical, procreation, everything ultimately should lead to well-being, if exercised correctly. Aristotle holds that it is obvious that well-being must be the ultimate goal of life because every person ultimately tries to achieve well-being. This kind of assumption of having an ultimate goal and having things that lead to it categorizes values in two different kinds of groups; namely values in-itself, intrinsic, or inherent values, and instrumental values. Intrinsically valuable are things that have values within themselves, without being an instrument for something else. Intrinsic value is contrasted with instrumental values, which are an instrument for attaining other things that are valuable in themselves, intrinsically, or inherently valuable.

To complement this concept, we have to add that there are also neutral values and negative values. Neutral values are those for which we have no positive or negative preference. An example of a neutral value might be the color of the taxi you are using on your way to the airport. You don't care if the taxi is red, orange, or yellow as long as it brings you to the airport safely and on time. Safety and punctuality, in contrast, are instrumentally important values. A broken taxi that leaves you stranded on the highway to the airport or a drunken taxi driver who doesn't find his way to the correct airport gate constitute negative values, especially if you miss your flight. However, things may change, and here we can see a certain relativity of the whole concept; for example, when the plane you intended to board crashes and the drunken taxi driver or the broken taxi prevented you from boarding this aircraft. Then, in this case, the drunken driver or broken taxi represent positive values for

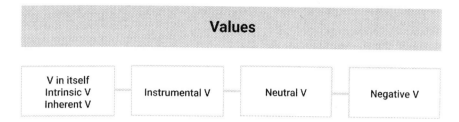

Figure 3.3 Instrumental vs intrinsic value

you, while the crashing plane represents a negative value. In this respect, it can be said that values are, so to speak, guard rails in our life for what is really important to us in order to be able to lead a good life; and what is ultimately important to us, such as justice, security, prosperity, integrity and the like, ultimately condenses from our own experience.

The important differentiation, for the Aristotelian theory discussed here, but also for the Kantian theory discussed below, lies between intrinsic, inherent values, or values in-itself on the one hand and instrumental values on the other. Because well-being represents an inherent value, while everything else that leads to well-being are instrumental values. In this regard education, nourishing food, good sleep, and good conversations that lead to well-being are all instrumental values that lead to the one intrinsic value: well-being in life. That is one of the most important aspects of Aristotle's theory of well-being or eudaimonia.

Before digging deeper into the details of Aristotelian virtue ethics we have to look more closely into the particular distinction between values in themselves and instrumental values. For example, we said that food is of instrumental value. The food on your plate, for example, meat, is instrumentally valuable for nourishing yourself (unless you are vegetarian or vegan), which, when consumed properly, should contribute to your well-being. However, the meat on the plate in front of you consists of flesh derived from an animal. If you are a meat-eater, the meat on your plate is of instrumental value for you. But if you are an owner of a pet and the meat derived from your slaughtered pet was served to you, even with very delicious sauces, you most likely will not appreciate the instrumental value that is represented by the meat gained from your pet, no matter how delicious the dish may taste. Why is that? Probably because our pet is more located in the direction of something that has intrinsic value or value in-itself or inherent value. This can be illustrated by a thought experiment, although an even less comforting one. Imagine you will be dying soon from a terminal disease and you have to decide the future of your pet; in this case you would still not eat it even with the most delicious sauce. You would rather give your pet to someone who you think would take good care of it. This idea that you would like to see your pet in good hands, even if you do not exist anymore, hints at the assumption that for yourself, at least, your pet may have something like a value in itself, which seems to be independent of your existence. Once the person who has adopted your pet behaves in the same way as you behaved in terms of valuation, the pet has intrinsic value for this person as well. However, if your pet is a nasty smelly dog who barks all night long and bites everyone who passes by your house, for most of those bitten or disturbed, your dog has negative value. While for those who drive past in cars, do not live close by and simply like cats, your dog may have neutral value. Animal rights activists and vegans will ascribe instrumental and maybe even intrinsic value to animals in general, at least to some particular ones, especially when it comes to endangered species which may disappear from the earth forever if not well cared for. From the perspective of wildlife management, the natural equilibrium in ecosystems has intrinsic value, not particular single components of nature. Animals or plants that overpopulate certain areas like possums in New Zealand, rats in cities, and camels in Australia thus become a threat to other species and thus a negative value from a wider (e.g. ecosystemic) perspective (cf. nt.gov.au/environment/animals/feral-animals/feral-camel). Eucalypt trees that are displacing indigenous pines in the mountains of Lesotho are considered of negative value for the ecosystem at large. The displaced plant or animal would have at least instrumental value for the eco-systemic balance, and if endangered, the species is getting closer to being intrinsically valuable.

Even though insurances actually ascribe a price tag to human life (instrumentally valuable), we normally assume that every human life has an infinite and unaccountable intrinsic value. However, it is a fact that different human lives have different monetary values, depending on the country, insurance, insurer's age, earning potential, and insurance policy. If a subject's or object's worth can be expressed in monetary value it could be argued that it cannot be "invaluable". However invaluable is not the same as intrinsically valuable, but the two concepts appear to be pretty close to each other. When Germans want to say that a person has a really bad character, not very much caring of

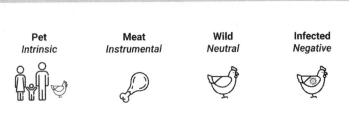

Figure 3.4 Value thought experiment

others, including his or her relatives, they say "she is such a bad person that she would even sell her grandmother", meaning that the grandmother only has instrumental (or even maybe negative) value for this person. Other candidates of examples for intrinsic value could be nature reserves, (precious or famous) artworks, memories, or dreams.

We can easily see with these examples that the act of ascribing values to, or valuation of, objects, beings, and other items or things, is something that seems to be relative, subjective, and not absolute. While for pious religious Hindus cows may be intrinsically valuable, for the average Western meat-eaters cows just have instrumental value. This means that ascribing instrumental or intrinsic value to something is highly debatable. Nevertheless, it makes sense to distinguish between things that are just useful for the help of achieving something and other things which we cherish so much that we wouldn't exchange them or sell them. Because we highly appreciate such things as they are in their current state or because a lot of things are needed for this situation, status, relation, or object that we cherish and appreciate so much. For example, we assume that for most people, health is considered intrinsically valuable, also because a happy life is closely associated with a healthy life. However, we have heard of persons who, for example in the Philippines, in very desperate situations sold an organ, e.g. a kidney or a liver, to make a living for their family (Yea, 2010). In this context, the particular sold organ just had instrumental value while the proper circumstances of living (well-being) for the family were valued as intrinsically valuable. Aristotle more than 2000 years ago also claimed that health contributes to well-being (Kraut, 2015). A longitudinal study over several decades by Harvard scholars (Diener, 2009) found out that there is one major factor that contributes to well-being which is even more important than health: friendships or significant relationships! The findings seem to be independent of gender, age, or generation (Diener, 2009).

3.2.2 Well-being, character, and virtues, a first approach

Other concepts are not quite synonymous with the concept of well-being but share a certain similarity, such as the concepts of happiness, the good life, flourishing, and the Ancient Greek notion of eudaimonia. Happiness is what is used in everyday language, but it is also a concept that is interdisciplinarily researched by economists, sociologists, psychologists, politicians, and so forth. One problem with the word "happiness" is its etymological relation to the word "happy" (www.etymonline.com). Being happy is considered to be a rather superficial state of mind that may not be long-lasting. However, Aristotle emphasizes in the *Nicomachean Ethics* that eudaimonia (translated often as "happiness") is in fact long-lasting, in contrast to pleasure, for example. Well-being is a broad concept that should not be confused with welfare, but the word well-being emphasizes that the existence or the life of a person or a group should be in good condition. But "good condition" is a rather vague statement. Nevertheless, the research on happiness has achieved significant recognition in the interdisciplinary World Happiness Report (Helliwell et al., 2020) or in the adoption of the concept by the Kingdom of Bhutan which measures gross national happiness (GNH) (Oxford Poverty & Human Development Initiative, 2020).

"Flourishing" is a word often employed by psychologists or from a pedagogical perspective (Lonka, 2013). This word emphasizes the aspect of development toward a certain possible optimum and this shows the etymological relation to flower (www.etymonline.com), which develops itself until it blooms. A better comparison would be an entire plant that grows and develops well, and for this development, conducive circumstances and environments are also needed – a theory especially emphasized by social psychology (Keyes, 2010).

More concretely, well-being nowadays is often empirically measured (Keyes et al., 2002). Measured dimensions, for example, can include safety and security, the quality and quantity of relationships, mental health, cognitive health, physical health, connectedness to a community, the purpose of life, freedom, and environmental quality. Safety and security can be measured with the help of crime rates, such as rates of break-ins or armed robbery per night in a city, road accidents, number of terrorist attacks within a year, and police response time in cases of emergencies. The quality of relationships can be measured by asking people how often they do meet friends and family members with whom they can have joyful, fruitful, and meaningful discussions, and trusted interactions. Mental health can be expressed by the fact persons can manage emotions constructively, including involving trusted others, if help is needed. The parameter of cognitive health includes intellectual health, education, how the environment corresponds to the need for fulfilling intellectual potentials, realizing creative growth potentials and development, the density of schools, museums, universities, e.g. per ten thousand citizens, and other cultural and educational facilities. Physical activity, as part of physical health, can be measured, for example, by asking participants how often they exercise per week and for how long. The density, quality, and area of parks in cities can be compared with the number of citizens. Community aspects are expressed in the sense of the feeling of belonging, for example.

One of the first studies researching happiness found that the happiest people were living in certain developing countries, for example Bangladesh (Mahmuda, 2003). But this research was biased because the study was mainly focused on asking participants regarding their subjective feeling of happiness which is usually quite high in cultures where people experience intensive social embeddedness in family contacts and the community. Due to a lack of financial resources and a lack of financial independence, family cohesion tends to be higher in such circumstances (Orthner et al., 2004). However, the interconnection between community members is something that is making a significant contribution to well-being; if this were not the case, and people did not gain a subjective sense of happiness from socializing with others

Normative ethical foundations 37

Figure 3.5 Indicators of well-being
Source: Redesigned from https://mch.umn.edu/resource-well-being-indicator-tool-for-youth-wit-y

frequently, in the Covid-19 crisis, people may not have complained so heavily about the lockdown measures by their governments. For a traditional African person, the concept of community plays the most significant role in all of these parameters (Auchter, 2017). Purpose has something to do with the meaning of life, orientation in life, future perspectives, and so forth. Nature or environment can be measured in environmental infrastructures such as water and air quality, the number of trees, green areas, gardens, and parks (e.g. within one square kilometer), and biodiversity in general. Freedom can be measured regarding press freedom, whistleblowing precautions by institutions, freedom of speech of citizens in general, and the freedom to express one's opinion in professional contexts.

Why is this important for business ethics? Because we can observe that companies that try to retain competent staff take the well-being of their workers seriously into account. At Google, now owned by Alphabet, initially workers were encouraged to spend 20% of their working time on personal ideas, developing innovative technology which could be beneficial for the company. Gmail and other Alphabet products were developed in such a context. This approach also contributes to a person's purpose, self-fulfillment, and well-being. Brunello Cucinelli gives his workers ample time for lunch (90 minutes) so that they can socialize, which contributes to their well-being in psychological, communal, and social terms. Cucinelli, Starbucks, and many other companies allow workers to further their education, which is a feature intended to foster cognitive well-being. Several companies nowadays design environmentally friendly and safe workplaces, such as Patagonia and Freitag.

Especially for the Western context, these empirically measurable dimensions of quality of life like healthcare, environment, education, freedom, and many others are important parameters for well-being. From an economic point of view, high income, high revenue, high GDP play important roles. In the Covid-19 crisis, we could observe discussions among virologists, epidemiologists, economists, and politicians regarding the tradeoff between human health and the sustainability of a country's economy. Focusing too much on virological and epidemiological related health issues, by social distancing and other measures such as lockdowns, has negative impacts on other psychological and social health parameters, and if the economy suffers, people lose their jobs and the tax shortfalls mean that urgent investments can no longer be made or can only be made decades later. In contrast, focusing too much on restarting the economy lets the virus spread faster. We can easily see, with this current example, that there are tradeoffs between different kinds and interpretations of well-being.

In the Southeast Asian context, well-being dimensions such as harmony and peace of mind play a particularly important role. In business meetings in some Asian contexts, agreements should reach a consensus, as a harmony ideal. In an African traditional context, communal and social embeddedness are crucial for social and personal well-being, while the individual only counts as part of the community.

We can summarize that the understanding of what constitutes well-being is multifaceted, diverse, and relative, depending on the historical context, current circumstances, and the respective culture. The concept of well-being employs diverse and various yet highly significant values. Due to the fact we have not solved the question of what constitutes well-being conclusively we have to highlight one particular approach that has dominated the ethical discussion since the Ancient Greeks. The Aristotelian account of eudaimonia (well-being or happiness) is still dominating the current ethical discourse on well-being and happiness.

In the business context the question is who is entitled to well-being, since providing well-being for particular stakeholders requires financial, human, and other resources. Therefore, we can see that the determinants of who is entitled to well-being also depend on the context. A liberal context will emphasize the individuals' entitlement to well-being, often based on merits. A rather collective, communitarian cultural context emphasizes families' or communities' entitlement to well-being. From the nation-states' perspective, the well-being of the society or the country is pertinent. And one should not misunderstand the Fridays for Future (FFF) movement's call for more environmental responsibility (see Chapter 4) as an eco-centric demand (centered only on the ecosystem). Because FFF's aim is to take humanity's well-being, especially future humanity's well-being, more seriously, besides the demand that the well-being of plants, animals, and the entire planet, and "the science behind it", needs to be considered more seriously. But of course, the dimension of "future" in Fridays for Future points in the direction of future generations' well-being.

Going back to the business perspective, what is at stake is the well-being of the company at large and in particular the well-being of stakeholders. If a company does not take the well-being of particular stakeholders into account it may get into serious trouble, even if the company may not have considered a certain group of persons or entities as stakeholders. The Boeing 737 MAX crashes point to the fact that the well-being of airline personnel and passengers was not taken seriously enough. Otherwise, safety and security would have been the main priority, not only for the sake of not risking the reputation of the company. But the economic dimensions, focused on TSR (rather than TSI), and research and development advances by competitor Airbus increased the pressure for a quickly sellable technologically overhauled bestselling 737, instead of designing and developing a new aircraft from scratch which would have taken several years plus completely new training programs for pilots.

3.2.3 An Aristotelian perspective on well-being, character, and virtues

Ethical theories and accounts of well-being and happiness try to tackle the questions of what constitutes well-being. This approach points to a collection or set of values, and the question regarding who is entitled to well-being. The Ancient Greek philosopher Aristotle, who lived in the 4th century BCE, focused his account of ethics on this phenomenon of eudaimonia, happiness, or well-being in one of his most important books, the *Nicomachean Ethics*. In a synthetic account on eudaimonia, Aristotle summarized, computed, and fused what had been considered significant for well-being by previous thinkers. A few ideas and concepts that Aristotle synthesized follow in the next paragraph, because many of these concepts represent values that are relevant in the business context.

Pythagoras, whom we know from mathematics lessons on the Pythagorean Theorem ($a^2 + b^2 = c^2$), considered knowledge and harmony as essential for well-being. That is not surprising because for Pythagoras, with the help of knowledge we can scientifically appreciate that everything, our whole life, the entire Cosmos, is based on harmony (Kepler, 1997). Harmonies can be detected in microstructures, such as atoms and cells, but also in music, e.g. as rhythms and chords, in mathematics, in nature, in terms of natural seasons, moon phases, high and low tides, hormonal cycles, but also in the macrostructure of the cosmos, such as the constellations and circulation of planets, and anywhere else. The understanding that harmony is essential for human life and underlies any observable phenomenon is something that can be extracted from the observation and understanding of the environment. Heraclitus made people aware that they need to accept and accommodate constant change (Diels & Kranz, 1903). This is a fact that is probably even more pertinent today than it was during Heraclitus' time. The Covid-19 pandemic and potential disruptive technologies are very obvious examples that businesses and citizens need to be prepared for constant change. Socrates, the teacher of Plato, but also Plato himself, emphasized the importance of wisdom, virtues, and an ideal state, meaning an ideal environment in which one has to actively participate to shape it into an ideal (Plato, 1997). The cynics, similar to Buddhist monks, emphasized that material things are of minor importance and practiced asceticism, at the same time emphasizing knowledge and virtue (Diels & Kranz, 1903). More or less of the opposite opinion regarding pleasure were the hedonists, who's founder Aristippos thought that we should focus on long-term, but not short-term, pleasures (Diels & Kranz, 1903). Zenon the founder of the stoics emphasized virtue and also political commitment (Diels & Kranz, 1903). His often misunderstood contemporary Epicure emphasized well-being, concentrating on pleasure, which he simply defines as the absence of pain or the attempt to work toward the minimization of pain (Diels & Kranz, 1903). Further down in this chapter, when dealing with utilitarianism, we have to come back to the Epicurean ethical theory because the Epicurean pleasure and pain account is an important foundation of utilitarian ethics. The Skeptics, like their founder Pyrrhon, emphasized peace of mind by the insight into the indifference of things in life (Diels & Kranz, 1903).

While one could claim that this is more a subject for an introductory philosophy or ethics class, one needs to acknowledge that all of the values communicated within these above-mentioned accounts are relevant within normative ethical theories applied to business contexts. We will now, and further down, cover issues such as knowledge and critical thinking, the ability to accommodate constant change, wisdom or making use of our intellectual faculties, virtues, creating and maintaining well-being, conducive environments, the dimension of pleasure, commitment, the well-being of stakeholders, the minimization of pain, or taking the harm principle seriously into account. These all are values that play a pertinent role in the business context.

For Aristotle eudaimonia or well-being is of intrinsic value, because it is the goal of all human affairs. It is long-lasting and continuous, not just short-term happiness, or pleasure, which is just a by-product of eudaimonia. But most importantly, eudaimonia or well-being is an activity of the soul and this needs more thorough and further explanation. For Aristotle, in the *Nicomachean Ethics*, there exist two kinds of eudaimonia. A primary form, which only a certain elite can achieve, and a secondary form that is achievable by everyone. The secondary form of eudaimonia can be achieved by exercising ethical virtues, which is potentially possible for everyone. The primary form of eudaimonia or exclusive form of eudaimonia is an activity under the virtue of the most divine element of the human soul, which is wisdom. Living a life in contemplation seems to be the most ideal life according to Aristotle's understanding of well-being. But not many people have this opportunity to live a life of contemplation; maybe monks, researchers, certain teachers, artists, some politicians, or entrepreneurs. But ordinary people will not have the means to live a life mostly dedicated to contemplation. Aristotle is well aware of this. However, everyone can live a life of well-being and eudaimonia as long as one can exercise the ethical virtues properly. On top of this, if one is in a position to increase the proportion of the contemplative aspects in one's life significantly, one can reach this higher form of eudaimonia. Nevertheless, a reasonable amount of external goods is essential for both forms of eudaimonia or well-being (Aristotle, 2018).

According to Aristotle, there are two categories of virtues, ethical (or character) virtues, and intellectual (or dianoetic) virtues (the Greek word *dianoia* means intellect or reason). The concept of virtue can also be translated as goodness or excellence. Ethical goodness and intellectual excellence are of outstanding importance for the fulfillment of the good life.

Aristotle does not see ethical virtues as ends in themselves; virtues are rather meaningful for character development and leading a good life. Aristotle has a comprehensive system of ethical virtues, although nowadays (after around 2500 years) it is by no means so clear which virtues are really useful and transferable to the present day. In any case, there is no clear ranking of ethical virtues. More important and helpful, however, is the idea that ethical

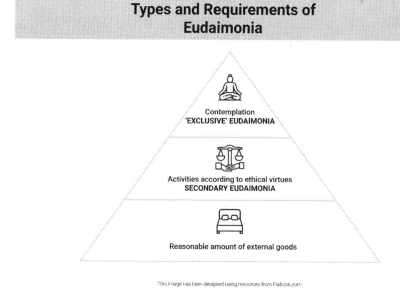

Figure 3.6 Types of eudaimonia

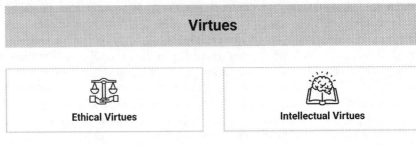

Figure 3.7 Ethical vs intellectual virtues

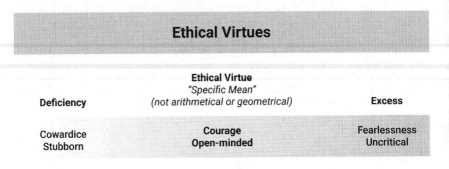

Figure 3.8 Ethical virtues

virtues are always an ideal mean, or a middle way, between the two extremes: excess and deficiency. This middle way or mean is a specific mean depending on the particular person and circumstances. It is not an arithmetic or geometric mean that could easily be calculated. An example is the ethical virtue of courage. An excess of courage would be fearlessness and its deficiency would be cowardice. Another ethical virtue is open-mindedness. An excess of this character trait is represented in an uncritical person, a deficiency of open-mindedness can be observed in a stubborn person. In the same way, the virtue of generosity can be viewed as the well-balanced middle way between avarice and wasteful behavior. All ethical virtues function according to this specific mean (Aristotle, 2018).

A simple example of how this specific mean depends on a particular person and circumstances can be displayed in the following thought experiment. Imagine that a person is drowning in a river with a rapidly flowing torrent. You happen to walk by on your way home from work, and you want to rescue the person. If you are a good swimmer, enjoying good health, you would be a coward if you did not jump in and rescue the person. But if you can't even swim, it would be fearless and stupid to jump into the river in this situation. In such given circumstances it would be better to find other means to rescue the person, for example by finding someone who can swim very well, or quickly getting a rope or a long stick for the drowning person to grab. This move would be prudent.

While in the case of ethical virtues this ideal or golden mean represents the correct and appropriate measure, the idea of maximization is at the center of intellectual or dianoetic virtues; more specifically, this means that the more a person possesses a particular virtue (such as cleverness, or certain economic, technical, medical, or intellectual skills and the like), the better. For example, think of a scientist or engineer who ultimately can never know enough about his or her scientific field. This also makes it clear that virtues are not a quality that people have from birth, but must first be acquired through concrete practice and experience. The more frequently a doctor has performed a certain surgical procedure, the more confidently they can act in unexpected and emergency situations. The same applies to ethical virtues: in order to be able to act virtuously, in order to be able to differentiate between excess and deficiency in certain actions, people must have gained a certain experience in life, which means nothing other than that they must have accumulated a certain virtue capital.

Even if one is not leading a contemplative life, nevertheless, the intellectual virtues, wisdom and prudence, guide a person to find a specific mean between excess and deficiency in the domain of the ethical virtues, like in the example of the drowning person. Everyone is in a position to practice prudence and wisdom, but not everyone is in a position to mainly concentrate on exercising prudence and wisdom most of the time. Such circumstances are rather constituent of an exclusive form of eudaimonia. One can imagine a person working in an ordinary job every day, such as a cashier or salesperson in a supermarket; such a person needs to be in a position to find a middle way between excess and deficiency in the domain of ethical virtues. However, they will usually not have the chance to exercise intellectual virtues such as prudence and wisdom in the same way as a monk who lives a life of contemplation and meditation, a musician who dedicated their life to music practice and performance, or an entrepreneur-engineer who is living for their inventions, or a diplomat whose prudence is challenged day-by-day in tricky political dilemmas, or a researcher who dedicated their life to the research of some very particular issue that may have a significant impact on humanity, like genetic engineering or just "blue sky research", that is the research which we do not yet know if it will have applicable dimensions or not, but which needs to be researched to test possible avenues of discovery. Examples would be deep sea or deep space exploration.

The idea of a hierarchical organization of essential things in life is also reflected in the Maslowian hierarchy of needs. While the physical needs are at the bottom of this pyramid, self-fulfillment is at the top (Maslow, 1943). Being in a position to live a highly self-fulfilled life comes relatively close to a life where contemplation and the intensive use of intellectual virtues are predominant. Another distinction that lets us better understand the relevance

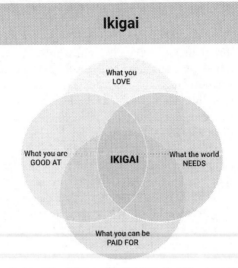

Figure 3.9 Ikigai
Source: Redesigned from twitter.com/ikigaibook

of the Aristotelian ethics of well-being in the business context is a distinction between job, career, and calling. While a job is work that is done on a day-to-day basis to earn a living that may or may not be sufficiently, that may or may not be rewarding in terms of self-fulfillment, a career, by contrast, is related to the person's progressing role and their self-development. A career may be intellectually more rewarding and challenging, but may not be fulfilling. The two forms of work are contrasted with what can be labeled a "calling" where one has a strong identification with the role one is fulfilling. This kind of occupation may or may not be rewarded or paid sufficiently, but is usually considered to be very self-fulfilling. Many artists, entrepreneurs, researchers, teachers, religious persons, etc. experience their professional life as a form of calling. Businesses can contribute to the people working for them having an increased sense of self-fulfillment.

A Western interpretation of the Japanese concept of Ikigai holds that we should do what we love, what the world needs, what we can be paid for, and what we are good at; trying to involve all four concepts at the same time will increase the likelihood of a happy life (García & Miralles, 2016; cf. Mogi, 2017).

Ethical toolbox 3.1: Aristotelian virtue ethics applied to stakeholders

Well-being, sometimes referred to as "happiness", is of significant importance for states and individuals but also corporations that try to attract a highly skilled and reliable workforce. Well-being is of the highest importance for all stakeholders of a corporation. The idea that well-being is of utmost importance for individuals and society at large can be traced back to Greek antiquity. The Greek philosopher Aristotle (384–322 BC), the most important philosopher of Western antiquity, besides Plato, wrote in his *Nikomachean Ethics*:

> of all the good things to be done, what is the highest? Most people … call it happiness [well-being], understanding being happy as equivalent to living well and acting well…[But] the masses think it is something straightforward and obvious, like pleasure, wealth, or honour … The masses, the coarsest people, see it as pleasure, and so they like the life of enjoyment… The masses appear quite slavish by rationally choosing a life only for cattle. [Note the animal-human comparison] … Wealth is clearly not the good we are seeking, since it is merely useful, for getting something else [instrumentally valuable]. (Aristotle, 2018)

Aristotle is criticizing that the masses of the people are simply seeking pleasure, gratification, and wealth. However, he thinks that the intelligent human person cannot be compared with an animal. Humans' nature, capacities, and talents are aiming at a higher goal.

> Things should be called good in two senses: things good in themselves, and things good for the sake of things good in themselves. So let us distinguish things good in themselves [intrinsic value] from those that are means to them [instrumental value]. Happiness [well-being, flourishing] in particular is believed to be complete without qualification, since we always choose it for itself and never for the sake of anything else. Honour, pleasure, intellect, and every virtue … we choose them also for the sake of happiness, on the assumption that through them we shall live a life of happiness; whereas happiness no one chooses for the sake of any of these nor indeed for the sake of anything else… Well-being, then, is obviously something complete and self-sufficient, in that it is the end [goal] of what is done.
>
> Living is obviously shared even by plants, while what we are looking for is something special to a human being. We should therefore rule out the life of nourishment and growth. Next would be some sort of sentient life, but this again is clearly shared by the horse, the ox, indeed by every animal. What remains is a life, concerned in some way with action, of the element that possesses reason. … As this kind of life can be spoken of in two ways, let us assume that we are talking about the life concerned with action in the sense of activity, because this seems to be the more proper use

> of the phrase. ... The characteristic activity of a human being is an activity of the soul in accordance with reason. (Aristotle, 2018)
>
> To utilize human intellectual capacity (a specific human virtue) is – according to Aristotle – essential for self-fulfillment and a happy life (Aristotle, 2018).

3.2.4 Guidelines for good conduct in business and elsewhere: Virtues

Corporations are interested in certain skills and virtues of their workforce. Certain Volkswagen engineers, responsible for the "Emission Possible" or "Dieselgate" scandal, although highly skilled in engineering, cannot be considered as virtuous in an ethical sense since these engineers developed software that gave the impression of a clean car while the cars were, in fact, contaminating the air. Not only did Volkswagen get into serious trouble, but so did the entire diesel engine industry and even the car industry at large, especially in Germany. Thus, virtues, intellectual as well as ethical, are equally important in business. In any case, a lack of virtues can lead to the collapse of entire companies and industries in international competition. Aristotle wrote the following about virtue.

> Some virtues ... are intellectual, such as wisdom, judgement, and practical wisdom, while others are virtues of character, such as generosity and temperance... Virtue, then, is of two kinds: that of the intellect and that of character. Intellectual virtue owes its origin and development mainly to teaching, for which reason its attainment requires experience and time; the virtue of character (ethos) is a result of habituation (ethos), for which reason it has acquired its name through a small variation on 'ethos'... [Character is] corrupted by deficiency and excess, as we see in the cases of strength and health; for both too much exercise and too little ruin one's strength, and likewise too much food and drink and too little ruin one's health, while the right amount produces, increases and preserves health. The same goes, then, for temperance, courage and the other virtues: the person who avoids and fears everything, never standing his ground, becomes cowardly, while he who fears nothing but confronts every danger, becomes rash. In the same way, the person who enjoys every pleasure and never restrains himself becomes intemperate, while he who avoids all pleasure – as boors do – becomes, as it were, insensible. Temperance and courage, then, are ruined by excess and deficiency, and preserved by the mean... In this way every knowledgeable person avoids excess and deficiency, and aims for the mean and chooses it; the mean... is ...relative to us... I am talking here about the virtue of character, since it is this that is concerned with feelings and actions, and it is in these that

we find excess, deficiency, and the mean… Virtue, then, is a state involving rational choice, consisting in a mean relative to us and determined by reason; the reason, that is, by reference to which the practically wise person would determine it. It is a mean between two vices, one of excess, the other of deficiency. (Aristotle, 2018).

> **Study questions 3.1**
>
> (1) According to Aristotle: What is the highest good in life and how do we achieve it? Do you agree? Why (not)?
> (2) How can business activities contribute to the good life/well-being?
> (3) What is virtue according to Aristotle? Explain in detail.
> (4) How can virtue be relevant in the business context?
> (5) What are the virtues of an entrepreneur, businessperson, and "custodian" like Cucinelli?
> (6) Research some up-to-date material on happiness and well-being.

3.3 Duty and critical thinking

3.3.1 Immanuel Kant's deontological ethics and "sapere aude"

The German 18th-century philosopher Immanuel Kant criticized eudaimonistic theory. According to Kant's interpretation "eudaimonism" meant pleasure-seeking (Kant, 1993). An ethical good life, according to Kant, cannot be guided by pleasure but must be guided by duties. Comparing this criticism with what is going on in the business context we can also recognize that business activities are usually more guided by duties, obligations, and contracts than by pleasure. The philosophical notion of deontology, meaning "ethical theory according to duty", comes from the Greek word *deon*, which means duty.

An entirely neglected feature of Kantian thought in business ethics discourse, somewhat contrasting with his duty ethics, is the insight that we always should utilize our capacity for critical thinking. We should thoroughly question existing procedures, methods, rules obligations, and laws. This is especially pertinent in a time in which fake news and deep fakes are part of our everyday online life.

A very interesting parallel needs to be pointed out here between the Aristotelian ethical theory and Kantian thought. We can combine these two mentioned components of Kantian thought, which are usually not brought together since the critical thinking, "dare to know", "sapere aude", dimension of Kantian thought does not feature very prominently when introducing Kantian ethics in business ethical contexts. But we can see that both Aristotle and Kant consider the combination of an ethical component with an intellectual reflective critical component as something essential in and a constituent

48 Normative ethical foundations

of human life. This is a striking, highly interesting, and pertinent parallel between Kantian and Aristotelian thought. In both theories, ethics is informed by rationality.

3.3.2 The hypothetical and categorical imperative

Kant's well known categorical imperative is a specification of the Golden Rule, which is one of the most prominent ethical rules. Variations of this Golden Rule or similar concepts can be found in many cultures and religions. Positively formulated it states that "we should do unto others as we would have them do unto us" (Mieder, 2001). Or to put it negatively: what you don't want someone to do to you, don't do to anyone else. The Golden Rule can be interpreted in two different ways: on the one hand as a strategic rule of prudence that expresses an economic point of view; on the other hand as an ethical rule that stands for a moral point of view in its purest form. In the first case we are dealing with the hypothetical imperative, in the second with the categorical imperative. Kant therefore assumes that man is a citizen of two worlds. The hypothetical imperative represents the world of wise advice, whereby it can be assumed that all people strive for their personal well-being and happiness. If individuals have a specific goal (e.g. the goal of pursuing a professional career or living healthy), then it is rational and a command of practical reason to behave in a certain way (e.g. by continually educating themselves, observing a healthy diet, doing regular sporting activities or the like). Hypothetical imperatives therefore always have an "if-then" structure, which is why Kant called it "hypothetical".

It should now be noted that most individuals not only pursue their own interests, which is quite legitimate, but also have moral interests and thus the willingness to put themselves into the shoes of others. As soon as one no longer only has one's own interests in mind, but also the interests of others, one has adopted the moral point of view according to Kant, which he calls the categorical imperative and which reads as follows: "Act only according to that maxim [rule] whereby you can, at the same time, will that this rule should become a universal law" (Kant, 1993). "Will" in this sentence means effort with all possible measures. In contrast to the hypothetical imperative, which is dependent on many conditions, the categorical imperative always applies categorically. "Imperative" is a rule that we must (!) follow; it is also categorical as a universally valid rule without any conditions or exceptions (no "ifs" or "buts"). In German the sentence reads:

> Handle nur nach derjenigen Maxime durch die du zugleich wollen kannst, dass sie ein allgemeines Gesetz werde. (Kant, 1993)

This means that we should act always in that manner that what we are doing could become a generally or universally acceptable and approvable law. Otherwise, if the action were not universalizable, then it would fail the moral test of the categorical imperative. "Cooking the books", speeding on a highway, crossing the traffic light during the red phase, cheating in exams, these are all things we would not accept as universal laws. The concept of universal law is the highest order norm, very closely related to a higher order norm, such as the concept of hyper-norm, but the categorical imperative is, so to speak, the mother of all ethical hyper-norms. We can easily see that many of the laws that have existed for long periods have probably been created with something like a categorical imperative consideration in mind. One of the problems with this demand for thinking whether our actions could be acceptable as universal laws are the time constraints. We do not always have sufficient time in every situation to think through this categorical imperative in detail with all its implications and ramifications. Likewise, realistically, we will never succeed one hundred percent in always taking into account the interests of all other actors impartially. However, if the Volkswagen managers and engineers had followed the categorical imperative and if they had been guided more strongly by moral interests, they would very likely have kept Volkswagen out of serious trouble.

3.3.3 The practical imperative and human resources

The distinction between intrinsic and instrumental values that we discussed above is also reflected in Immanuel Kant's so-called *practical imperative*, which reads: "act in such a way that you treat humanity, whether in your own person or in that of any other [person], never only as a means to an end, but always at the same time as an end [in itself]" (Kant, 1993). If we only treat people as a means to an end, but not as a means in themselves, then we use these people simply as instruments. When companies are accused of not taking the human dimension of people working for them seriously into account then it is feared that these companies only use workers as a means to an end. Press reports claimed that between 2010 and 2016 several Foxconn employees were so desperate with their exhausting working conditions and cramped unsanitary living conditions in factory-run dorms that some of them committed suicide by jumping from the roof of a Foxconn building. It could be argued that, at least from those worker's perspective, these employees were only used as a means to an end, as an instrument, as a (human) resource (Barboza, 2010). In 2018 undercover journalists claimed that some Amazon warehouse workers were wearing diapers or urinating in bottles during peak hours in high shipping seasons in order to save time in high-demand working environments (Ghosh, 2018). It can be claimed that such working environments neglect the human dimension of human resources.

When Brunello Cucinelli emphasizes his understanding of conducting business as humanistic capitalism he wants to make clear that he is not treating stakeholders, especially not his workers, as a means to an end, but that he recognizes the humanity in humans, and the human resources dimension of his business. From the above-mentioned Foxconn worker's perspective, the workers were just used as resources, and thus only as a means to an end to increase TSR. In light of these positive and negative examples, we have to descriptively acknowledge the difference between intrinsically valuable "*human* resources" and "human *resources*", which are only seen as instrumental value.

In a chapter on objectification in her seminal book on *Sex and Social Justice*, Martha Nussbaum, an American philosopher, emphasizes that it is not a problem if we treat people as a means to an end, meaning when we objectify people, as long as we see the humanity behind or in the human person. To objectify persons is acceptable as long as we do not only treat people as a means to an end, meaning not only treating people as instrumentally valuable, but intrinsically valuable at the same time. She gives a straightforward example in an essay on objectification in *Sex and Social Justice* (Nussbaum, 1999). She mentions that she may use her lover as a pillow or backrest to lean on when she sits in bed reading a book. But at the same time, she is aware that what she uses as a pillow or as a backrest is a human person, for her a very important person, that she loves. The interesting aspect is that it seems to be ethically acceptable to her to use people as a means to an end if we appreciate the person as an end in itself at the same time! And this is exactly what the practical imperative states, namely that we should treat humans always at the same time as an end in themselves and never only as a means to an end. The application to the business context is obvious: when people work for us, we inevitably use them as a means to our own ends, since we have an interest in making money with their help. At the same time, however, we have to see these persons not only as instruments, of instrumental value, but also as valuable in themselves. In terms of the human resources, we need to appreciate and not forget about the *human* dimension of this specific resource. The Tycoon Music company in its catalogue of percussion instruments features on each introductory page for a specific type of percussion instrument a well-known musician (Tycoon, n.d.). Juxtaposed on the same page, the workers who craft this type of instrument are shown as well. In this context the workers, the human (re)source (efficient cause) of the instrument, are given the same dignity as the receiver who is playing the instrument (the final cause), the artist.

Case study 3.1: The Harvey Weinstein case

Research the Harvey Weinstein case, which sparked the "#MeToo" movement. The case illustrates how the instrumentalization of women, and actors in general, is an industry systemic problem that grew in a context which globally promotes freedom of speech, democracy, and human rights. The Harvey Weinstein scandal is not a singular case but stands for the systemic instrumentalization of women in certain industries, such as the film industry.

(1) Have you heard of similar cases in your own cultural or professional context? Share and discuss your findings with others.
(2) Depending on culture and legal frameworks, what are differences regarding "consent" for consensual sex in different cultures?
(3) What can be done from different stakeholders' perspectives to deal with and prevent such cases?

3.3.4 Ignorance is not bliss: "Dare to know!"

Ignorance is not bliss! In a small essay entitled *An Answer to the Question: "What is Enlightenment?"* (Kant, 1784), Immanuel Kant tries to figure out what enlightenment means in Germany during his time. The period in European cultural history from the 17th to 19th century, the Enlightenment is the age in which it was thought that rationality, reason, and science should govern all human affairs (Kant, 1784). Enlightenment in this historical scientific context is not related to the Buddhist understanding of enlightenment, although both forms of enlightenment imply spiritual, intellectual, and rational advancement, and a comparison between the two would be a highly desirable research topic. Kant's essay is not only interesting for the particular German age of Enlightenment context, but also for one specific dimension in general, which is the claim that we should dare to make use of our intellectual capacity. The Enlightenment creed, according to Immanuel Kant, is "Sapere aude! Have the courage to make use of your own intellect". The Latin phrase, *sapere aude*, originating in the Roman poet Horace's First Book of Letters (Holt & Hond, 2013), means "dare to know", dare to be wise, dare to "think for yourself", which also connotes "dare to question", "dare to challenge", "dare to ask", "dare to discuss", and "dare to initiate changes". This is highly important in today's business world. For example, in the context of fake news, sometimes insufficient legislation on social media content, unethical regulations, and whistleblowing. Even if there exist habits, procedures, and rules in business contexts set up by authorities, we still need to think and reason on our own.

Ethical toolbox 3.2: "Sapere aude!", whistleblowing and rule-based ethics

Whistleblowing is an example of where certain individuals act against rules and regulations by leaking information that needs to be disclosed to inform the public about ethical wrongdoing. This may happen in corporations or other organizations. Edward Snowden is an example of a famous whistleblower. He leaked confidential information about the US NSA's data-collecting activity (Poitras, 2014). Practically any internet-connected person around the world can be spied on. Snowden was doing what the German 18th-century philosopher Immanuel Kant had in mind when writing about "sapere aude!" and "enlightenment" ("Aufklärung"): enlightenment is:

> the human being's emancipation from its self-incurred immaturity; Immaturity is the inability to make use of one's intellect without the direction of another [person]. This immaturity is self-incurred when its cause does not lie in a lack of intellect, but rather in a lack of resolve and courage to make use of one's intellect without the direction of another. ...
> "Sapere aude! Have the courage to make use of your own intellect!" is hence the motto of enlightenment. Laziness and cowardice are the reasons why such a large segment of humankind remains immature for life; and these are also the reasons why it is so easy for others to set themselves up as their guardians. It is so comfortable to be immature... The guardians who have kindly assumed supervisory responsibility have ensured that the largest part of humanity ... understands progress toward maturity to be... dangerous... It is thus difficult for any individual to work himself out of the immaturity that has almost become second nature to him. He has even become fond of it and is, for the time being, truly unable to make use of his own reason, because he has never been allowed to try it. Rules and formulas ... are the shackles of a perpetual state of immaturity. (Kant, 1784)

Study questions 3.2

(1) There are many laws and rules that guide our everyday life. Why is it still important to make use of one's intellect?
   a. As a consumer
   b. As a decision-maker in a business situation
(2) Can you think of examples of how the Golden Rule (or the categorical imperative) applies in your everyday life in general or in a business context in particular?
(3) Research some up-to-date material on:
   a. Deontology and business ethics
   b. The categorical imperative and codes of ethics and codes of conduct
   c. The practical imperative and objectification of women and children in the business context
   d. Whistleblowing and "sapere aude"

3.4 Utilitarianism

3.4.1 Epicurean roots

The ancient Greek philosopher Epicure was strongly influenced by both hedonism and cynic asceticism. The ascetic cynics did not value possessions and were focused on the moment in time. Contemporaries claimed that a student of the school's founder Antisthenes, Diogenes of Sinope, lived in a discarded wine barrel, dressed in a piece of cloth and infamously urinated and relieved himself of other bodily urges everywhere in public, because he neither cared about possessions nor what others thought about him (Diels & Kranz, 1903). Ancient Greek ascetics, similar to Jain and Buddhist nuns and monks, minimized possessions as much as possible to concentrate on more important spiritual and intellectual values. In contrast, the hedonists claimed that whatever increases our long-term pleasure is beneficial for the further development of our well-being. Both hedonists and ascetics had convincing arguments, and Epicure could be seen as synthesizing asceticism and hedonism in his account on eudaimonism (Diels & Kranz, 1903). He held that happiness is achieved through pleasure, as the hedonists claimed, but Epicure defined pleasure simply as the absence or minimization of pain (Diels & Kranz, 1903). Thus, Epicure synthesized eudaimonistic, hedonic, and ascetic accounts of ethics into a consistent theory. We should enjoy the small things that we can easily access and develop, like significant friendships, health, education, meaningful conversations, simple and healthy food, which inevitably leads to happiness or eudaimonia for ourselves and those who live a similar lifestyle. Maybe the Covid-19 crisis in 2020 and 2021 reminded some people to appreciate the little and essential things they had when they stayed at home with their loved ones or with friends during lockdowns, even if they had little at their disposal.

3.4.2 Utilitarianism

Utilitarianism recognizes itself in the Epicurean eudaimonistic ethical tradition, especially regarding the important values of pleasure and pain which determine a happy or unhappy life (Mill, 2017). In contrast to the Kantian theory of ethics discussed above, utilitarianism does not focus on the motives of the persons or the actions themselves in the course of ethical assessment, but exclusively on the consequences and results of certain actions or rules. For this reason, in utilitarianism, unlike in non-utilitarian ethical theories, there are no actions that are categorically prohibited. In this respect, utilitarianism represents an ethical theory that is relatively close to economic reasoning, although it must not be equated with an economic theory. According to the British philosopher Jeremy Bentham, who is also considered the founder of utilitarianism, happiness is constituted as an experience of pleasure and a lack of pain. For Bentham, the fundamental axiom of utilitarianism is "the greatest happiness of the greatest number [of people] that is the measure of right and wrong" (Bentham, 2009). In other words, the solution that produces the highest average utility for all actors is morally correct. Bentham was also one of the first to consider the ethical treatment of animals (Bentham, 2009). Bentham's student, John Stuart Mill, was the one who promoted and popularized utilitarianism. Utilitarianism is derived from the Latin word *utilitas* which means usefulness (www.etymonline.com). According to John Stuart Mill, the good life is constituted by the greatest benefit for the greatest number of people. And this can be achieved by following the rule of utility (Mill, 2017). But this means that good and ethical is what is useful, a doctrine which Aristotle had denied when he stated that "to consider everything in terms of usefulness is least appropriate for great souls or free spirits" (Aristotle, 2018).' According to John Stuart Mill, the greatest happiness principle is an existence as far as possible from pain and as rich as possible in enjoyment, both – and this is important – in terms of quantity and quality (Mill, 2017). Here is a significant difference between Bentham's account of utilitarianism and Mill's form of utilitarianism. While Bentham only propagates the increase of the quantity of pleasure as significant for happiness, John Stuart Mill states that both quantity and quality of pleasure are important for the promotion of happiness. This means that, in contrast to Bentham, Mill makes differences between different types of utility, between culturally higher, integral forms of utility on the one hand and simpler, more primitive forms of utility on the other, whereas for Bentham the only thing that matters is how much overall utility results from an action.

Importantly, we have to note, that this happiness or utility is not the happiness of a single individual and especially not one's own happiness (in that regard utilitarianism could be interpreted as altruistic) but the happiness of the greatest number of people and, if the circumstances allow, the greatest well-being of all sentient beings. This standard of morality was novel during John Stuart Mill's time because if taken very seriously, this account takes all sentient beings into consideration, thus utilitarianism is less human-centric than previous ethical theories. In this context, it must also be taken into account that utilitarianism is anything but a soft ethical concept – it places high ethical demands on individuals: a true utilitarian would (for moral reasons) agree to a certain action or rule that maximizes average utility even if she herself would be disadvantaged by this action or rule. For this reason alone, utilitarianism should not be confused with a simple form of economic personal utility maximization.

Utilitarianism is a form of consequentialist theory, this means that the consequences and the results determine if an action is ethical or not (Sinnott-Armstrong, 2019). The intentions (the "will"), as in the case of Immanuel Kant's categorical imperative, do not play a significant role in the consequentialist utilitarian type of thinking. Thus, one of the moral problems with utilitarianism arises from the fact that in utilitarianism intentions do not play an important role, but rather the outcome of an action. If you rescue a drowning person not because it is your duty as a good swimmer, but because you do not want to be bothered by a nightmare, if you think about the drowned person haunting you during dreams at night, your rescue action is still ethical from a consequentialist and utilitarian perspective. At the same time, it should not be overlooked in this context that there can also be situations in which there is nothing left but to make utilitarian decisions, namely within tragic situations. Let us imagine that two overcrowded refugee boats are floating in the open sea, threatening to sink, but for certain reasons we are only able to save the occupants of one of the two boats. In this case we are faced with a real dilemma in which the options for action are severely limited and in which there is nothing left but to carry out a utilitarian benefit calculation and, for example, to evacuate the ship on which more people are sitting in order to save more human lives.

Another critical point with utilitarianism is that it does not cater for minorities. Utilitarianism lacks a principle of justice that takes the interests of disadvantaged individuals into account. Act utilitarianism, as suggested by John Stuart Mill, focuses on aggregate well-being, on the maximization or aggregation of happiness for the greatest number of people, no matter if there may be individuals or minorities who may experience an unhappy life. This means the harm suffered by individuals or minorities is offset against the luck or benefit of the greatest number. In that regard, it is justifiable to (slightly) reduce the overall amount of happiness of a minority group as long as the overall well-being of the majority increases (significantly) at the same time. For John Stuart Mill's form of act utilitarianism an action is morally correct, is morally good, and is ethical, if it maximizes pleasure, utility, well-being, and happiness for the greatest number of people and, if possible, for all sentient beings. Utilitarianism thus takes non-sentient beings into account and holds that their well-being also needs to be maximized, although this could be detrimental to a minority group of humans or detrimental to humans in general. Therefore, this theory is highly important in environmental ethics and climate change considerations.

Ethical toolbox 3.3: Utilitarianism as guideline in business ethics

Utilitarianism is an ethical theory that goes hand-in-hand with common sense and economic reasoning. The 19th-century English economist and utilitarian philosopher John Stuart Mill, the most important utilitarian philosopher and student of Jeremy Bentham, wrote the widest read and most famous book on utilitarianism. The general idea of this theory is that usefulness and pleasure are the yardsticks of ethics. Mill writes:

> The creed which accepts as the foundation of morals, Utility, or the Greatest Happiness Principle, holds that actions are right in

proportion as they tend to promote happiness, wrong as they tend to produce the reverse of happiness. ... happiness is ... pleasure, and the absence of pain; ... unhappiness [is] pain, and the privation of pleasure ... Pleasure, and freedom from pain, are the only things desirable as ends; ... all desirable things ... are desirable either for the pleasure inherent in themselves or as means to the promotion of pleasure and the prevention of pain. ...

Some kinds of pleasure are more desirable and more valuable than others. ... If I am asked, what I mean by difference of quality in pleasures, or what makes one pleasure more valuable than another ... there is but one possible answer. Of two pleasures, if there be one to which all or almost all who have experience of both give a decided preference, irrespective of any feeling of moral obligation to prefer it, that is the more desirable pleasure. ... It is better to be a human being dissatisfied than a pig satisfied. ... That standard is not the agent's own greatest happiness, but the greatest amount of happiness altogether ... According to the Greatest Happiness Principle ... the ultimate end ... is an existence exempt as far as possible from pain, and as rich as possible in enjoyments, both in point of quantity and quality .... This ... is necessarily also the standard of morality; which may accordingly be defined, the rules and precepts for human conduct, by the observance of which an existence ... to the greatest extent possible, secured to all mankind; and not to them only, but, so far as the nature of things admits, to the whole sentient creation. (Mill, 2017)

Study questions 3.3

(1) How does Mill explain the foundation of morals/ethics?
(2) When you think of Bentham and Mill, what is the difference between higher and lower pleasures, happiness, well-being, flourishing (this question is also looking back to Aristotle's theory)?
(3) How are such distinctions relevant in the business context?
(4) What does Mill mean by "better to be a human being dissatisfied than a pig satisfied"?
(5) What does Mill mean by the "greatest amount of happiness altogether"?
(6) How does this apply in the business context in which we have to deal with various stakeholders?
(7) Do you see any problems with this theory?
(8) Research some up-to-date material on this theory.

3.4.3 Negative utilitarianism, rule utilitarianism, and preference utilitarianism

A slight variation of John Stuart Mill's form of act utilitarianism is negative utilitarianism. Negative utilitarianism does not focus on the maximization of pleasure, but mainly on the minimization of harm or the reduction of pain (Acton & Watkins, 1963). Also, for negative utilitarianism, Epicurean philosophy could be seen as a precursor, since Epicure focused closely on the minimization of harm or the reduction of pain as defining pleasure and fostering well-being. Another example of an approach that is in line with negative utilitarianism is Jainism.

A prominent example of the application of this theory can be found in the work of many help organizations around the world, the purpose of which is not the maximization of pleasure, but the minimization of harm. The Bill & Melinda Gates Foundation attempts to reduce pain and harm by fostering research and development on HIV, AIDS and malaria medicine for example (www.gatesfoundation.org). Another very prominent and straightforward example is represented by the "Safety First" sign at many building sites, which is an indication that the reduction of pain and the minimization of harm is of utmost importance for the organization, although it may be that this strategy exists mainly because the management has fears regarding their safety records and reputation. Furthermore, many parts of the traffic laws could be seen as an approach to minimize pain and harm, e.g. laws regarding compulsory helmet and seatbelt usage.

Rule utilitarianism can be interpreted as utilitarianism with deontological guidelines. Act utilitarianism is then morally correct if the individual actions taken maximize pleasure, utility, and well-being for the greatest number of people, or all sentient beings. However, act utilitarianism, according to which the utility maximization paradigm applies to every single action, can also lead to certain counterintuitive consequences. For example, investments in environmentally friendly technologies would basically not be possible at all, since investments generally do not represent anything other than a form of temporary waiver in the hope of a higher return later on. Rule utilitarianism, in contrast, states that the ethically correct rule is the one that results in the greatest amount of utility, pleasure, or well-being for everyone affected by this rule. The crucial point is therefore that, according to rule utilitarianism, not every single action has to be utility-maximizing. Rather, such rules are morally correct and thus to be implemented, the observance of which leads to the greatest benefit in the medium and long term. In that regard, again, traffic laws could be seen as an application of the combination of rule utilitarianism and negative utilitarianism, because traffic laws represent those rules which result in the greatest minimization of harm.

The most interesting form of utilitarianism for the business context is preference utilitarianism. Prominent representatives of the theory are R.M. Hare and Peter Singer (Singer, 2011). In contrast to the classical utilitarianism

Types of Utilitarianism

Type of Utilitarianism	Philosopher	Criteria
Act U.	Mill	Action is right if it maximizes pleasure / utility / well-being for the greatest number (of sentient beings)
Rule U.	Critics of Mill	The correct rule is the one that results in the greatest amount of utility / well-being for everyone affected
Preference U.	R.M. Hare, Peter Singer	Promoting actions that fulfill interests / preference of beings / stakeholders involved
Negative U.	Jainism, Karl Popper	Minimizing harm / pain (no focus on pleasures)

Figure 3.10 Types of utilitarianism

according to Bentham and Mill described above, preference utilitarianism no longer focuses only on increasing well-being and reducing suffering of the majority as a basis for decision-making, but on promoting those actions or rules that will result in the maximization of the interests and preferences of certain people involved, and in the business context these persons, groups, or entities are the stakeholders. Preference utilitarianism applied to the business context means that the company should promote actions and establish rules that consider and foster the interests and the preferences of all stakeholders involved.

If we again look at the larger picture of a society and consider Total Societal Impact, it seems that TSI is more an act utilitarian approach, because the business is considering the overall benefit for the majority of the society. When setting up certain internal company rules such as codes of conduct or selected ethical regulations that try to minimize accidents and harm in general or set certain compliance goals, then this is a combination of rule and negative utilitarianism. But when taking the utility, benefit, and well-being of all stakeholders into consideration and when we try to promote the well-being of the stakeholders affected by a company's actions, this is an example of preference utilitarianism.

Case study 3.2: The Ford Pinto case

(1) Research the Ford Pinto case.
(2) How can act utilitarian considerations justify Ford's strategy at that time?

(3) What would be the consequences if the Ford management had applied other forms of utilitarianism (negative, rule, and/or preference utilitarianism)?
(4) What would be the consequences if the Ford management had applied other ethical theories such as the Kantian deontological ethics?
(5) Did you come across similar cases in other companies or industries during your research?

3.5 Care ethics

Care ethics based on feminist considerations will be presented here in the context of two other closely related theories: African Ubuntu ethics and Arthur Schopenhauer's claim that compassion is the foundation of ethics.

3.5.1 Feminine foundation of care

A feminist account of philosophy and ethics can claim that there are biologically significant differences between men and women. While the first wave feminists claimed equality between women and men (Freedman, 2007), certain feminists also emphasized the differences between women and men (Fuss, 2013). One of these undeniable differences lies in the potential to bear children and the fact that only women can conceive children. This biological fact and the anthropological difference between men and women result in social-cultural consequences. One of the consequences of the potential of childbearing is that women have to exercise care for another organism within their own body for nine months and then this newborn organism will be existentially dependent on a woman for survival, at least in typical

Care / Compassion / Community

Key Term	Movement / Philosopher	Characteristics
Compassion	Schopenhauer	Compassion is the foundation of ethics
Care	Feminism	Caring for people / beings close to us: not neutral / not impartial
Community	e.g. African Ethics	A human being is only a person due to her / his embeddedness in a community

Figure 3.11 Care, compassion, community

60 Normative ethical foundations

circumstances. During these nine months, but also thereafter, for several months, the child's existence heavily depends on the mother, which implies a special relationship between mother and child that is biologically different than the relationship between a child and a father. There exists a dependency of the child or the potential child on the mother and from the mother's side care needs to be exercised to secure the survival of the child. Thus, there is an empirically provable different account regarding care between women and men based on their undeniable anthropological difference.

Jack Ma, the co-founder of Alibaba, the largest online marketplace in the eastern hemisphere, claims that he observed a difference regarding care in the many years when evaluating, planning, and conducting business at Alibaba. In an interview given at the World Economic Forum (WEF) in 2018, Jack Ma claims that female colleagues at Alibaba, on average, care more about customer satisfaction and harmonious constructive working relationships with colleagues than men (World Economic Forum, 2018). With the help of data and statistics collected from the Alibaba online marketplace, Ma can provide data-driven evidence that women, when shopping, buy mainly for their spouses and their children or other family members, while when men order online, they mainly do so for themselves. Jack Ma deduces from his experience and the data available at Alibaba that women do "care more".

However, in business as anywhere else, the account of caring does not need to be a specifically female domain. It is observable that Brunello Cucinelli is exercising care ethics by especially taking care of his colleagues and the citizens in his village. Care ethics tries to make a difference for those persons to whom we are related or connected by blood, relationship, profession, or inclination and for whom we can make a significant difference. Thus, there is a certain undeniable bias that comes with the ethics of caring.

However, care ethics does not demand that the caregiver is altruistic. A person can only care for another person if she or he takes care of herself or himself well enough first. A very illustrating example is the direction given in announcements by flight attendants regarding the use of oxygen masks in an emergency. Adults should first fit the oxygen masks to themselves and then to the child/ren beside them. In this example, we can see that proximity plays an important role in caring properly for others, as well as the differential between a person that can help themselves and another person or a group that requires help. Even though there may be another person in need of help fitting an oxygen mask at the very end of the aircraft, a person in the middle of the plane would not be required to help the person at the end of the aircraft because there is not sufficient proximity, the caregiver and the person to be cared for are not close enough; helping in this context would not make any sense, because it would be completely detrimental for the helper.

3.5.2 Compassion as meta-ethical foundation

The German philosopher Arthur Schopenhauer defined compassion as the meta-ethical foundation of ethics. According to him, there is only one explanation of why we act ethically and that is compassion (Schopenhauer, 1998).

Compassion must be understood as putting oneself into the position of a suffering person and experiencing the suffering as if it would be one's own suffering. Due to this identification with the other's suffering, we can feel like the other, and therefore we will be willing to help since we can imagine how it would be if we were in this situation. For Arthur Schopenhauer, in our deepest inner feelings, we almost become the other (Schopenhauer & Saunders, 2004). We can see with this example that emotional proximity plays an important role in caring contexts even if geographical proximity is not given. That is the case for example if people on one side of the globe help other persons on the completely opposite side: the person can identify with, or feel compassion for, another person at a very different location. This applies, for example, in a context where persons become godfathers of a school child in a developing country. In the business context, Toms, a certified B corporation, initially started with a "one for one" approach in which they donated one pair of shoes for every sold pair of shoes to a child in need (Toms, 2020). This approach, also coined "caring capitalism", influenced many other companies to adopt similar CSR models, based on an ethics of care (Schermerhorn, 2011).

3.5.3 African Ubuntu ethics as social and political foundation

The famous Kenyan philosopher John Mbiti stated that a traditional African is only a full person if embedded in a community (Mbiti, 1990). His famous statement "I am because we are and, since we are, therefore I am" (Mbiti, 1990) indicates that humans cannot be thought of as individuals only, and at the same time we are always social beings. A claim that can be traced back to Aristotle's *Politics* where he elaborates on the *zoon politikon* (Aristotle, 2009), a living creature that exists in a polis (a city-state), meaning in a social context, more generally speaking. By nature, humans are socio-political creatures, who need to organize themselves politically and act ethically in order to get along with each other peacefully, be socially successful and culturally constructive. From the traditional African perspective, a single person, without contacts, not meeting other people, is a living creature, but not a fully human being.

While Schopenhauer and feminism supplied meta-ethical, motivational, emotional, anthropological, and bio-ontological and foundations of care ethics, Aristotle and Mbiti connect the fact that we do care, and have to care for each other, with our social-political situatedness. The practice of care ethics is very predominant within family contexts, but has its manifestations in a professional context as well, such as in the oxygen mask example, and in examples of caring capitalism or humanistic capitalism as that of Brunello Cucinelli, which includes care for future generations as well, at least to a certain extent, as we will see in Chapter 4.

3.6 Environmental ethics

The fifth and last standalone normative ethical theory, namely environmental ethics, needs separate and thorough treatment due to its urgency, not only for businesses but for humanity in general. Environmental business ethics,

62 *Normative ethical foundations*

corporate environmental responsibility, and businesses' responsibility toward future generations will be developed in Chapter 4. While environmental ethics for some time has been treated or understood as one of many disciplines within the area of applied ethics, nowadays it is evident that due to our planetary emergency – and also for ontological reasons which are understood not only by philosophers, but also by imminent politicians and even bankers and many other leading business persons – environmental ethics is and must be one of the five normative standalone ethical theories.

3.7 Fairness, justice, power, and responsibility

In the following, we will deal with two further theories that may not be regarded as standalone theories, but which make sense to consider seriously for business contexts. The first is John Rawls's theory of justice and the second is Amartya Sen's account on power and responsibility.

Justice is a very broad or wide philosophical, ethical, and juristic concept. It may be contrasted with equality (Greek: *isotes*; Latin: *aequitas, aequalitas*; French: *égalité*; German: *Gleichheit*) which means treating everyone in the same way, although in a somewhat quantitative way. For example, each person living in an apartment complex is entitled to one (designated) parking spot. While the first wave of feminism was very much concerned with equality, the concepts of fairness or equity, in contrast, take specific circumstances into account, for example, the input, the output, surrounding conditions, and needs (qualitative and quantitative). This more detailed perspective on specific circumstances may be applied to well-off, pregnant, female, or handicapped persons who are then, based on these specific backgrounds, entitled to special parking. In Thailand's shopping malls, visitors not only find specific parking spots for handicapped persons, pregnant women, families, or

Figure 3.12 Supercar parking (only)

Figure 3.13 Forms of justice

women in general, but also for owners of "superbikes" and "supercars". All of these mentioned parking lots are located near the mall entrance. It is not uncommon that in many hotels around the world, highly expensive vehicles may be parked in front of a hotel entrance, since this is meaningful marketing for the hotel.

Justice may also be seen in different forms, for example, as compensatory justice, distributive justice, and retributive justice. Retributive justice can simply mean punishment. Distributive justice is the justice that is concerned with the distribution of scarce economic goods and monetary resources, e.g. when paying salaries or dividends. Compensatory justice regulates compensation such as salaries, for example, the amount insurance companies need to pay as compensation for something lost, stolen, or damaged, but also what compensation companies have to pay in cases of wrongdoing. For example, Volkswagen had to pay compensation to customers for vehicles affected by the Dieselgate affair. Another form of compensation in this context was that the car dealers had to handle reimbursements for cars given back by their customers.

3.7.1 Fairness and justice

The 20th-century Harvard University philosophy professor John Rawls wrote a seminal book, *A Theory of Justice*, that he developed over various editions. In this book, John Rawls tries to resolve the conflict between freedom and equality. The book can be seen in the tradition of social contract philosophy, and our interest is to apply this political philosophy or philosophy of law to the business context. Rawls addresses his approach to all persons who have an interest in justice and who ask themselves the question of what is fair and what is not. One of the key passages in this book contains a thought experiment that anyone should use who wants to know what conditions can be considered fair.

In this context, it should also be pointed out that thought experiments regarding ideal states, societies, and laws can be traced back to ancient Greek times starting with Plato's books *Politeia* and *Nomoi* and Aristotle's *Politics*. Adam Smith, Immanuel Kant, and John Stuart Mill had already employed concepts of impartiality in situations in which justifiable long-term planning for a society should be accomplished. Rawls and the utilitarian Harsanyi disagreed for a long time as to which of the two ultimately invented the thought experiment. However, since Harsanyi published his version some years before Rawls, there are some indications that Harsanyi is the real inventor: "My equiprobability model was first published in 1953, and was extended in 1955. [...] Later John Rawls again independently proposed a very similar model [...]. But while my own model served as a basis for a utilitarian theory, Rawls derived very nonutilitarian conclusions from it" (Harsanyi, 1982).

In this thought experiment, the reader will be brought into what John Rawls calls "original position", a position that corresponds to a fictitious starting point in human history (Rawls, 1999). One of the basic assumptions of the original position is that humanity could start all over again. A crucial point regarding the thought experiment is that persons who will live at a later point in human history gather in this original position and debate and decide on future legislations, laws, and regulations that they want to give themselves for their later life in society (Rawls, 1999). All participants in the original position are therefore confronted with the question of which laws they would consider just (fair) and capable of consensus, with Rawls assuming that all people are risk averse. In this situation, the original position, people wear the so-called "veil of ignorance", whereby Rawls proceeds from the following assumptions: first of all, he assumes that the people in the original position have a certain general knowledge. For example, they should know about what democracy, capitalism, socialism, etc. are. Otherwise, they would not even know what alternatives they are talking about in the original position. In any case, in order to be able to compare different social arrangements with one another, a certain basic knowledge must be available. What the individuals in the original position should not be aware of, however, is personal information about themselves in later life in society (Wenar, 2017). Such personal information is hidden by the veil of ignorance. The veil of ignorance thus means the persons in the original position lack knowledge such as their nationality, race, sexual or political orientation, gender, level of intelligence, ability or disability, health status, age, religion, skills, education, and many other genetic, character, and personal traits. Each possibility is equally likely to occur, meaning decision-makers could be among the most disadvantaged and vulnerable in society in relation to certain laws, which at the same time makes it clear that the veil of ignorance forces people to adopt an impartial point of view (or perception) when debating later laws. Crucially important is also the fact that these people will not even know when they will be born (Rawls, 1999). While the account of care ethics may involve bias toward a person or a group and discriminate toward other persons or other groups, justice as fairness in the understanding of John Rawls tries to remove bias, with the help of the veil of ignorance. This veil of ignorance in the original position requires each and every person not only to put her or himself in the shoes of another person, but also in the shoes of any other possible person including those who are not yet alive. Thus, this account on justice requires us to not only think in terms of justice within our current living generation (intra-generational or intra-generative justice), but additionally regarding justice across the coming generations, which is called intergenerational justice or inter-generative justice. We will come back to inter- and intra-generational justice in Chapter 4 on corporate environmental responsibility.

As described above, Rawls assumes that all persons involved in the original position have an aversion to risk, which is why they always orientate themselves to the possible worst-case scenario. This risk aversion can be described and illustrated somewhat more technically and numerically with the so-called "maximin principle". According to the maximin rule, all available alternative options that can be identified in a certain context should be assessed according to their worst possible consequences. The next step is to choose the alternative for which the worst possible result or outcome is still better compared to all other alternatives. According to Rawls, people in the original position behind the veil of ignorance would choose the maximum among the minima (this is precisely why the principle is called the "maximin principle"). As a precautionary measure, all rules must be laid down in such a way that, in the worst-case scenario, potential harm is minimized from the outset. This also makes clear that Rawls always has the weakest milieus and individuals in society in mind, who may be hit by fate and have to deal with the worst case (Wagner, 2019).

This kind of thinking approach could be interpreted in the business strategy of Starbucks whose management probably considered what kind of preferences farmers, but also customers, have. As soon as you put yourself neutrally in the position of farmers and consumers, as Rawls's theory suggests, the following becomes clear: if you are a farmer you want to be well paid and not physically exploited, and you also do not want to deal with chemical substances on a day-to-day basis that ruin your health. As a consumer, you may have the same perspective as the farmer regarding unhealthy substances or residuals that may be left as chemical traces in the coffee and you may also want to contribute to environmental responsibility, but you would also prefer to have a high-quality coffee, and it seems that Starbucks customers are prepared to pay a fair, but premium, price for such a coffee.

We also see this approach in modern software design (Newell & Gregor, 2000). For example, for the visually impaired, many use screen reader tools that render text into audio speech. However, what happens when the website such as an e-commerce platform has multiple images of their products? Many programmers now use "alternative texts", which is similar to tagging an image with the description of the image. This way, when the visually impaired person comes to an image with their screen reader, the person can recognize this is an image and understand the context. Although this feature is time-consuming since it requires manually adding descriptions for the images, and more than 99% of the user base will never see it, it is crucial for an ethical platform to be inclusive towards all users. In any case, in the original position, if we imagined that we would later be born as a visually impaired person, we would speak out in favor of the development and implementation of such technologies, as they would drastically simplify our lives in later society and enable inclusion.

Ethical toolbox 3.4: An ethical thought experiment: The veil of ignorance

If there is a conflict situation between the interests of different stakeholders of an organization, and if we would like to judge the situation from a neutral position (if something like that exists at all), the veil of ignorance used by the US American 20th-century Harvard professor John Rawls in his famous book *A Theory of Justice* (1971) may help to clarify such different interests.

> persons in the original position are rational. ... The notion of the veil of ignorance is implicit ... in Kant's ethics ... The idea of the original position is to set up a fair procedure so that any principles agreed to will be just. ... I assume that the parties [people] are situated behind a veil of ignorance. They do not know how the various alternatives will affect their own particular case and they are obliged to evaluate principles solely on the basis of general considerations. ... It is assumed, then, that the parties do not know certain kinds of particular facts. First of all, no one knows his place in society, his class position or social status; nor does he know his fortune in the distribution of natural assets and abilities, his intelligence and strength, and the like. Nor, again, does anyone know his conception of the good, the particulars of his rational plan of life, or even the special features of his psychology such as his aversion to risk or liability to optimism or pessimism. More than this, I assume that the parties do not know the particular circumstances of their own society. That is, they do not know its economic or political situation or the level of civilization and culture it has been able to achieve. The persons in the original position have no information as to which generation they belong. ... They must choose principles the consequences of which they are prepared to live with whatever generation they turn out to belong to. (Rawls, 1999)

Study questions 3.4

(1) What does Rawls mean by "original position" and "veil of ignorance", and how are these two concepts related?
(2) How can the concepts of "veil of ignorance"/"original position" be useful in the business context? Give examples.

(3) What does the last sentence imply for the business domain: "They must choose principles the consequences of which they are prepared to live with whatever generation they turn out to belong to"?
(4) Are there certain types of business decisions where Rawls's theory of justice is particularly helpful? In what kind of decisions does it seem more sensible or even inevitable to make utilitarian decisions?
(5) Research some up-to-date material on this theory.

3.8 Power and responsibility

The Nobel prize-winning economist Amartya Sen in his 2009 book *The Idea of Justice* stated one very simple but important fact for business contexts. There exists an asymmetry of power between two unequal persons, groups, or entities which implies corresponding obligations, duties, and responsibilities. This asymmetry of power exists, for example, between parents and children, between companies and their employees, but also between more and less advanced countries and economies. This positive correlation between power and responsibility can be expressed in a diagram. The more power a person, a group, or an entity has, the more responsibility this person, group, or entity should exercise.

Since the birth of the corporation as a legal entity or legal "person" (Achbar & Abbott, 2004), an increase in the power of corporations, especially multinational corporations, has been observed. The power of large multinationals is comparable to state entities. We will discuss different forms of power in Chapter 5 on stakeholders. This increasing power is often manifested in the size and shape of buildings. It is for example claimed that Apple Park's "Spaceship", Apple Inc.'s headquarters in Cupertino, is larger than

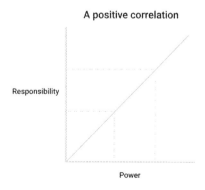

Figure 3.14 Power and responsibility correlation

68 *Normative ethical foundations*

the US Department of Defense's headquarters, The Pentagon. While these buildings manifest the symbolical power of companies, corporations can also be compared to states in terms of their users. Facebook is larger in terms of monthly active users than the two largest countries by population together, China and India. The number of Foxconn employees equals the population size of Estonia, Switzerland, or East Timor. The number of Walmart employees equals the population size of Botswana. The revenues of certain large corporations equal some countries' GDP PPP, the gross domestic product based on purchasing power parity. Walmart's revenue roughly equals the GDP PPP of Hong Kong, Samsung's revenue roughly equals the GDP PPP of Israel, and each of Apple's or Volkswagen's revenues equal the GDP PPP of Finland (all data 2020).

At the World Economic Forum (WEF) in 2017, Klaus Schwab, the founder of the WEF, joked in a conversation with Sergey Brin, the co-founder of Google and at that time president of Alphabet, that there are only three powers left in the world: the US, China, and Alphabet, meaning that being the president of one of the largest multi-national corporations is equal to being the president of the largest or the second-largest country in terms of economic power.

Ethical toolbox 3.5: Responsibility is implied in power asymmetry – Amartya Sen, *The Idea of Justice*

Sergey Brin stated in an interview at the World Economic Forum in Davos 2017 that powerful corporations such as Google, can no longer be "purely profit-motivated", this is "not really a reasonable position to take" (World Economic Forum, 2017). Large multinational corporations have revenues, subscribers, and human resources that make these businesses comparable to smaller states. Due to this power over financial means, data, and human resources, a corresponding responsibility exits, argues the Indian contemporary economist and philosopher Amartya Sen, utilizing ethical reasoning by the Buddha:

> Freedom to choose gives us the opportunity to decide what we should do, but with that opportunity comes the responsibility for what we do – to the extent that they are chosen actions. Since a capability is the power to do something, the accountability that emanates from that ability – that power – is a part of the capability perspective, and this can make room for demands of duty... As a contrast let me consider another line of reasoning that takes the general form of arguing that if someone has the power to make a change that he or she can see will reduce injustice in the world, then there is a strong social argument for doing just that ... The perspective of obligations of power was presented powerfully by Gautama Buddha in *Sutta-Nipata*. Buddha argues there that we have the responsibility to animals precisely because of the asymmetry between us, not because of any symmetry that takes us to the need

> for cooperation. He argues instead that since we are enormously more powerful than other species, we have some responsibility towards other species that connects exactly with this asymmetry of power. Buddha goes on to illustrate the point by an analogy with the responsibility of the mother towards her child, not because she has given birth to the child ... but because she can do things to influence the child's life that the child itself cannot do. The mother's reason for helping the child, in this line of thinking, is not guided by the rewards of cooperation, but precisely from her recognition that she can, asymmetrically, do things for the child that will make a huge difference to the child's life and which the child itself cannot do. The mother does not have to seek any mutual benefit – real or imagined – nor seek any as if contract to understand her obligation to the child. That is the point that Gautama was making... The justification here takes the form of arguing that if some action that can be freely undertaken is open to a person (thereby making it feasible), and if the person assesses that the undertaking of that action will create a more just situation in the world (thereby making it justice-enhancing), then that is argument enough for the person to consider seriously what he or she should do in view of these recognitions. (Sen, 2011)

Using exactly this line of argumentation, Dr. P. Roy Vagelos, the chairman of Merck, announced in 1987 that Merck & Company would distribute a drug against river blindness free of charge to countries that request it (The New York Times, 1987). The drug had been developed at Merck's expense, based on a previously developed drug against worms in livestock and dogs. Vagelos was aware of Merck's potential ("power") and its related obligation to help in this context, even if the development and distribution of the drug was a financial loss for Merck. However, Merck gained trust, customers, and market share in the long run. We can also see with this example of how a concentration on TSI impacted significantly on TSR. It should be noted that trust and trust-building are essential virtues and values for sustainable business relationships (Udomkit et al., 2020).

Study questions 3.5

(1) Where does responsibility come from, according to Amartya Sen; how is responsibility ethically implied in relationships?
(2) What does the context of power, obligation, and responsibility mean for the business context? Give further examples of how particular businesses deal with power and responsibility.
(3) Research recent business issues regarding power and responsibility.

Case study 3.3: The Facebook–Cambridge Analytica scandal

Research the Facebook–Cambridge Analytica scandal.

(1) Identify and explain the important stakeholders which were affected by this incident, and how they have affected Facebook.
(2) Use ethical theories to analyze the ethical implications of this incident.
(3) How should Facebook, especially the CEO and a CIO (Chief Information Officer), have reacted to this incident?
(4) Research recent data protection and data privacy issues.

Ethical Theories Applied to Business

Ethics	Philosopher	Criteria
Virtue & Holistic Well-Being	Aristotle	- Mediation between conflicting standpoints/stakeholder interest - Consider holistic well-being of involved stakeholders - What would a person with a commendable character do?
Duty Rule Principle	Kant	- Reflect, reason on your own! (Think! It's not illegal) - Is a particular decision universalizable as part of corporate culture/Code of Conduct/corporate responsibility?
Utilitarianism	Mill	- Maximize benefits & minimize harms for all involved stakeholders - Consequences for all involved stakeholders
Responsibility	Sen	- Power (automatically/inherently) implies responsibility
Impartiality Justice Fairness	Rawls	- How would a neutral/uninvolved person judge? - (Outsider/alien/expert perspective)
Compassion Care Ubuntu	Feminism African Philosophy	- Caring for persons/beings close to use (not impartial/not neutral) - CSR
Environmental Ethics	Environmental Movement	- Sustainability/responsibility towards future communities - Corporate environmental responsibility

Figure 3.15 Overview: Ethical theories applied to business

Key takeaways

(1) Virtue ethics aims at developing societies' and individuals' virtue and well-being.
(2) Kant is prominently known for formulating the most famous ethical "axiom" of rule-based ethics, the categorical imperative: "Act only according to that maxim whereby you can, at the same time, will that it should become a universal law".
(3) Practical imperative: "Act in such a way that you treat humanity, whether in your own person or in that of another, always at the same time as an end and never merely as a means".
(4) For utilitarianism, actions that result in the greatest happiness for the greatest number of people are ethical actions.
(5) Care ethics highlights the importance of care, interpersonal relationships, and compassion.
(6) The theory of justice aims to eliminate injustices – also in later societies – through an impartiality perspective.
(7) The theory of power and responsibility explains how higher power automatically implies higher responsibilities.
(8) For environmental ethicists, societal entities have the responsibility of seriously considering the eco-environment and future communities.

References

Achbar, M., & Abbott, J. (2004, June 4). *The Corporation* [Documentary; History]. Big Picture Media Corporation.
Acton, H.B., & Watkins, J.W.N. (1963). Symposium: Negative utilitarianism. *Proceedings of the Aristotelian Society, Supplementary Volumes*, 37, 83–114.
Aristotle. (2009). *Politics* (R.F. Stalley, Ed.; E. Barker, Trans.; Reissue ed.). Oxford University Press.
Aristotle. (2018). *Nicomachean Ethics*. The Internet Classics Archive. http://classics.mit.edu/Aristotle/nicomachaen.1.i.html
Auchter, L. (2017). An African view on global business ethics: Ubuntu – a social contract interpretation. *International Journal of Business & Economic Development*, 5(2), 1–14.
Barboza, D. (2010, June 6). After Foxconn suicides, scrutiny for Chinese plants. *The New York Times*. www.nytimes.com/2010/06/07/business/global/07suicide.html
Bentham, J. (2009). *Utilitarianism*. BiblioBazaar.
Cucinelli, B. (2020). *My Idea of Humanistic Capitalism*. www.brunellocucinelli.com/en/humanistic-capitalism.html
Diels, H., & Kranz, W. (1903). *Die Fragmente der Vorsokratiker griechisch und deutsch*. Weidmannsche buchhandlung. http://books.google.com/books?id=xQYrAAAAMAAJ&oe=UTF-8

Diener, E. (2009). Subjective well-being. In E. Diener (Ed.), *The Science of Well-Being: The Collected Works of Ed Diener* (pp. 11–58). Springer Netherlands. https://doi.org/10.1007/978-90-481-2350-6_2

Freedman, E. (2007). *No Turning Back: The History of Feminism and the Future of Women*. Random House Publishing Group.

Fuss, D. (2013). *Essentially Speaking: Feminism, Nature and Difference*. Routledge.

García, H. & Miralles, F. (2016). *Ikigai: The Japanese Secret to a Long and Happy Life*. Random House.

Ghosh, S. (2018, March 16). UK Amazon warehouse workers "peed in bottles", undercover author finds. *Business Insider*. www.businessinsider.com/amazon-warehouse-workers-have-to-pee-into-bottles-2018-4

Harsanyi, J.C. (1982). Morality and the theory of rational behaviour. In A. Sen & B. Williams (Eds.), *Utilitarianism and Beyond* (pp. 39–62). Cambridge University Press. https://doi.org/10.1017/CBO9780511611964.004

Helliwell, J., Layard, R., Sachs, J., & De Neve, J.E. (2020). *World Happiness Report 2020*. Sustainable Development Solutions Network. http://worldhappiness.report/

Holt, R., & Hond, F. den. (2013). Sapere aude. *Organization Studies*, *34*(11), 1587–1600. https://doi.org/10.1177/0170840613502293

Kant, I. (1784). An answer to the question: "What is enlightenment?" In Mary J. Gregor (Ed.), *The Cambridge Edition of the Works of Immanuel Kant* (pp. 11–12). Cambridge University Press. doi: 10.1017/CBO9780511813306.005.

Kant, I. (1993). *Grounding for the Metaphysics of Morals: With On a Supposed Right to Lie Because of Philanthropic Concerns* (J.W. Ellington, Trans.; 3rd ed.). Hackett Publishing Company, Inc.

Kepler, J. (1997). *The Harmony of the World*. American Philosophical Society.

Keyes, C. (2010). Flourishing. In *The Corsini Encyclopedia of Psychology*. Wiley. https://doi.org/10.1002/9780470479216.corpsy0363

Keyes, C., Shmotkin, D., & Ryff, C.D. (2002). Optimizing well-being: The empirical encounter of two traditions. *Journal of Personality and Social Psychology*, *82*(6), 1007–1022. https://doi.org/10.1037/0022-3514.82.6.1007

Kraut, R. (2015). *The Routledge Handbook of Philosophy of Well-Being* (1st ed.). Routledge.

Lee, M. (1998). The Ford Pinto case and the development of auto safety regulations, 1893–1978. *Business and Economic History*, *27*. www.researchgate.net/publication/237286809_The_Ford_Pinto_Case_and_the_Development_of_Auto_Safety_Regulations_1893-1978

Lonka, K. (2013). *Esa Saarinen: Elämän filosofi*. Aalto-yliopisto.

Mahmuda, F. (2003). *Understanding People's Perceptions of Subjective Well-being in a Rural Area in Bangladesh: A Gender Perspective*. Department of Economics and International Development, University of Bath.

Maslow, A.H. (1943). A theory of human motivation. *Psychological Review*, *50*(4), 430–437.

Mbiti, J.S. (1990). *African Religions & Philosophy*. Heinemann.

Mieder, W. (2001). "Do unto others as you would have them do unto you": Frederick Douglass's proverbial struggle for civil rights. *The Journal of American Folklore*, *114*(453), 331–357. https://doi.org/10.2307/542026

Mill, J.S. (2017). *Utilitarianism*. Coventry House Publishing.

Mogi, K. (2017). *The Little Book of Ikigai: The Secret Japanese Way to Live a Happy and Long Life*. Hachette UK.
Newell, A.F., & Gregor, P. (2000). "User sensitive inclusive design": In search of a new paradigm. In *Proceedings on the 2000 Conference on Universal Usability – CUU '00* (pp. 39–44). https://doi.org/10.1145/355460.355470
Nussbaum, M.C. (1999). *Sex and Social Justice*. Oxford University Press.
The New York Times (1987, October 22). Merck offers free distribution of new river blindness drug. *The New York Times*. www.nytimes.com/1987/10/22/world/merck-offers-free-distribution-of-new-river-blindness-drug.html
Orthner, D.K., Jones-Sanpei, H. & Williamson, S. (2004), The resilience and strengths of low-income families. *Family Relations*, 53: 159–167. https://doi.org/10.1111/j.0022-2445.2004.00006.x
Oxford Poverty & Human Development Initiative. (2020). *Bhutan's Gross National Happiness Index*. https://ophi.org.uk/policy/national-policy/gross-national-happiness-index/
Plato. (1997). *Republic*. Wordsworth Editions.
Poitras, L. (2014, October 31). *Citizenfour* [Documentary; Film]. Artificial Eye Film Co. Ltd.
Rawls, J. (1999). *A Theory of Justice* (2nd ed.). Belknap Press.
Schermerhorn, J.R. (2011). *Introduction to Management*. John Wiley & Sons.
Schopenhauer, A. (1998). *On the Basis of Morality*. Hackett Publishing.
Schopenhauer, A., & Saunders, T.B. (2004). *The Wisdom of Life*. Courier Corporation.
Sen, A. (2011). *The Idea of Justice* (Reprint ed.). Belknap Press.
Singer, P. (2011). *Practical Ethics*. Cambridge University Press.
Sinnott-Armstrong, W. (2019) Consequentialism. In E.N. Zalta (Ed.), *The Stanford Encyclopedia of Philosophy* (Summer 2019). Stanford University Press.
Toms. (2020). *The TOMS Story*. www.toms.com/about-toms
Tycoon. (n.d.). *Tycoon*. https://tycoonpercussion.com/about-us/
Udomkit, N., Ensslin, V., & Meinhold, R. (2020). Three stages of trust building of international small- and medium-sized enterprises. *Global Business Review*, 21(4), 906–917. https://doi.org/10.1177/0972150919856990
Wachowski, A., & Wachowski, L. (1999). *The Matrix* [Film]. Warner Home Video.
Wagner, C. (2019). *Managementethik und Arbeitsplätze: Eine metaphysische und moralökonomische Analyse*. Springer-Verlag.
Wenar, L. (2017). John Rawls. In E.N. Zalta (Ed.), *The Stanford Encyclopedia of Philosophy* (Spring 2017). Metaphysics Research Lab, Stanford University. https://plato.stanford.edu/archives/spr2017/entries/rawls/
Wong, J.C. (2019, March 18). The Cambridge Analytica scandal changed the world – but it didn't change Facebook. *The Guardian*. www.theguardian.com/technology/2019/mar/17/the-cambridge-analytica-scandal-changed-the-world-but-it-didnt-change-facebook
World Economic Forum. (2017). *Davos 2017—Conversation with Sergey Brin at the World Economic Forum 2017*. www.youtube.com/watch?v=ffvu6Mr1SVc
World Economic Forum. (2018, January 24). *Jack Ma: Love Is Important in Business | Davos 2018*. www.youtube.com/watch?v=4zzVjonyHcQ
Yea, S. (2010). Trafficking in part(s): The commercial kidney market in a Manila slum, Philippines. *Global Social Policy*, 10. https://doi.org/10.1177/1468018110379989.

4 Sustainability and organizations' environmental responsibility

Trash and treasures

Abstract

In this chapter, two main topics are covered; environmental business ethics and sustainability. In this context newly considered stakeholders need to be discussed: future communities, ecosystems, and non-human species are becoming key factors in businesses. This addition of stakeholders to the stakeholder discourse also arises from the changing demands of environmentally conscious consumers, businesses, and investors. Then, shifting the focus onto sustainability, we will explore the dimensions and the concepts of sustainability and the effects of environmental issues on future generations. We will also assume certain non-human perspectives. Further concepts explored are ecological economics' internalization of external effects and precautionary and pre-actionary decision-making approaches. This chapter includes case studies, e.g. on Patagonia, Rubber Killer, and the 5G network.

Chapter keywords

(1) Internalization of external effects
(2) Intra-generational
(3) Intergenerational
(4) Sustainable Development Goals
(5) Ecological economics
(6) Integrative dependency model
(7) Anthropocentrism
(8) Biodiversity
(9) Precautionary approach

Study objectives

After studying this chapter readers will be able to:

(1) Explain the relevance of organizations' environmental responsibility for business sustainability.

DOI: 10.4324/9781003127659-4

(2) Explain the relevance of sustainability concepts and sustainable development for businesses.
(3) Understand how businesses can affect and are affected by eco-environments, non-human species, and representatives of future generations.
(4) Analyze ethical issues in specific business contexts in regard to sustainability, corporate environmental responsibility, and environmental business ethics.

Case studies

4.1 Micro- and nanoplastic in water, animals, food, and humans
4.2 Rubber Killer
4.3 Patagonia
4.4 The 5G network: Between pre-actionary and precautionary considerations

Films

(1) *Bottled Life*
(2) *Watermark*
(3) *Manufactured Landscapes*

Thought experiments

(1) Weighing a skyscraper
(2) Water on a bald head and in the desert
(3) Why is there no business on Mars?
(4) The last person argument
(5) Spaceship earth

4.1 Business ethics and the natural environment

Due to concerns regarding human health issues, such as increasing cancer rates and climate change, consumer awareness and business responsibilities for natural ecosystems have increased (DesJardins, 2005). In the Monsanto-Glyphosate case, for example, Monsanto, a subsidiary of Bayer, was held responsible for not labeling the herbicide Roundup and its ingredient Glyphosate as possibly carcinogenic. This conveys the message that businesses will be held responsible for unethical actions, moral shortcomings, and even potential but ignored risks (Reuters, 2019). Also, investors these days invest more responsibly, supporting environmentally friendly and ethically responsible companies (BCG, 2017). According to research by the Boston Consulting Group (BCG), companies nowadays are more engaged in the production of ethical products and offer services that have ethically positive impacts on the society – Total Societal Impact (TSI) – if they have a choice. By focusing

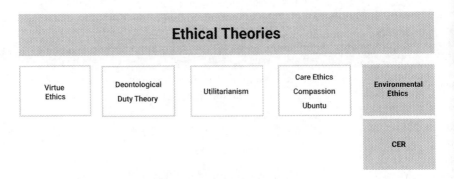

Figure 4.1 Environmental ethics and CER

on TSI such companies, in many cases, will also increase their revenue in the long run – Total Shareholder Return (TSR) (BCG, 2017). On the public side, civil society forces, such as the Fridays for Future movement, have gained worldwide momentum by claiming that past and present businesses, political entities, and consumers have not taken serious action against climate change, eco-systemic degradation, and intergenerational injustice (www.fridaysforfuture.org/).

4.2 Environmental ethics and stakeholders

The major issues in this chapter will be partly linked to environmental issues and environmental ethical theory which is construed as one of the most recent and topical approaches within normative ethics, besides the already presented classical approaches, such as virtue ethics (Aristotle, 2018), deontology (duty ethics) (Kant, 1993), and consequentialist theories including utilitarianism (Mill, 2017) and care ethics (Held, 2006). Topics in the environmental business ethics domain also involve new types of stakeholders that become relevant in the sustainability context, namely: 1) future communities, 2) natural ecosystems, and 3) non-human species (Carroll et al., 2017).

4.3 Key concepts

All business activities are essentially dependent on natural resources – be they renewable or non-renewable. The following concepts will be addressed in this chapter:

- Internalization of external effects (Wiesmeth, 2011)
- Environmental and human health impacts (Wani et al., 2019)
- Intra-generational and intergenerational justice or equity (Cottier et al., 2019; Meyer, 2017)

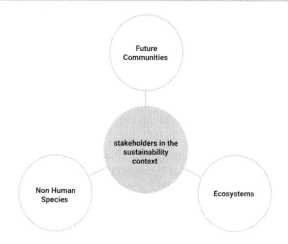

Figure 4.2 Stakeholders in the sustainability context

- Sustainability (World Commission on Environment & Development, 1990)
- The triple bottom line (Szekely et al., 2017)
- The circles of sustainability (James, 2014)
- The United Nations Sustainable Development Goals (United Nations, 2016)
- Ecological economics (Spash, 2017)
- Integrative dependency model of ecology, society, and economy (Daly & Farley, 2004)
- Anthropocentrism and non-anthropocentrism (Moore, 2017)
- Last person argument (thought experiment) (Routley, 1973)
- Biodiversity (Lanzerath & Friele, 2014)
- Pre-actionary and precautionary approach (Steel, 2015)
- Spaceship earth concept (thought experiment) (Boulding, 1966)

4.4 Business ethics, environmental and health concerns

In recent years business ethics books started to include chapters on "environmental ethics" (Fernando, 2010), "sustainability" (Ferrell et al., 2018), "business and environmental sustainability" (Hartman et al., 2017), or "business and corporate environmental responsibility" (DesJardins, 2013). As indicated above, the reasons for taking environmental issues and sustainability concepts seriously are manifold and include legal obligations, increasing environmental and health awareness, severe environmental and health issues, increasing demand for environmentally friendly and healthy choices, and considerations regarding health and environmental responsibility on the part of consumers, businesses, and investors. On the theory side, normative ethics has been expanded by the theory of environmental ethics besides the normative ethical theories such as virtue ethics, deontological ethics, utilitarianism, and care ethics, with each of these normative ethical theories being helpful and applicable to a different extent depending on the locally observed environmental or sustainability problem.

DesJardins already stated in 2005 that "creative businesses and entrepreneurial individuals will not wait for consumer demand (for healthy and environmentally friendly products) to magically appear" (DesJardins, 2005), meaning that businesses and entrepreneurs need to anticipate demands and cater to them. Steve Jobs anticipated the demand of a device that combines several highly useful features and functions such as mobile phone, photo and video camera, address book, pocket computer with an internet browser, GPS-maps combination, and music and video player into one single device – the iPhone. Similarly, entrepreneurs should anticipate what health and environmentally conscious consumers need and want. In the future, even more consumers will buy environmentally friendly and healthy products. On the other hand, there is a growing awareness of ecological and health harms that "virtually guarantee that future businesses will be judged negligent for failing to take steps to prevent easily foreseeable harms" (DesJardins, 2005), which leads to the conclusion that corporate environmental responsibility needs to be taken more seriously in theory, e.g. when teaching business ethics, drafting CSR campaigns, and in practice, in everyday business planning and executing CSR activities.

On the managerial side, the classical or simplified stakeholder models need to be expanded for taking corporate environmental responsibility into account. The classical stakeholder theory consisting of the five primary stakeholders – customers, employees, financiers, communities, and suppliers (Freeman et al., 2010) – does not sufficiently reflect the impacts that businesses have on future communities, ecosystems, and non-human species. Once again, this classical stakeholder model does not consider the impacts that non-human species and ecosystems can have on current businesses and future business activities. One example is the ongoing mass extinction of insects by insecticides and other impacts on ecosystems (Youngsteadt et al., 2019) which leads to significant changes in agricultural practices. Certain plants formerly pollinated by insects now need to be pollinated manually by humans or machines. Deteriorating ecosystems will have a very significant impact on industries such as tourism (Foulkes, 2017).

There are many examples of how businesses need to consider stakeholders in the sustainability context, but it is very obvious that businesses have been depending on natural resources such as water and wood for millennia. Water and wood are especially interesting examples of renewable resources because roughly 45–65% of human bodies are made up of water, and we usually cannot survive much longer than three or four days without it. Wood, also a renewable resource, leads us to the exploration of the sustainability model, a long-term planning perspective. If we want people in the future to enjoy and harvest trees, we need to plant them now. Behind the idea of sustainability is the concept of intergenerational ethics, ethics along the line of generations, which already poses significant economic challenges, especially when it comes to non-renewable resources such as rare earths, metals, and those minerals like tantalum and indium which are used in electronic devices like mobile phones, tablets, and laptops.

For all these reasons, this chapter (and the business cases contained within it) will also explain how renewable and non-renewable resources have deteriorated and how this deterioration has a significant impact not only on the business sector but also on human health. Furthermore, as we will see later, methods of rethinking product cycles bring a lot of entrepreneurial opportunities.

4.5 Water, a renewable but highly essential resource

One negative example of a company that has been accused of deteriorating resources is Nestlé with its bottled water business, in particular the "Pure Life" brand. The documentary *Bottled Life* (Schnell, 2012) claims to reveal how Nestlé in some cases had extracted water beyond the renewal rate of the sources' watershed, causing (un)sustainable environmental impacts, deteriorating natural ecosystems. Among Nestlé's stakeholders in economically developing countries are certain local communities who, after Nestlé started its operation, no longer have access to drinking water due to the sinking groundwater level. But for Nestlé this is a highly lucrative business because in some instances – the film claims – it buys a tanker load of water for ten dollars, but once the water is bottled Nestlé sells the same volume of water for fifty thousand US dollars (Schnell, 2012). Another negative side effect in the water bottling business is the amount of plastic produced and disposed of to bottle the water, especially in cases in which the bottles are not or cannot be recycled.

Film case study 4.1: *Bottled Life*

Watch the film *Bottled Life* and research Nestlé's current drinking water business.

(1) What is your opinion regarding Peter Brabeck's business strategies from a business ethical perspective?
(2) Who are Nestlé's stakeholders and how are they affected by its water business?

> (3) How could those stakeholders affect Nestlé?
> (4) Who owns the water of this planet and how should the drinking water on our planet be distributed/utilized?
> (5) Apply the ethical theories discussed earlier in trying to tackle the problems related to (un)just drinking water distribution/usage.
> (6) What has Nestlé done and what should/could Nestlé do further to rescue its reputation?

Edward Burtynsky in his documentary *Watermark* shows impressively how water is shaping the life of human civilization and how we, in turn, are shaped by water (Burtynsky, 2019). One scene in the documentary shows footage of a boy swimming in a pool. The camera zooms out and the viewer can see that the pool in which the boy swims belongs to a house that, besides many other houses with pools, is located in a gated community that in turn is located in a swamp in Florida. The housing community is shaped by this transformation of the swamp and by the fact that it is built in the water, but also the swamp has been landscaped, "manufactured", and transfigured by the housing community. This example illustrates Burtynsky's main concern in the *Watermark* documentary, "how water is shaping us and how we are shaping water" (Burtynsky, 2019).

This statement is an explanatory example of the relationship between humans, businesses, and stakeholders. Natural ecosystems are shaping businesses, and businesses are shaping natural ecosystems. In more general terms, businesses are influencing ecosystems and ecosystems are influencing businesses. In the Nestlé Pure Life water case study, for example, we can see how water resources are found in natural ecosystems such as forests and why high water quality attracts companies like Nestlé. Nestlé sets up water extraction facilities and builds roads to extract, bottle, market, and distribute the drinking water. With these business activities the ecological environment is altered, for example, by building roads and factories, and in some cases by lowering the groundwater table (Schnell, 2012). In turn, ecosystems have impacts on businesses. If the groundwater level is depleted beyond the renewal rate, water-extracting companies may close the facilities and set up extraction facilities elsewhere. However, due to the exploitation of water which leads to the sinking groundwater table, local businesses such as fish farms may be heavily affected, due to the declining population of fish or dying out of particular species of trees, the roots of which cannot reach the lower groundwater table. In such cases, the business activities of water-extracting companies may negatively impact the timber and fish farming industries.

In 2011 one of the most impactful floods in Bangkok halted operations for many local businesses. They were no longer in a position to direct the water where it was supposed to flow. There was water everywhere around the citizens, but many stores, like convenience stores, had no further drinking water. That was a situation reminiscent of the English poet Samuel Taylor Coleridge's *The Rime of the Ancient Mariner* in which one stanza reads "water, water everywhere, nor any drop to drink" (Coleridge, 2009).

Some experts fear that Bangkok, for many years counted as one of the most visited cities in the world, may be underwater by 2030. The city has an approximate average elevation of 1.5 meters above sea level and is sinking about 2 centimeters every year. Already some areas within Bangkok, parts of the suburb Ramkhamhaeng, for example, are below sea level. Bangkok could be underwater by 2030 because of the excessive pumping of groundwater, the weight of city buildings, and rising sea levels due to global warming, resulting from melting ice caps. To imagine the weight of the city buildings we can conduct thought experiments such as imagining that we are carrying one 10-liter water bucket in each hand. The weight of concrete is more than double the weight of water, meaning more than 20 kg. The average car weighs about 1,000 to 1,500 kilograms or between 1 and 1.5 tons. We can imagine how many buckets of cement are needed to build a high-rise building. Skyscrapers are estimated to weigh between 200,000 and 500,000 tons. Bangkok is close to housing 100 skyscrapers, buildings higher than 150 meters, and many more high-rise buildings. All those buildings, and also bridges and roads, weigh the city down.

These examples illustrate how we are dependent on water as a resource and how water can have an impact on our lives, including business activities. The film *Bottled Life* claims that Nestlé, in some instances, monopolizes drinking water access, which in ethical terms is an equity problem, and water extraction beyond the renewal rate in particular areas causes environmental problems.

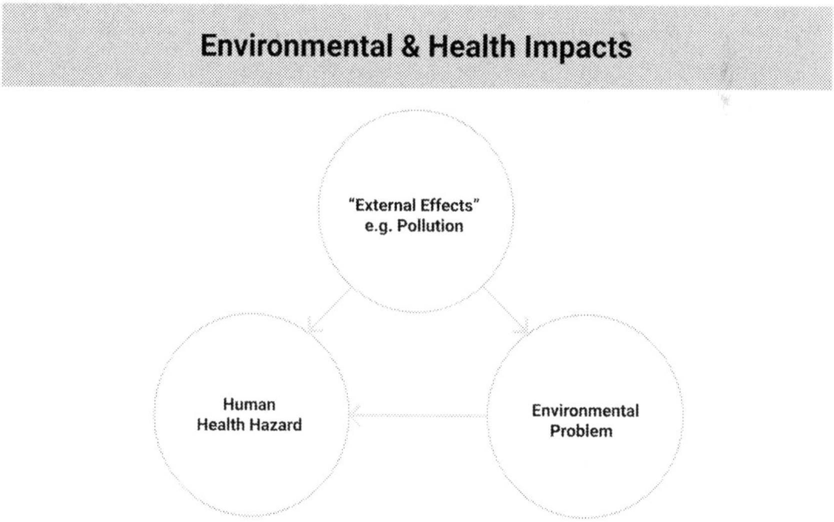

Environmental & Health Impacts

"External Effects"
e.g. Pollution

Human
Health Hazard

Environmental
Problem

Figure 4.3 Environmental and health impacts

Besides the water issues already mentioned, we also have problems with water in terms of drinking water pollution because of contamination with micro- and nanoplastics. As mentioned, human bodies consist of roughly 45–65% water, and cannot survive three or four days without it. The water we drink everyday usually comes in containers or through pipes which are made of different kinds of plastics, PET (polyethylene), PVC (polyvinyl chloride), or PC (polycarbonate), for example. Some of these plastics contain hormone-mimicking substances or are suspected to be toxic, carcinogenic (i.e. causing cancer), or have other adverse human health effects. PC is leaching (releasing) BPA (bisphenol A), which, for example, can mimic the action of estrogen. PVC seems to be one of the most problematic plastics because it is considered to contribute to cancer over long-term exposure, and it has been banned for food packaging in a number of countries; even some car manufacturers have eliminated PVC in the interior of their cars.

Case study 4.1: Micro- and nanoplastic in water, animals, food, and humans

Microplastics are plastic particles smaller than 5 mm, and nanoplastics, unintentionally produced plastic particles ranging from 1 to 1000 nm (Gigault et al., 2018). The oceans are full of micro- and nanoplastics and some researchers claim that in a few years there will be more microplastic in the oceans than plankton (Suaria et al., 2016). Plastic pollution concentrations in the ocean are reaching 580,000 pieces per square kilometer (Worm, 2015). Birds, fish, and other water animals are ingesting these small plastic particles. Many organisms digest these particles, and we are then eating these plastic particles in the food we consume. Plastic and its traces can meanwhile be found everywhere in the oceans, including the Mariana Trench, the deepest valley in the ocean that is about 11 kilometers deep (deeper than Mount Everest is high). BPA is meanwhile found in human blood and urine (Markham et al., 2010; Owczarek et al., 2018).

Research nanoplastic and microplastic, and answer the following questions:

(1) What exactly are nano- and microplastics?
(2) Where do they originate?
(3) How can we control the amount of plastic that enters the oceans and later the food chain?
(4) What should 1) consumers, 2) governments, and 3) businesses do to minimize the health and environmental impacts of nano- and microplastic?
(5) Research what is currently done by NGOs and corporations regarding nano- and microplastics.

4.6 Entrepreneurial opportunities for environmentally conscious businesses

Following the business activity of Rubber Killer, an upcycling business in Thailand, we can understand that there is a need to prevent, reuse, reduce, recycle, and recover rubber and plastics. Entrepreneurs find out what different stakeholders can do to avoid plastic and come up with business ideas that could make use of recycled plastics. Besides entrepreneurial plastic recycling innovations, downcycling and upcycling of recyclable materials needs to be considered as well. The fact that plastic or rubber recycling can be used as a sustainable business idea is shown by the case studies of Freitag (Chapter 1) and Rubber Killer.

Upcycling means "process[es] in which used materials are converted into something of higher value and/or quality in their second life" (Sung, 2015), while down-cycling converts materials into something of lower value. One example is the upcycling of elephant excrement near Chiang Mai in Thailand. Elephant excrement is mixed with paper maché and upcycled to create gift wrapping or greeting cards. Many companies such as Patagonia offer to

---

Case study 4.2: Rubber Killer

Research Rubber Killer and answer the following questions (see Rubber Killer, 2019):

(1) What is the philosophy of the founder of Rubber Killer? How does this business idea differ from the Freitag company?
(2) What do customers think about the brand? In which countries are the brand and its products successful? Why there?
(3) Which ethical theories would suggest that this is an ethical and sustainable business and why?
(4) What can other entrepreneurs learn from Rubber Killer?

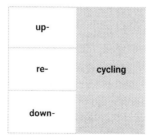

Figure 4.4 Up-, re-, and downcycling

> **Case study 4.3: Patagonia**
>
> Patagonia is a paradigmatic example of a company that is relatively consistent in considering future communities, ecosystems, and non-human species as stakeholders. The company reduces its impact on the environment by reducing their ecological footprint. Patagonia repairs products which in turn encourages customers to use their products long term and recycle them when no longer in use. In many countries, a 7-R strategy (refuse, refill, return, repair, reuse, recycle, and reduce) is gaining ground, especially when it comes to protecting nature reserves. 7-R billboards can be seen in some nature reserves, even in less environmentally conscious countries like Thailand, encouraging consumers to rethink their consumption patterns, and in several places separating trash bins which are labeled according to the different types of trash.
>
> Research the apparel company Patagonia and answer the following questions:
>
> (1) What kind of customers does Patagonia attract? Explain.
> (2) Why is for Patagonia the environment/nature a stakeholder?
> (3) What are the differences between Patagonia and other clothing companies?
> (4) How can we understand/interpret the marketing campaign "Don't buy this jacket"?
> (5) Is Patagonia's growth a contradiction in the context of the company's environmental responsibility culture?

manage the full life cycles of their products. Customers can bring products into shops for repair or products can be given back for secondhand sale or recycling. These kinds of cyclic business models are becoming more and more popular in Europe, Australasia, and North America. Entrepreneurs in other parts of the world need to anticipate such trends of more environmentally friendly and healthy consumer products. Adidas is meanwhile successfully selling running shoes made from recycled plastics intercepted from coastal communities and beaches before the plastic reaches the ocean (Morgan, 2019).

Patagonia is a paradigmatic example of a highly successful company that has taken corporate environmental responsibility as its business philosophy. Caring about the environment and being responsible for future generations is at the core of the company's DNA. Patagonia is a certified B corporation, a business that balances profit and purpose. B corporations are legally required to scrutinize their impact on any kind of stakeholder, including the environment (https://bcorporation.net/). Other examples of well-known B corporations are the ice cream manufacturer Ben and Jerry's (www.benjerry.com) and the German, Berlin-based, search engine Ecosia (www.ecosia.org/). We can learn from Patagonia that caring about the environment and future communities can even increase profit, despite the fact that huge profits were not intended by its founder, Yvon Chouinard, who unintentionally started this business by handcrafting reliable climbing gear for himself and his friends.

External effects such as constant air pollution with toxic substances not only have direct human health impacts, such as respiratory complications, but pollutants may also enter the human body indirectly via environmental contamination through water that is contaminated, for example, with microplastics. Fish then ingest the microplastic and, once humans consume the fish, a part of the micro- or nanoplastic is indirectly ingested by humans. This indicates that water contamination has an indirect impact on human health.

Toxic substances enter the human body via contaminated products that we are consuming, for example, food, water, or other consumer products, including non-food items. These may be toxic substances in everyday consumer products, but also building materials such as asbestos. Health hazards range from air pollution, caused by traffic and factories, to water pollution, due to micro- and nanoplastics that reach the human body via the pollution of

Figure 4.5 Environmental issues and business

drinking water, groundwater, water in rivers, lakes, and oceans. Soil polluted with pesticides, insecticides, and fertilizers may lead to the contamination of food. Not often considered as a serious hazard is noise pollution coming from highways, airports, and factories, which may lead to psychological and psychosomatic side effects. All these are human health hazards which may result from business activities and our personal consumption.

The number of environmental issues we are facing are multiple; overpopulation of the planet, the question of the carrying capacity of the planet, the overconsumption of goods and energy, the depletion of non-renewable and renewable resources, the potentially irreversible degradation of ecosystems, such as deforestation and overfishing, the reduction of biodiversity, the degradation of food quality, and so forth.

When considering the utilization of resources, tools have been developed to compare the resource usage of similar or different products and services. Two well-known concepts are the ecological rucksack (Schmidt-Bleek, 2004 and the ecological footprint (Wackernagel & Rees, 1998). These concepts help us to compare the use of resources, especially for two comparable products, to estimate or measure resource utilization (e.g. the utilization of two or more different mobile phones).

4.7 Sustainability

Ethical discourse features many controversies regarding justice, but the recent Fridays for Future movement in particular brought one form of justice to the attention of the public: *intergenerational* justice (www.fridaysforfuture.org/). Justice can be considered within one generation, which is called intragenerational justice, or it can be considered between different generations, which has been termed intergenerational justice. Sometimes the terms "intergenerational equity" or "inter-generative equity" are also used. It is of utmost importance to understand that currently we do not take intergenerational equity and intergenerational justice sufficiently into account, because we are over-consuming resources which we are not entitled to from an intergenerational fairness perspective.

Some resources we are using will be depleted within the current century, such as tantalum and indium, and some rare earths, minerals, and metals will no longer be available for future generations at a certain point in time. However, we desperately need, or in some cases just "want", these non-renewable resources for the production of mobile phones, computers, tablets, and other devices. And we may even need more of these non-renewable resources in the near future if we think about the Internet of Things, self-driving cars, and the hardware and electricity used for Artificial Intelligence (AI), cryptocurrencies, blockchain, and other technologies. The only option left for saving the environment and advancing technology would be a neat and comprehensive recycling program so that these non-renewable resources will also be available for generations in the future. We already have enough difficulties

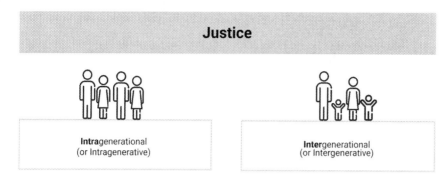

Figure 4.6 Intergenerational vs intra-generational justice

dealing with renewable resources, sometimes simply called "renewables", like wood and water. Also, sun, wind, and plants are considered renewable resources, while non-renewables are resources such as oil, gas, minerals, and so forth. It needs to be noted that these resources are called non-renewable resources because they are not naturally renewable from a perspective of a single human lifetime, because many of the non-renewables take millions of years to replenish or rebuild, while renewable resources are usually available in abundance, like sun and wind. Other renewables such as trees and other plants are renewed automatically in the natural cycle as long as humans do not interfere negatively.

The so-called Hubbert curve, named after Marion King Hubbert, renders an approximation of the production rate of a non-renewable resource over time, predicting the depletion of natural resources (Hubbert, 1956). The symmetrical Hubbard curve is pagoda shaped and predicts that resource extraction starts slowly, accelerates exponentially, peaks, decelerates at the same rate as it accelerated, and then runs out at the same rate as extraction started. Based on this curve, there exists the prediction that humans may never completely extract all non-renewable resources from the earth because at one point in time the extraction of non-renewable resources would be so expensive that it would not be economically feasible to extract them anymore. It follows that engineers and businesses would rather search for more abundant resource substitutes that could replace scarce metals, minerals, and earths, or mine similar resources on other planets, satellite moons, or meteorites in the future.

Businesses and humans individually depend heavily on water for almost all kinds of activities. This is why we have used water in different circumstances as an example of an indispensable renewable resource. This partially explains why water is one of the five phases (wuxing) in Chinese philosophy, together with wood, fire, earth, and metal. The phases ("elements") of wood and water are closely connected. Water nourishes plants which in turn contain and retain water. Trees in a forest need water to grow and at the same time the leaves, the branches, the trunk, and the roots contain water. The mass of a tree very roughly contains about 50% water. The roots of plants prevent soil erosion and the soil ("earth") absorbs and contains water. Thus, there exists a vice-versa dependency or interdependence between water and wood. Water nourishes plants, and plants and earth contain water. Areas without plants, like deserts, cannot contain water for a very long time.

For illustrative purposes, we can imagine that a desert, in terms of water retention, is a bit similar to a bald head that dries very easily when washed, compared to a head with dense and long hair which takes a longer duration for air drying. The Greeks, Romans, and medieval populations already deteriorated many natural forests in Europe beyond the renewal rate. Thus, the majority of Greeks were not living according to the rules of nature, as stoic philosophers propagated. At least, this philosophical wisdom was not applied to forests. Between 1600 and 1900 about 50% of the forest in the US had been cut, because wood used to be the major building material. And currently, we are experiencing a progressing large-scale depletion of the native Amazon rainforest in Brazil, and with this comes a significant reduction of biodiversity. The relationship between water and wood brings us to the concept of sustainability and sustainable development.

4.7.1 Sustainable development

The idea of sustainably planting trees can be traced back to the year 1560 and German forestry rules as stipulated in Hans Carl von Carlowitz's book *Sylvicultura Oeconomica* (von Carlowitz, 2018). The book is the first treatise formulating the concept of sustainability in forestry. Part of the subtitle of the book reads *"the economic news and instructions for the natural growing of wild trees, [...] requires the careful management of sustainable forestry resources"*. Carlowitz recommends the conservation and plantation of trees in such a way that the utilization of trees and forests will be "continuously enduring and sustainable" (von Carlowitz, 2018). The general ecologic-economic idea was that we should not plant fewer trees than we cut, meaning that we should always leave sufficient resources for the next generation. This is a key issue and idea of intergenerational justice or intergenerational equity.

There exist roughly three trillion trees on our blue-green planet and every year 10 billion more trees are logged than planted (Crowther et al., 2015). So far, we have done the opposite of sustainable forestry: we plant fewer trees than we cut. However, the idea of planting trees has come to the center of mitigating, decelerating, or even halting climate change. A *Science* study claims that a 25% increase in forest areas, planting more than 500 billion trees on an available area of almost one billion hectares, could increase the planet's canopy cover in order to store more than 200 gigatonnes of carbon, thereby reducing the atmospheric carbon pool by around 25% (Bastin et al., 2019).

Some businesses, such as Ecosia, have made it their mission to "cultivate a more environmentally, socially and economically sustainable world" by reversing deforestation and by "planting a billion native trees" (www.ecosia.org/). There are some examples of Thai companies that have incorporated sustainable business practices in their everyday business activities, especially in regard to sustainable wood sourcing, such as "Double A paper" and "Tycoon percussion". Double A paper does not use recycled paper, but claims that their paper "consists of 94% eucalyptus (hardwood pulp) from Double A Paper from Farmed Trees (PFFT) and 6% pine and spruce (softwood pulp) from FSC-certified [Forest Stewardship Council] suppliers" (Double A Global, n.d.). PFFT is sourced from trees that are cultivated and grown along Thai rice paddies. Farmers make use of an otherwise unutilized space and it is claimed that these trees even keep the soil in place, preventing soil erosion. Tycoon music uses sustainable rubberwood for the majority of its instrument production. The rubberwood, or Siam Oak, is taken from rubber tree plantations where the rubber trees can no longer be used for rubber production (Tycoon, n.d.).

The classical definition of sustainable development stems from the so-called "Brundtland Report" entitled *Our Common Future* (World Commission on Environment & Development, 1990). Development is sustainable if it "meets the needs of the present without compromising the ability of future generations to meet their own needs". This report is named after Gro Harlem Brundtland, a former prime minister of Norway (1990–1996). Development which meets the *needs* of the present without compromising the ability of future generations to meet their own *needs* emphasizes *needs*, not *wants*. Current generations should of course meet their needs, but a lot of goods and services purchased in the so-called developed world go beyond what is essentially needed. Many things are simply wanted. However, it could be also argued that a new mobile phone every two to three years is not straightforwardly a want, but an essential tool today that needs to be updated with a frequency that keeps pace with the technological advancement of the professional business world. We can see with this example that it is not simple to differentiate between the concepts of needs and wants. For most professionals a frequent replacement of their mobile phone is essential for their business activities; for non-business users, an up-to-date mobile phone is rather a want. What is a need and what is a want depends on circumstances and it may become quite subjective, depending on a person's perception. The differentiation between needs and wants can also be linked to what is considered the minimum rate for social welfare in different countries. It is important to add that even if the differentiation between needs and wants was theoretically clear, most people would not be happy to only satisfy their needs, forfeiting all other wants.

On the one hand, the Brundtland definition seriously takes future communities' needs into account, because from the perspective of intergenerational ethics this kind of development intends to not leave future generations worse off than current generations are. But on the other hand, current lifestyles and corresponding business activities would be impossible to maintain if we followed the prescriptive implications of the Brundtland definition. Our current behavior will certainly leave future generations worse off in terms of environmental conditions and renewable and non-renewable resources. Also, we were worse off in terms of environmental conditions and natural resources than previous generations; trees were given as an example before, but clean water and clean air are other examples.

4.7.2 Domains and dimensions of sustainability

In the context of sustainability discussions, it is often claimed that businesses, governments, and citizens need to consider the so-called triple bottom line (People, Planet, Profit) regarding three aspects of sustainability (Szekely et al., 2017). The three spheres, aspects, domains, or dimensions can be rendered in a Venn diagram: the eco-environmental, the social, and the economic/business dimensions overlap in reality, and only if we consider all three spheres and their interdependent nature do we account for sustainability.

In recent years the "circles of sustainability" have been developed, which bring together four sustainability spheres or quadrants, namely ecology, culture, politics, and economics (James, 2014). The circles of sustainability are used to measure the sustainability of cities and communities. At the same time, they could also be used for measuring the sustainability of businesses because the tools are clear and easily communicable to customers. The Swedish outdoor company Fjällräven adopted a four directions sustainability compass "[N] Nature and Environment; [E] Economy and Business Processes; [S] Social Responsibility; [W] Wellbeing" from Alan AtKisson (2008). With the motto "Leaving basecamp in better condition than we found it", Fjällräven interestingly goes beyond the Brundtland definition (Fjällräven, 2019).

Figure 4.7 Triple bottom line

Inducing or abstracting a sustainability definition from this motto, sustainable development would meet the needs of the present generation but while "*improving*" the ability of future generations to meet their own needs".

The United Nations Sustainable Development Goals (SDGs) developed 17 criteria that are used for indicating and measuring sustainability: no poverty, zero hunger, good health and well-being, quality education, gender equality, cleaner water and sanitation, affordable and clean energy, decent work and economic growth, industry innovation and infrastructure, reduced inequalities, sustainable cities and communities, responsible consumption and production, climate action, life below water, life on land, peace, justice and strong institutions, and partnership for the goals (United Nations, 2016). Some of the businesses in the context of their corporate social responsibility actions are indicating why and how they meet one or the other of these Sustainable Development Goals.

However, ecological economists claim that the three spheres ecology, society, and economy or business need to be seen from a different perspective, namely from an ontological perspective that renders these three spheres in their integrated existence. A thought experiment can tangibly illustrate this positioning. As far as we know, there is no business on Mars, because there is no society on Mars that could engage in business activities. But why is there no society on Mars? Because there is no ecosystem on Mars. As soon as an artificial ecosystem is created on Mars, people will start moving to the planet. As soon as a society is established on Mars, business activities will be launched. With the help of this thought experiment, we can understand that ecological economists must be correct by claiming that businesses and the economy are a subset of the society and the society is a subset of the ecosystem. Businesses depend on society and society depends on the ecosystem. According to ecological economists, this ontological fact can by no means be

Figure 4.8 Integrated sustainability model

ignored because if the ecosystem is destroyed, a society can no longer survive. Without society, there will be no business activities either.

Against this background, the following statement by Michael Schramm on the term "sustainability" and its two components "sustain" and "ability" needs to be highlighted: if we want to preserve our ecosystem, "our social creativity must develop the 'ability' to promote the ability and creativity of natural things to 'sustain' themselves" (Schramm, 2020).

4.7.3 Challenges regarding future generations' claims

The sustainability demands from the Brundtland definition confront us with a number of issues, especially if we take the needs of future generations very seriously. If non-renewable resources were shared among the current and an infinite or indefinite high number of future generations nothing would be left for any of these generations, including the present generation. This is a very powerful logical argument that requires us to rethink the implications of the Brundtland definition. Nevertheless, future generations' needs in regards to non-renewable resources can theoretically be met, but only if the respective current generation strictly and consistently recycles non-renewable resources.

There are two rather weak arguments that discount future generations' needs. The first argument stipulates that the further we try to estimate future generations' needs in the far future, the less we may estimate or predict them. That is not completely incorrect if we try to imagine how our grandparents, for example, could have predicted what kind of products and services we need. Our grandparents would not have imagined that we would need or want iPhones, tablets, fully autonomous cars, and AI-assisted devices. But on the other hand, it is evident that they would have known that we want clean air, clean water, and resources that satisfy our needs. The second weak argument is that we may not even be sure about the existence of future generations because the current style of life may make the earth unlivable for future generations, or humanity may become extinct because of disasters. Such disasters could be pandemics, worse than Covid-19, natural disasters or anthropogenic disasters, caused by humans, e.g. excessive global warming beyond a point of no return, or a dystopian singularity scenario, like in the film *The Matrix*, in which an AI system takes over humanity and even paralyses human beings (Meinhold, 2009).

Due to this unpredictability of future generations' wants, needs, and even existence, some economists claim that we should discount values that project into the future. Based on the relative unpredictability of future generations' preferences, e.g. concerning non-renewable resources, it could be claimed that values in the future are worth less than they are worth today. This idea is based on a psychological assumption: myopia. The medical term myopia means shortsightedness. In economic psychology, myopia means shortsightedness in a metaphorical sense. Discounting future values is the economic consequence of shortsightedness in terms of knowledge or acceptance about future values, but it is also explainable by a philosophic-anthropological condition that persons have a present preference for positive values. We would prefer to have positive things now rather than sometime in the future and we would prefer negative things far in the future rather than right now. This is why people would usually prefer to grow old gracefully. The worst negative value for an individual is death, or being severely handicapped, which is why we often try to ignore the topic or wish the occurrence of death to remain as far in the future as possible (Meinhold, 2014).

Assume that we knew that there will be an earthquake in the future and we could choose when the earthquake may occur. Most likely, people would prefer the earthquake to happen in the far future. This would also make sense in terms of personal and infrastructural disaster preparation for the earthquake. The further away the earthquake occurs in the future, the better it would be. This kind of present preference is not myopic. But if the earthquake would occur beyond a person's possible lifespan, this person would discount the (negative) value ascribed to the importance of the earthquake, since the earthquake will not affect this person and thus the threat of the earthquake has limited relevance to them. Similar reasoning is behind the fact that many people are ignoring the looming (potential) climate catastrophe.

But if it comes to receiving positive services or goods, for example a gold coin, most people would prefer to receive the gold coin right now rather than some time in the future. Because nobody *knows* if the respective person will be given the gold coin in the future. There is a certain uncertainty regarding the objects or services we may receive some time in the near or far future. This is why we have a preference for positive things happening or being received in the present, and prefer negative things to occur in the far future.

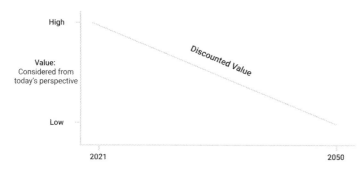

Figure 4.9 Discounting values

4.7.4 Reasons for considering future generations' claims

While economic myopia and present preference are understandable from a behavioristic perspective, there are very powerful arguments for considering future generations' or future communities' moral standing and taking intergenerational justice, equity, fairness, and responsibility very seriously. The German philosopher Hans Jonas wrote in his 1984 book *The Imperative of Responsibility* that along with technologically pertinent advancements humans also developed the potential to annihilate the entire planet. With this potential of destruction comes the imperative of responsibility (Jonas, 1984). In his book *The Idea of Justice* Amartya Sen stated that power implies a corresponding amount of obligation, duty, and responsibility (Sen, 2011). The more power a person, group, business, or entity has, the more responsibility is naturally tied to this power or potential power. This idea applies, for example, to parent–child relationships, to the relationship between more and less advanced economies, and to large multinational corporations and their relationships to stakeholders, such as employees, other (smaller) businesses, communities, customers or users, and governmental entities (see also Chapter 3).

Combined with the previously mentioned argument of Hans Jonas, it becomes obvious that if a group or an entity has the power to annihilate the entire planet, then this group or entity has a corresponding unimaginably high responsibility. This does not only apply to the firepower of weapons, but also the destructive power of anthropogenic environmental pollution caused by societies and businesses, such as microplastic waste and CO_2 emissions. John Rawls in his 2001 book *Justice as Fairness* (Rawls, 2001) claims that members of any generation would adopt principles they would want preceding generations to have followed. For instance, today's generations wish that previous generations had issued stricter rules and laws to limit CO_2 emissions. Rawls uses a thought-experimental retro-perspective approach projected from the future into the present and from the present into the past (see also Chapter 3). We imagine living in the future and look back to the present and we ask ourselves what would we like this current generation to do for generations living in the future or we would ask ourselves the question what would we have liked our grandparents to have done in terms of intergenerational justice or intergenerational equity. According to Rawls, people in the original position would opt for a fair savings principle due to their risk aversion in order to prevent the risk that no generation at a certain point in time consumes all non-renewable resources at the expense of subsequent generations. By agreeing on such a just savings principle in the original position, the problem of future discounting discussed above could also be counteracted. As it should have by now become clear, this kind of thinking makes current youth protests around the globe against climate change and environmental destruction, such as those of Fridays for Future, highly tangible.

4.8 Anthropocentrism

Another important concept that is pertinent for a wider understanding of organizations' stakeholders is that of anthropocentrism vs non-anthropocentrism. The word anthropocentrism is derived from the Greek "anthropos" meaning human and "kentron" meaning center. As humans we consider ourselves at the center or peak of the creation or evolution. Following this anthropocentric perspective, we make environmental and climate regulations and laws compatible with current convenient lifestyles without seriously taking into account the current climate crisis and environmental emergency. In contrast, if we adopt a non-anthropocentric perspective we should then consider stakeholders in the sustainability contexts such as non-human species and ecosystems.

There exist three forms of anthropocentrism, which need to be disambiguated: 1) ontological anthropocentrism, 2) epistemological anthropocentrism, and 3) ethical anthropocentrism. Ontological anthropocentrism assumes a superior existence of human beings compared to non-human species. While this ontological fact cannot be denied, for example, if species are compared in regard to intelligence or the creation of culture and technology, ontological anthropocentrism is rather descriptive than normative and does not necessarily imply human chauvinism or the ethical instrumentalization of other species. Epistemological anthropocentrism refers to the fact that humans cannot entirely avoid human-generated perspectives on the rest of nature. Neither ontological nor epistemological anthropocentrism implies necessarily ethical normative anthropocentrism, which may claim superior treatment of humans in terms of mainly ascribing intrinsic or inherent value only to humans and some of their products (Dzwonkowska, 2018).

Normative ethical anthropocentrism becomes a problem because a large portion of nature has been instrumentalized to the extent that the overemphasis on human "wants" has resulted in the large-scale destruction of nature that we are facing now. Since normative ethical anthropocentrism should at least save nature for the sake of humanity, there is a further component that exacerbated the destruction of nature: the myopic collective behavior, mentioned above, meaning non-sustainable behavior, which includes disregarding potential stakeholders such as non-human species and ecosystems.

4.9 Last person argument

One such thought experiment which makes a non-anthropocentric vantage point tangible is the so-called last person argument (Peterson & Sandin, 2013), which was published in its first variation by Richard Routley (Routley, 1973). Imagine the following scenario: you are the last person on the planet, and you are going to die because you have contracted a disease that has so far killed all of humanity, except for you. You start feeling the first symptoms and will probably die within a few days. Also, you do not want

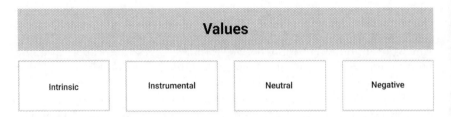

Figure 4.10 Instrumental vs intrinsic value

to live any longer because the symptoms of the disease in its final stages are unbearable. There exists a device which you can use to blow up the entire planet. No other humans would be negatively affected, you would only shorten one human life, your own.

This thought experiment evokes an intuition where it seems to be wrong to annihilate the entire planet, despite the fact that no other human will be negatively affected, since humans may not be the only beings of value in this world. We indirectly ascribe intrinsic value to the planet, even a planet without humans, by strongly feeling that it is not justifiable to annihilate the planet. Planet earth has not only instrumental value but intrinsic value. According to the distinction of intrinsic value and instrumental value, not only humans or human life may be of intrinsic value but species, ecosystems or even individual animals or plants, depending on the interpretation of the term intrinsic value, inherent value, or value in itself. Instrumental value, by contrast, is a value or an object that is valuable or useful for something else.

For example, the classroom's whiteboard is useful for rendering ideas in the educational environment. Intrinsic value is something that has inherent worth, it is valuable on its own or by itself. Besides human beings, we may ascribe intrinsic value to artworks, thoughts, memories, and other irreplaceable objects or things. We can easily see that we make a distinction between our pets and the animals that we have killed and prepared for the meat that some of us eat. There is a difference between the animal which has been the source of the meat on the plate and the animal that is waiting for us at home, a pet. We may consider that the pet has a higher value than the animal which has been killed for the meat on our plate. Even if we may be starving, in ordinary day-to-day conditions, we may not consider eating our dog or our cat even though we are very hungry (unless in a disastrous emergency). Our pet may have something more than simple instrumental value; it may have, for us personally, higher value, which may not be intrinsic but at least close to something like intrinsic value, that we would ascribe to other human beings.

A non-anthropocentric perspective claims that we need to consider ascribing intrinsic value not only to human persons, but to planet earth at large, to ecosystems, to certain non-human species, and other non-replicable entities.

4.10 Ecotopian innovations

Ernest Callenbach in his 1975 novel *Ecotopia* already had the idea that businesses should consider sustainability, environmental ethics, and ecological economics in everyday life and business activities (Callenbach, 2009). In this direct interactive democratic system recycling is strictly enforced. Callenbach opined that we need comprehensive renewable energy production with tidal, wind, and solar electricity production. Cars without combustion engines, free electric public transport systems, such as electric high-speed trains and slow jump-on trams, combined with public bicycles as we can find them in some environmentally friendly cities and university campuses today. He imagined the de-concentration of living space in green cities where trees and water surfaces signify the cityscape (Meinhold & Stasi, 2021). Callenbach had the idea of developing smart plastics of three types: immediately self-recycling plastics (e.g. for packaging), slowly self-recycling plastics, and highly durable plastics (e.g. for building and construction or medical purposes). More prominent than plastics was a revival of natural sustainable and long-lasting materials such as wood, stone, metal, and glass as the main materials for building and usage in everyday life. Clothes were made of either natural materials such as cotton, hemp, wool, and leather or from high-tech recyclable synthetic materials (Meinhold, 2013). This kind of fabric philosophy described in *Ecotopia* is reflected in two exemplary business ethics cases we have studied, the American outdoor company Patagonia and the Swiss bag company Freitag.

4.11 Manufactured nature and ecological economies

Edward Burtynsky in his documentary *Manufactured Landscapes* depicts large-scale photos and footage of industrial landscapes. These photos very impressively render the deep and devastating non-sustainable environmental impacts industries have on ecosystems. In 1968 the Apollo 8 mission for the first time made citizens aware of the fragility of their own planet. The so-called "earthrise" image of the earth from a lunar orbital perspective intensified the awareness of environmental responsibility that was growing slowly all over the world. The environmental movement made us aware that we had treated non-human sentient beings such as animals and plants as "the other". This, so far, has been a very anthropocentric perspective and approach.

Several religions, tribal philosophies, but also ecological economics and environmental ethics explain that we need to understand humans' embeddedness in nature, its connectedness with the environment, and its dependency on natural resources (George, 2015). This ontological fact explains how ecological economics comes up with the dependency or integrated model of the economy, society, and ecology where business and society depend on the ecosystem. Patagonia, an American outdoor attire company, has integrated sustainability in a very serious way into its business model. Ecological economists (Daly & Farley, 2004) claim that renewable resources have to be used in such a way that they can regenerate, for example when fishing or cutting trees. Non-renewable resources should be used extremely carefully at least until we find replacements or if technology can guarantee that future generations have the same benefit from the limited resources we leave them behind. Emissions from factories, for example, or due to traffic, must be limited in such a way that ecosystems can regenerate. Biodiversity must not decline – in particular endangered species should not disappear. And the human population growth must be limited. When it comes to innovations, they must be compatible with eco-systemic sustainability, such as solar power or algae harvesting. And the prices must reflect the "ecological truth".

4.12 Internalization of external effects

That prices should reflect the "ecological truth" means that currently, most product or service prices do not reflect environmental or health impacts. Environmental and health impacts are also called "external effects". The "internalization of external effects", or the polluter-pays principle, means that health and environmental impacts, in particular the costs thereof, need to be included in prices of products or services. When we reflect on the market prices of products such as cars and petrol, we usually calculate all costs that car and oil companies have to produce cars or petrol, plus markup and taxes. But these costs do not reflect all costs that result from the usage of cars and petrol: human health impacts and environmental pollution are omitted. However, adding all these costs to cars and fuel leads us to what ecological economists call "real costs". Such prices "speak the ecological truth", as ecological economists put it. The private costs plus the cost of external effects equals the social costs or real costs. In order to make prices reflecting real costs, many environmentalists, but also entrepreneurs such as Elon Musk, CEO of Tesla and SpaceX, opt for a carbon tax. A carbon tax could internalize external effects, i.e. the environmental impacts, in the price of energy, services, and products.

This so-called internalization of external effects leads to higher prices, for example cigarettes would be significantly more expensive if they included the costs of cancer treatments that result from smoking those cigarettes. According to the market principles of supply and demand, the demand for cigarettes automatically would decrease due to the higher cigarette prices. If all our products and services included external effects in their prices, we would have real costs and ecological economists would claim that these product prices speak the ecological truth. Besides, as some customers are willing to pay higher prices for organic and fairly produced and traded products (e.g. when customers buy coffee from Starbucks), then it can be claimed that such customers are willing to pay, at least a part, of the external effects their products cause or pay for preventing external effects because the exploitation of workers, as well as soil and water pollution, are avoided.

Another example of the internalization of external effects can be illustrated with the noise around airports being internalized in ticket prices. Imagine that we asked a random group of inhabitants in a one-kilometer radius around an airport how much they would spend per year so that they no longer have to suffer from the noise pollution from airplanes. We could calculate how many people live in this one-kilometer radius and we could then calculate the average of how much every asked person would be willing to spend to avoid that noise. The number of people living in the one-kilometer radius would be multiplied with the average amount a person would spend for noise avoidance. This amount could be added to all tickets purchased for planes that depart and land at this airport within one year. Broken down to each ticket, the higher ticket price would internalize the external effect, namely the noise. The ticket price would increase slightly, and slightly fewer tickets would be purchased. People living in this one-kilometer radius around the airport could be compensated with the money gotten from the travelers. Residents in this one-kilometer radius could either spend the money on noise proofed windows, save the money for vacations, or buy a house somewhere else in the long run.

4.13 Precautionary vs pre-actionary considerations

In order to avoid highly dangerous external effects, careful or conservative scientists suggest following the precautionary approach. The precautionary approach is based on deontological demands. If practices or technologies carry catastrophic risks or unknown irreversible consequences the practice or the technology must be rejected until the risk is significantly diminished or disproved. The application of the precautionary approach is extremely important, for example in the case of nuclear power generation, having in mind nuclear disasters of the scale of Fukushima (2011) and Chernobyl (1986). In the light of these nuclear disasters, residents of affected areas, and not only them, would have, at least retrospectively, opted for a precautionary approach. To take another example, on the basis of the precautionary principle one could argue that AI technology should be carefully managed. From a utilitarian perspective, however, AI technology should be massively developed, since aggregately seen, AI will most likely benefit the greatest number of humans. In this sense, following a pre-actionary approach, risk-taking is essential in order to pave the way for new inventions that may change the world positively. Examples are fully autonomous driving which will in the long run decrease the number of deadly accidents, digital currencies, which will ease payments and transactions, and genetic design and engineering which will combat, cure, eliminate, and maybe prevent diseases such as cancer, HIV, malaria, and Alzheimer's.

> **Case study 4.4: The 5G network: between pre-actionary and precautionary considerations**
>
> It is quite difficult to balance the sustainability of steadily progressing digital critical infrastructure that is very much needed for future technologies, such as the Internet of Things or fully autonomous driving, on the one hand and health concerns regarding such new technologies on the other. It is difficult to balance between pre-actionary and precautionary approaches. There is fierce competition between providers of high-tech software and hardware which demands pre-actionary approaches by corporations. Daily life in advanced economies is neither convenient nor normally manageable without intensive information and communication technology utilization, but yet we are still not sure about the health implications of these new technologies, such as the 5G network.
>
> Research 5G's technological opportunities and potential health threats.
>
> (1) What are the potential health threats that are being discussed?
> (2) Imagine a fully operating 5G network covering all areas is in place. Given the potential health threats above, who are the stakeholders that could be affected, directly or indirectly?
> (3) Which of the ethical theories discussed in this chapter could help prevent these potential threats?
> (4) Imagine you were a CEO in the mobile phone/wireless industry. What actions would you take after you are informed about the scientific findings of the potential threats?

Key takeaways

(1) Modern stakeholder theory includes the environment, non-human species, and future communities as stakeholders.
(2) Environmental responsibility and consciousness have become a successful business model.
(3) Sustainability encompasses multiple domains and dimensions.
(4) The scope of sustainability spans multiple generations.
(5) Internalization of external effects should be added to business products and services.
(6) Precautionary actions are key in preventing future harm.
(7) Pre-actionary approaches are essential for paving the way for new technology.
(8) Pre-actionary and precautionary approaches need to be balanced.

References

Aristotle. (2018). *Nicomachean Ethics.* The Internet Classics Archive. http://classics.mit.edu/Aristotle/nicomachaen.1.i.html

AtKisson, A. (2008). *The ISIS Agreement: How Sustainability Can Improve Organizational Performance and Transform the World.* Earthscan.

Bastin, J.-F., Finegold, Y., Garcia, C., Mollicone, D., Rezende, M., Routh, D., Zohner, C.M., & Crowther, T.W. (2019). The global tree restoration potential. *Science, 365*(6448), 76–79. https://doi.org/10.1126/science.aax0848

BCG. (2017). *Total Societal Impact: A New Lens for Strategy.* www.bcg.com/publications/2017/total-societal-impact-new-lens-strategy.aspx

Boulding, K. (1966). *The Economics of the Coming Spaceship Earth.* http://dieoff.org/page160.htm

Burtynsky, E. (2019). *Watermark.* www.edwardburtynsky.com/projects/films/watermark

Callenbach, E. (2009). *Ecotopia.* Random House Publishing Group.

Carlowitz, H.C. von. (2018). *Sylvicultura Oeconomica.* Franklin Classics Trade Press.

Carroll, A.B., Brown, J., & Buchholtz, A.K. (2017). *Business & Society: Ethics, Sustainability & Stakeholder Management* (10th ed.). South-Western College Pub.

Coleridge, S.T. (2009). *Rime of the Ancient Mariner: And Select Poems.* The Floating Press.

Cottier, T., Lalani, S., & Siziba, C. (2019). *Intergenerational Equity: Environmental and Cultural Concerns.* Brill.

Crowther, T.W., et al. (2015). Mapping tree density at a global scale. *Nature, 525*(7568), 201–205. https://doi.org/10.1038/nature14967

Daly, H.E., & Farley, J. (2004). *Ecological Economics: Principles and Applications.* Island Press.

DesJardins, J.R. (2005). Businesses and environmental sustainability. *Business and Professional Ethics Journal, 24*(1–2), 35–59.

DesJardins, J.R. (2013). *An Introduction to Business Ethics* (5th ed.). McGraw-Hill Education.

Double A Global. (n.d.). *Sustainable Sourcing.* www.doubleapaper.com/index.php/sustainable

Dzwonkowska, D. (2018). Is environmental virtue ethics anthropocentric? *Journal of Agricultural and Environmental Ethics, 31*(6), 723–738. https://doi.org/10.1007/s10806-018-9751-6

Fernando, A.C. (2010). *Business Ethics and Corporate Governance.* Pearson Education India.

Ferrell, O.C., Fraedrich, J., & Ferrell, L. (2018). *Business Ethics: Ethical Decision Making & Cases* (12th ed.). Cengage Learning.

Fjällräven. (2019). *Sustainability.* www.fjallraven.com/us/en-us/sustainability

Foulkes, I. (2017, August 25). Switzerland landslide: Are the Alps melting? *BBC News.* www.bbc.com/news/world-europe-41049827

Freeman, R.E., Harrison, J.S., Wicks, A.C., Parmar, B.L., & Colle, S. de. (2010). *Stakeholder Theory: The State of the Art.* Cambridge University Press.

George, S.K. (2015). Earth's the limit: The sense of finiteness among the hill tribes of northeast India. In KAS (Ed.), *Environmental Values Emerging from Cultures and Religions of the ASEAN Region.* Konrad Adenauer Foundation. doi: 10.13140/RG.2.1.2636.8480

Gigault, J., Halle, A. ter, Baudrimont, M., Pascal, P.-Y., Gauffre, F., Phi, T.-L., El Hadri, H., Grassl, B., & Reynaud, S. (2018). Current opinion: What is a nanoplastic? *Environmental Pollution, 235*, 1030–1034. https://doi.org/10.1016/j.envpol.2018.01.024

Hartman, L.P., DesJardins, J.R., & MacDonald, C. (2017). *Business Ethics: Decision Making for Personal Integrity & Social Responsibility* (4th ed.). McGraw-Hill Education.

Held, V. (2006). *The Ethics of Care: Personal, Political, and Global*. Oxford University Press.

Hubbert, M.K. (1956, January 1). *Nuclear Energy and the Fossil Fuel*. Drilling and Production Practice. www.onepetro.org/conference-paper/API-56-007

James, P. (2014). *Urban Sustainability in Theory and Practice: Circles of Sustainability* (1st ed.). Routledge.

Jonas, H. (1984). *The Imperative of Responsibility: In Search of an Ethics for the Technological Age*. University of Chicago Press.

Kant, I. (1993). *Grounding for the Metaphysics of Morals: On a Supposed Right to Lie Because of Philanthropic Concerns* (J.W. Ellington, Trans.; 3rd ed.). Hackett Publishing Company, Inc.

Lanzerath, D., & Friele, M. (2014). *Concepts and Values in Biodiversity*. Routledge.

Markham, D.A., Waechter, J.M., Wimber, M., Rao, N., Connolly, P., Chuang, J.C., Hentges, S., Shiotsuka, R.N., Dimond, S., & Chappelle, A.H. (2010). Development of a method for the determination of Bisphenol A at trace concentrations in human blood and urine and elucidation of factors influencing method accuracy and sensitivity. *Journal of Analytical Toxicology, 34*(6), 293–303. https://doi.org/10.1093/jat/34.6.293

Meinhold, R. (2009). Being in the matrix: An example of cinematic education in philosophy. *Prajna Vihara, 10*(1–2), 18.

Meinhold, R. (2013). Ecotopia. In P.B. Thompson & D.M. Kaplan (Eds.), *Encyclopedia of Food and Agricultural Ethics* (pp. 1–4). Springer Netherlands. https://doi.org/10.1007/978-94-007-6167-4_295-5

Meinhold, R. (2014). *Fashion Myths: A Cultural Critique* (J. Irons, Trans.). Transcript-Verlag.

Meinhold, R., & Stasi, A. (2021). "Eco-polis": Environmental sustainability in ecotopian cities. *Interdisciplinary Studies in Literature and Environment*. https://doi.org/10.1093/isle/isab002

Meyer, L.H. (2017). *Intergenerational Justice*. Routledge.

Mill, J.S. (2017). *Utilitarianism*. Coventry House Publishing.

Moore, B.L. (2017). *Ecological Literature and the Critique of Anthropocentrism*. Springer.

Morgan, C. (2019, September 2). Adidas is turning plastic ocean waste into sneakers and sportswear. *Business Insider*. www.businessinsider.com/adidas-sneakers-plastic-bottles-ocean-waste-recycle-pollution-2019-8

Owczarek, K., Kubica, P., Kudłak, B., Rutkowska, A., Konieczna, A., Rachoń, D., Namieśnik, J., & Wasik, A. (2018). Determination of trace levels of eleven Bisphenol A analogues in human blood serum by high performance liquid chromatography–tandem mass spectrometry. *Science of the Total Environment, 628–629*, 1362–1368. https://doi.org/10.1016/j.scitotenv.2018.02.148

Peterson, M., & Sandin, P. (2013). The last man argument revisited. *The Journal of Value Inquiry, 47*(1), 121–133. https://doi.org/10.1007/s10790-013-9369-x

Rawls, J. (2001). *Justice as Fairness: A Restatement*. Harvard University Press.

Reuters. (2019, July 19). Bayer welcomes judge's call for reduced damages in $2 billion... www.reuters.com/article/us-bayer-glyphosate-lawsuit-idUSKCN1UE0KN

Routley, R. (1973). Is there a need for a new, an environmental ethic? *Proceedings of the XVth World Congress of Philosophy, 1*, 205–210. https://doi.org/10.5840/wcp151973136

Rubber Killer. (2019). *About Us.* https://rubberkiller.com/pages/about-us

Schmidt-Bleak, F. (Ed.) (2004) *Der ökologische Rucksack.* Hirzel.

Schnell, U. (2012). *Bottled Life.* www.bottledlifefilm.com/home

Schramm, M. (2020). *A Worldview for a Sustainable Bioeconomy.* University Hohenheim.

Sen, A. (2011). *The Idea of Justice* (Reprint ed.). Belknap Press.

Spash, C.L. (2017). *Routledge Handbook of Ecological Economics: Nature and Society.* Taylor & Francis.

Steel, D. (2015). *Philosophy and the Precautionary Principle.* Cambridge University Press.

Suaria, G., Avio, C.G., Mineo, A., Lattin, G.L., Magaldi, M.G., Belmonte, G., Moore, C.J., Regoli, F., & Aliani, S. (2016). The Mediterranean plastic soup: Synthetic polymers in Mediterranean surface waters. *Scientific Reports, 6*, 37551. https://doi.org/10.1038/srep37551

Sung, K. (2015). A review on upcycling: Current body of literature, knowledge gaps and a way forward. In *The ICECESS 2015: 17th International Conference on Environmental, Cultural, Economic and Social Sustainability.* www.waset.org/conference/2015/04/venice/ICECESS

Szekely, F., Dossa, Z., & Hollender, J. (2017). *Beyond the Triple Bottom Line: Eight Steps Toward a Sustainable Business Model.* MIT Press.

Tycoon. (n.d.). *About Us.* https://tycoonpercussion.com/about-us/

United Nations. (2016). *Sustainable Development Goals Report 2016.* UN.

Wackernagel, M. & Rees, W (1998) *Our Ecological Footprint: Reducing Human Impact on the Earth.* New Society Publishers.

Wani, K.A., Ariana, L., & Zuber, S.M. (2019). *Handbook of Research on Environmental and Human Health Impacts of Plastic Pollution.* Engineering Science Reference.

Wiesmeth, H. (2011). *Environmental Economics: Theory and Policy in Equilibrium.* Springer Science & Business Media.

World Commission on Environment & Development. (1990). *Our Common Future.* Oxford University Press.

Worm, B. (2015). Silent spring in the ocean. *Proceedings of the National Academy of Sciences, 112*(38), 11752–11753. https://doi.org/10.1073/pnas.1513514112

Youngsteadt, E., López-Uribe, M.M., & Sorenson, C.E. (2019). Ecology in the sixth mass extinction: Detecting and understanding rare biotic interactions. *Annals of the Entomological Society of America, 112*(3), 119–121. https://doi.org/10.1093/aesa/saz007

5 Ethical stakeholder analysis and ethical SWOT analysis

Abstract

This chapter centers the discussion around the concept of stakeholders. Stakeholders will be defined and the different types of stakeholders explained, including how stakeholders can be mapped. The account taken in this chapter expands the theory and practice of stakeholder analysis and management to include future generations, non-human species, and eco-environments as stakeholders and, especially, considers the often-neglected impact of those stakeholders on businesses. The text supplies and discusses tools to map, assess interests, assess power, understand responsibilities, develop strategies, and monitor stakeholder activities. Recognizing the relationship between stakeholders and businesses is crucial in ethical decision-making. The text also explains how to analyze stakeholders' interests, power, urgency, proximity, and legitimacy, their willingness to cooperate and the potential and actual threats they pose. Finally, the ethical SWOT analysis will be briefly explained in its relevance for the ethical decision-making process. The chapter includes case studies on the Volkswagen's Dieselgate Affair and on Fjällräven's intergenerational responsibility.

Chapter keywords

(1) Ethical stakeholder analysis
(2) Corporate stakeholder responsibility
(3) Stakeholder value creation
(4) Ethical SWOT analysis

Study objectives

After studying this chapter readers will be able to:

(1) Utilize the stakeholder concept from an ethical perspective.
(2) Understand how companies create values for stakeholders.
(3) Analyze businesses' impacts on stakeholders.

DOI: 10.4324/9781003127659-5

(4) Assess stakeholders' impacts on organizations.
(5) Create SWOT analyses focused on ethical issues.

Case studies

5.1 Volkswagen's Dieselgate scandal
5.2 Fjällräven's commitment to the environment and future communities

5.1 Stakeholders

This chapter introduces the stakeholder theory and ethical stakeholder analysis. It explains how to map stakeholders and how to understand and analyze their influence, interest, various forms of power, and potential to cooperate or to pose a threat. The account taken in this chapter expands the theory and practice of stakeholder analysis and management to include future generations, non-human species, and eco-environments as stakeholders, and especially considers the often neglected impact of those stakeholders on businesses. This chapter also briefly introduces the ethical SWOT analysis (Strengths, Weaknesses, Opportunities, and Threats). The tool of SWOT analysis is practiced in many business domains but is rather neglected from an ethical perspective. The 5G network is an example of how the entire population of a city or a country can become affected by business activity. On the one hand, 5G will finally enable the Internet of Things and fully autonomous driving and therefore safer traffic. On the other hand, some stakeholders, such as certain city councils, prefer to halt 5G implementation due to some as yet unresolved security issues regarding the health impacts of radiation. The Volkswagen Dieselgate scandal showcases that neglecting even remote or not easily recognizable stakeholders can have severe implications on TSR. The case of Fjällräven's environmental responsibility demonstrates how future generations and ecosystems are considered as stakeholders.

5.1.1 Stakes (not steaks)

The stakeholder approach is interpreted and implemented in different forms both in literature and in practice (this aspect is dealt with in more detail below). It gained notoriety mainly through the pioneering work *Strategic Management: A Stakeholder Approach* by the American management theorist Robert Edward Freeman in 1984 (Freeman, 1984). Although Freeman did not invent the term "stakeholder", he was the first to place it in a book title. The most important aspect of the stakeholder concept is very convincingly explained by him in an interview regarding stakeholders (corporateethics, 2009). Freeman stated in this interview that if a company has an impact on someone or something, it would not be a smart decision by the business to ignore that impact and that person or entity. On the other hand, a company will not be able to ignore something or someone that/who has an impact on its business activities, no matter how this entity or person is named. This is, for example, how even a hacker may become a "stakeholder" (in the wider and – some would maybe opine – perverted sense). A common convention of naming people or entities upon which the business activity has an impact or who/which can have an impact on an organization's activities is as "stakeholders". Stakeholder engagement and its management should not be seen as an alternative to corporate governance but as an essential component. Within the context of the engagement or management of a company's stakeholders, ethical implications need to be considered; this is why ethical stakeholder analysis is essential when studying business ethics cases. A number of authors prefer the term "stakeholder engagement", or "stakeholder engagement management" instead of "stakeholder management", because some stakeholders do not feel comfortable being "managed". They would like to be given a voice, their values need to be considered seriously, so managers have to treat stakeholders responsibly (Shams et al., 2019). Frameworks on how to engage stakeholders are, for example, provided by the Global Reporting Initiative (GRI) (www.globalreporting.org/Pages/default.aspx) and the International Organization for Standardization (ISO). The ISO has designed a stakeholder engagement requiring a framework for sustainability (ISO, 2010) and the GRI is a network-based entity providing a sustainability reporting framework that is internationally widely utilized.

The word "stake" (not steak), literally refers to something that is pointed, like a pillar or a post, something that is stuck into the ground and is holding something else in place, for example, a tent. In English we also have the phrase "something is at stake", meaning that something is at risk. If we don't prepare well for exams, for example, our grades are at stake. We can imagine one of those heavy Bedouin tents in Northern African deserts: the canopy of these tents is made from wide strips of thick and heavy camel wool cloth. Such a tent needs to be fixed to the desert ground with many deep and spiked or pointed wooden or metal pillars, posts, and stakes to prevent it collapsing or being blown away by a desert storm. If you remove one of those stakes the tent's stability is "at stake".

A stake is a claim, a share, or interest which a person, a group, or an entity has in the activities and outcomes of an organization's actions, procedures, and policies (cf. Freeman, 1984). Customers that are buying airline tickets are (secondary) stakeholders of Boeing and Airbus. If an airplane manufacturer tends to neglect certain values and preferences of passengers, such as safety and security, and puts TSR before TSI, plane tickets purchasers may become more vigilant in the future when choosing the category "equipment" when booking a flight ticket and thus may be able to boycott certain manufacturers' aircrafts. Following German news between 2016 and 2020, many Volkswagen customers decided to boycott Volkswagen when buying their next vehicle due to the "Dieselgate" scandal (Reuters, 2017). In this case, it seems that some Volkswagen managers and engineers neglected the fact that the United States Environmental Protection Agency (EPA) and the Center for Alternative Fuels, Engines, and Emissions, at West Virginia University, must be considered as stakeholders of Volkswagen, because these entities found out that there existed significant discrepancies between real-world on-road emissions tests with portable emissions measurement systems and laboratory or garage emissions tests (Hotten, 2015). As of June 2020 this scandal, also triggered by not recognizing relevant (potential) stakeholders, has cost Volkswagen around 33 billion USD. The important lesson to learn from such cases is that not only definitive and easily detectable stakeholders need to be recognized, but also remote or potential stakeholders, such as NGOs, hackers, civil rights groups, environmental movements, and labor unions.

Business ethics deals with businesses' responsibility towards stakeholders. Edward Freeman, therefore, holds that the abbreviation CSR, the acronym for Corporate Social Responsibility, should better be used as an acronym for Corporate *Stakeholder* Responsibility (CSR) (Freeman, 2004). Beyond that, businesses should create values for their stakeholders. And as we have learned in Chapter 1, these kinds of values may not simply be monetary values but could be environmental health, cultural sustainability, educational infrastructure, or well-being, just to name a few. During a certain timeframe in the Boeing company's history, security and safety were regarded as a rather secondary value by the top management of Boeing and clean air was not regarded as a primary value by some Volkswagen engineers and managers. In both cases, the primary focus was to increase TSR as a major priority, neglecting certain values that would have increased TSI. These examples show that taking values and preferences of stakeholders as important guidelines for good governance is pertinent for business sustainability.

To summarize: businesses have responsibilities toward their stakeholders, also referred to as corporate stakeholder responsibility (CSR), as proposed by Ed Freeman. Businesses create values and affect their stakeholders, but can also be affected by their stakeholders. Stakeholders are persons, groups, or entities that are affected by or affect businesses and organizations.

The basic strategy when thinking in terms of stakeholder management or engagement tries to figure out how a decision is perceived from different

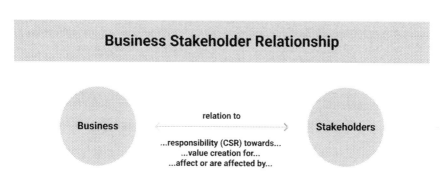

Figure 5.1 Business stakeholder relations

perspectives of all persons or entities involved. This is quite similar when thinking through possibilities and consequences of decisions in an original position, with the veil of ignorance in place, according to John Rawls's understanding of fairness and unbiasedness (see also Chapter 3). Then after thinking through how decisions are perceived and received by different stakeholders, it is important to consider the interests and preferences of the different stakeholders and how those interests and values could be joined or fused in a win-win setting.

This compromising, synthetic, and synergetic approach, becomes clear in one of the ethics definitions of Edward Freeman: ethics is a "conversation about how we can reason together and solve our differences, recognize where our interests are joined and need development, so that we all can flourish without resorting to coercion and violence" (TEDx Talks, 2014). While there may be a trace of the Rawlsian approach in the first part of the sentence, where Freeman talks about the conversation regarding how we can reason and jointly solve differences, there are three detectable ethical theories that are embedded in this definition: Freeman states that we need to "recognize where our interests are joined". When we try to join interests, we have a simultaneous value creation for all stakeholders in mind, which follows a preference utilitarian account (see also Chapter 3). Stakeholder management should not be a zero-sum game. A zero-sum game is a situation where what is gained by one person, group, or entity is lost by another, especially in contested settings or situations with limited resources. The part of the definition which reads, "so that we can all flourish", refers to the theory of well-being, flourishing, and happiness on the one hand (see also Chapter 3) and to preference utilitarian accounts on the other, because the greatest value creation for all affected stakeholders should be achieved. The final part of the quote, "without resorting to coercion and violence", refers to negative utilitarian or a negative hedonist approaches because this part of the definition intends to minimize harm and minimize pain.

Daryl Koehn writes about the application of ethics in business that ethical judgment does not mean subsuming under a universal rule, but identifying "the many goods at play in a contested situation and [realizing] as many of these goods as possible" (Koehn, 1995). Translated to the stakeholder perspective, it becomes clear that in situations where compromises are demanded, there almost always will be tradeoffs, but positive outcomes should be sufficiently realized for any involved stakeholder. Or as Mike Clayton phrases it: "You can please all of your stakeholders some of the time, and some stakeholders all of the time, but you can't please all stakeholders all of the time" (Online PM Courses – Mike Clayton, 2019).

5.1.2 Who are stakeholders?

In the interview mentioned in Chapter 3, Jack Ma emphasizes three important "values" of the Alibaba group. These three values are customers,

Three Important Stakeholders for Alibaba

Figure 5.2 Alibaba's three important stakeholders

employees, and shareholders. But what Jack Ma means, in fact, are stakeholders. These three groups are the most important stakeholders for Alibaba. Jack Ma indicates that shareholders may not like this hierarchy of stakeholders or values, but for him it is obvious that customers are the foundation of everything because without customers a company is in no position to pay employees or generate revenue (TSR); moreover, shareholders will sell their shares. However, without professional and caring employees, customers will buy their products and services somewhere else. This is why the shareholders are the last stakeholder category within this triangular prioritization.

The classical map of stakeholders, also called "primary stakeholders", consists of the five following stakeholder types: customers, employees, financiers, for example shareholders, communities, and suppliers (cf. Freeman, 1984). In this context, it should always be taken into account that one and the same person can assume multiple stakeholder roles at the same time. For example, an employee can at the same time be a consumer, possibly an investor (shareholder), and always part of a certain community.

An extension of this stakeholder map would include further subcategories of stakeholders such as the board of directors, management, staff, and secondary stakeholders, like geographic neighbors, industry organizations, lobby groups, unions, competitors, regulatory bodies, media, and the government, just to name a few. Other possibilities concerning stakeholder maps may distinguish between internal and external stakeholders. Internal stakeholders are employees, managers, board members, and owners, while external stakeholders are suppliers, the society at large, the government, creditors, shareholders, customers, and many other external entities. Another possibility for a stakeholder map is one that clearly distinguishes between primary and secondary stakeholders. The primary stakeholders, the five classical ones, are

110 *Ethical stakeholder analysis*

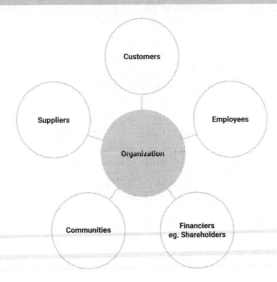

Figure 5.3 Primary stakeholders

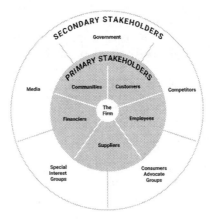

Figure 5.4 Primary and secondary stakeholders
Source: Redesigned from Freeman et al. (2007)

the ones mentioned before: customers, employees, suppliers, financiers, and communities (not necessarily geographical ones). Secondary stakeholders are, for example, the government, competitors, consumer advocate groups, special interest groups, and the media. This kind of stakeholder map is frequently used in several business ethics books.

However, if we take the aforementioned definition of stakeholders seriously, then we cannot neglect further pertinent stakeholders: future communities, ecosystems, and non-human species (Starik, 1995; Carroll & Buchholtz, 2005). The evidence that these stakeholders need to be taken into consideration seriously is provided by several factors. The Fridays for Future movement (FFF) has an impact on politics and current companies due to their worldwide demonstrations. Members of the FFF movement claim that a lot of business activities will harm the future communities they represent. That businesses have an impact on ecosystems is evident, but that – conversely – ecosystems can also have an impact on businesses becomes clear when looking at examples like fishing grounds that have been overfished beyond their renewal rate, so that the deteriorated ecosystems can no longer serve as a habitat and thus fisheries have to give up the harvesting of fish. Other examples are coastal land loss due to climate change and sea-level rise, or regions where rock and mudslides occur caused by melting permafrost that destroys facilities and businesses catering for tourists. Non-human species are also affected by business activities, and, the other way round, non-human species can affect businesses. One example is the declining bee population, which leads to fruit trees, formerly pollinated by bees, now having to be pollinated manually (Khoury et al., 2011).

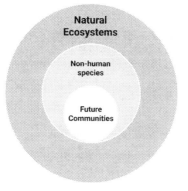

Figure 5.5 Ontological dependency: Nature, non-human species, future communities

If we situate these three stakeholders within their bio-ontological context we need to recognize that the natural ecosystems are home to non-human species. Both (natural) ecosystems and non-human species will be essential for the sustainable existence of future communities. Future communities depend on non-human species, which in turn depend on ecosystems. While non-human species and ecosystems can survive without humans, humans can neither survive without ecosystems nor non-human species.

5.1.3 Stakeholder analysis, engagement, and management

The first step in the ethical stakeholder analysis is to map the stakeholders, their relationships, and their coalitions, which should also include potential, remote, and not easily detectable stakeholders. Then the stakeholders' interests and power need to be assessed. It is usually very helpful to construct a stakeholder responsibility matrix. In a further step, strategies and tactics need to be developed, which in turn should be monitored (Weiss, 2021).

The interests of the stakeholders are an indication of how an organization can create values for particular stakeholders. In the Boeing 737 MAX case, it can be noted that aircraft passengers have low power or relative low power because in many cases there is only a very limited possibility of choosing the specific type of aircraft under the category "equipment" when booking an air ticket and when flying in a particular timeframe is required. In addition, it can never be ruled out that the aircraft type may change shortly before departure. However, passengers have a high interest in their safety. The civil or federal aviation administration regulatory bodies of nation-states have high power and high interest concerning the security of airplanes. Depending on the interpretation and on the individual shareholders, who are holding just a few shares or only have a short time horizon, they may have limited interest in how Boeing handles safety issues, and they do also have low power because not much will change if some of them sell their shares. Majority shareholders

Steps in Stakeholder Analysis & Management

1	2	3	4	5	6
Map stakeholders relationships and coalitions (may include potential stakeholders)	Assess each stakeholder's interest	Assess each stakeholder's power	Construct a stakeholder responsibility matrix	Develop strategies and tactics	Monitor

Figure 5.6 Steps in stakeholder engagement

may have high power but could have low interest in specific safety issues of Boeing, at least in the short term.

In the Volkswagen Dieselgate scandal the customers of cars may have a high interest in what happens to their cars or their cars' emission controlling system. At the same time, they only have very limited power to exert pressure on Volkswagen. The United States Environmental Protection Agency (EPA) detected Volkswagen's illegal emissions during real-world driving on the road. The EPA has a high interest in clarifying the Dieselgate affair, because the EPA represents the citizens' interests for clean air and, in hindsight, it appears to be very obvious that the organization has a high level of power because they ultimately brought Volkswagen's illegal emission handling strategy to worldwide media attention.

There are different forms of power of stakeholders (Weiss, 2021), for example, the voting power of board members or the political power of the government, the media, or NGOs. There is also economic power from shareholders, financiers, and competing companies that could consider a hostile acquisition of a firm. Technological power can be represented by hackers, competing technology firms, and suppliers. Legal power could be executed by courts, NGOs, and indirectly by lobbyists. Environmental power can be construed as the positive or negative impact companies may have on the environment and ecosystems. Companies such as Patagonia do have environmental power, but ecosystems can have environmental power as well as mentioned in the examples above. Cultural power is the power of media, celebrities, NGOs, and movements such as FFF, Extinction Rebellion, Human Rights Watch, and Greenpeace. In 2020 after the killing of George Floyd by a US policeman (Shammas et al., 2020), the actor George Clooney wrote an open letter against racism, claiming that racism in the US is a longer-lasting pandemic than Covid-19 (Clooney, 2020). India's most famous actor Shah Rukh Khan uses his cultural power to empower acid-attack survivors (Kanyal, 2019).

What makes stakeholders important is their power, their legitimacy, their urgency, and their proximity (Carroll et al., 2017; Gössling & Buiter, 2017). Powerful stakeholders are, for example, majority shareholders, but labor unions can also be quite powerful stakeholders, because strikes can bring the production or service of an entire economic sector to a standstill, such as

Stakeholder's Form of Power

Voting	Political	Economic	Technological
Legal	Environmental	Cultural	

Figure 5.7 Stakeholders' forms of power

strikes by pilot unions. Legitimate stakeholders are stakeholders that are officially recognized or usually easily recognizable as stakeholders such as students, employees, future employers, and the management of a university. While a hacker is not a legitimate stakeholder, they may become a stakeholder due to an imminent hacking incident, thus, in this case, urgency is a signifier of stakeholdership. Proximity can also constitute stakeholdership. A community living around a factory that emits harmful fumes, for example, is a stakeholder simply because of their proximity.

These dimensions that constitute stakeholdership are quite important because sometimes stakeholders may not be recognized until they create a serious problem for a company. Apparently, Volkswagen had not recognized the EPA that undertook independent exhaust testing on cars on the road as a stakeholder. But this urgent and imminent threat positioned the EPA as an urgent stakeholder which proved to be a major problem for Volkswagen, its management, and its engineers. Ikea did not recognize children as their stakeholders in the case of the Ikea Malm drawers, but since a child unexpectedly utilized these furniture pieces as climbing toys, the urgency of the incident made toddlers a stakeholder of Ikea, because some of the children died when the drawers collapsed on them (BBC, 2020).

Regarding the legitimacy of stakeholders, views range from a very narrow understanding that only shareholders and owners are legitimate stakeholders (Friedman, 1970), to anyone or any entity that can be affected by the business or can affect the business.

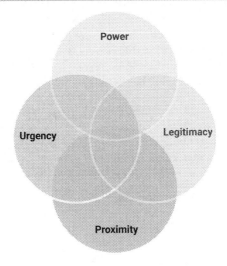

Figure 5.8 Stakeholder relevance
Source: Redesigned from Gössling & Buiter (2017)

The views of what constitutes a stakeholder range quite widely. The liberal Economist Milton Friedman held that the "business of business is business" (Friedman, 1970); other stakeholders than shareholders do not really matter from such a perspective. Robert Edward Freeman, a pioneer of the stakeholder approach, pointed out that stakeholders are those "groups that are vital to the survival and success of the organization" (Freeman, 2004). A wider definition Freeman proposed reads that stakeholders are any "group or individual who can affect or is affected by the achievement of the organization's objectives" (Freeman 1984). Mark Starik suggested that stakeholders are "individuals or groups with which business interacts who have a 'stake, or vested interest, in the firm'" (Starik et al., 1994), but beyond that any "natural entity which affects or is affected by organizational performance" is a stakeholder too (Starik et al., 1994).

Freeman initially assumed a primarily economic-strategic understanding of stakeholders, which in some ways was even close to the shareholder value approach:

> I believe that first we must understand the weaker sense of "stakeholder legitimacy": if you want to be an effective manager, then you must take stakeholders into account. [...] The point of strategic management is in some sense to chart a direction for the firm. Groups which can affect that direction and its implementation must be considered in the strategic management process. (Freeman, 1984)

As the quote illustrates, the core idea of this "strategic" stakeholder approach is that from the perspective of a company it appears strategically smart and advisable to take the interests of all relevant stakeholders into account, even if the company or the company's management itself has no moral interests at all. This applies even more to those stakeholders who can negatively influence the company's success and thus the interests of its shareholders. However, as is also obvious, the strategic stakeholder approach has nothing to do with (business) ethics. Rather, it aims at strategic success, i.e. at increasing or at least not reducing profit by taking into account the interests of certain stakeholder groups. In short, it's about TSR.

Just a few years after Freeman wrote his initial work on stakeholder management, he expanded his stakeholder approach beyond the strategic question in the direction of a greater consideration of ethical demands in management.

On the one hand, as described above, he continues to assume that, for strategic and economic reasons, it is indispensable to take the interests and concerns of all relevant stakeholders into account. In order to survive in the market, companies need to generate shareholder value: "Surely there are lots of ways to run a firm. [But] All of these ways have to ultimately generate profits and satisfy some set of stakeholders" (Freeman, 2004). There can be no doubt that companies can only achieve shareholder value if they cooperate with all relevant stakeholders and build strategic and profitable relationships with them. For this reason alone, the shareholder value approach in its pure form is not feasible at all, since shareholder value can only be generated or increased if the interests of the stakeholders are taken into account and served.

At the same time, however, Freeman also states that it appears necessary to take moral aspects into account in stakeholder relationships in order to arrive at a more universal stakeholder approach. This means that the consideration and inclusion of stakeholder interests in corporate decisions is not only a strategic question, but is also related to the fact that there are legitimate moral interests and demands of certain stakeholders that have to be considered in some form in the management process. With that in mind, Freeman has stated that he deems it necessary "to revise this [strategic] concept along essentially Kantian lines. That is, each of these stakeholder groups has a right not to be treated as a means to some end, and therefore must participate in determining the future direction of the firm in which they have a stake". "Thus, property rights are not absolute, especially when they conflict with important rights of others. The right to property does not yield the right to treat others as means to an end. Property rights are not a license to ignore Kant's principle of respect for persons" (Chryssides & Kaler, 1993). Companies clearly do have property rights that allow them to act entrepreneurially. However, and this is a clear ethical issue, these property rights should not obscure the fact that companies must observe and respect the dignity of the people who are potentially or actually affected by their business activities, which also applies to the concerns of future communities.

Stakeholder Responsibility Matrix

	Economic	Legal	Ethical	Voluntary / Philanthropic
Customers				
Employees				
Financiers				
Suppliers				
Future Generations				
Non-Human Species				
Eco-Environments				
Etc...				

Figure 5.9 Stakeholder responsibility matrix

When considering the values and preferences of stakeholders, it is very helpful to construct a stakeholder responsibility matrix. With such a table we can figure out economic, legal, ethical, and voluntary or philanthropic responsibilities toward our stakeholders. This stakeholder responsibility matrix is aligned with the CSR pyramid (Carroll & Buchholtz, 2005). The CSR pyramid is based on the assumption that the company first needs to fulfill economic responsibilities in order to be profitable, which is seen as the foundation on which everything else is built. Nevertheless, the company needs to fulfill all legal responsibilities, but on top of that there are all the ethical responsibilities, and beyond that even philanthropic or voluntary responsibilities the company may want to address. An example of a voluntary responsibility is, for example, Brunello Cucinelli's restoration of medieval buildings in the company headquarters in Solomeo.

Furthermore, when analyzing stakeholders' interests and when developing strategies and tactics, the stakeholder's potential for threat and their potential for cooperation need to be assessed.

A stakeholder whose potential for threat is very high but whose willingness to cooperate is very low is a very dangerous stakeholder. If the potential to cooperate is rather high while at the same time the potential for threat is very high, this stakeholder can be and must be engaged for fruitful collaboration. The ideal case for a company exists when a stakeholders' potential for threat is very low, but their interest in cooperation with a company is very high. Stakeholders whose potential for threat is very low while their potential for corporation is also very low do not need to be concentrated on but still need monitoring.

In the Volkswagen Dieselgate affair the EPA had a very high potential for threat, and only a very limited interest in cooperation, whereas in the Boeing 737 MAX case, the Boeing 737 pilots and Boeing engineers had a high interest in cooperating with Boeing, but could pose a very high threat at the same time because they could expose safety loopholes in Boeing engineering.

Figure 5.10 CSR pyramid
Source: Redesigned from Carroll & Buchholtz (2005)

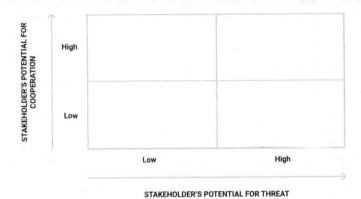

Figure 5.11 Stakeholders' potential for cooperation and threat
Source: Redesigned from Savage et al. (1991)

5.2 Ethical SWOT analysis

A SWOT analysis is a strategic planning technique that investigates the strength, weaknesses, opportunities, and threats of an organization or a project. SWOT analyses are utilized in the context of strategic planning, competitive advantage building, and marketing, just to name a few examples. The origin of this analysis tool is uncertain, some researchers credit it to work at the Stanford Research Institute, others trace the SWOT analysis back to a research team at the Harvard Business School. There are several variations, adaptations, and alternatives for the SWOT analysis, but due to its simplicity and its applicability as a business ethical device, the classical SWOT analysis remains a meaningful strategic tool.

The standard usage of SWOT construes strengths and weaknesses as internal characteristics and opportunities and threats as external. But from a business ethical analysis perspective, opportunities and threats can also be located within an organization. The real ethical threat in Volkswagen's emissions scandal was an internal decision-making failure resulting in the development of a device that switches emissions testing and filtering on and off, depending on the condition – driving condition (emission reduction mostly switched off) or testing condition (emission reduction switched on). The ethical threat preceding the two Boeing 737 MAX crashes was Boeing's long-term strategy of placing TSR before TSI, which also needs to be seen in the context of

Ethical SWOT Analysis

	Present / Actual	Future / Potential
+	Strengths	Opportunities
−	Weaknessses	Threats (Risks)

Figure 5.12 Ethical SWOT

external threats whereby competitor Airbus had already built new energy-efficient planes.

Therefore, in our approach here the ethical SWOT analyses investigate the ethical strengths, weaknesses, opportunities, and threats or risks as follows: while the strengths and opportunities represent the positive ethical dimensions of a company, the weaknesses, threats, and risks cater for the ethically negative side. Strengths and weaknesses are usually either present and/or internal, while opportunities, threats, and risks are either lying in the future, or are external, or represent a positive or negative potential.

Case study 5.1: Volkswagen's Dieselgate scandal

Research the Volkswagen Dieselgate scandal.

(1) Who are Volkswagen's stakeholders? Draw a detailed stakeholder map.
(2) What does "emission possible" mean? What could be the meaning of the wordplay "emission possible" – "Mission Impossible"?
(3) Why did Volkswagen ignore those stakeholders that detected the emission discrepancies?
(4) What happened after the Dieselgate affair surfaced on public and social media?
(5) What would you do as Chief Engineer and as CEO to rescue Volkswagen's reputation?
(6) Create an ethical SWOT matrix for Volkswagen.

Case study 5.2: Fjällräven's commitment to the environment and future communities

Research Fjällräven.

(1) Why and how is Fjällräven committed to the environment and future generations?
(2) What can other companies in your region learn from Fjällräven's CSR and CER?
(3) Create an ethical SWOT matrix for Fjällräven.

Key takeaways

(1) Businesses can have an impact on various stakeholders.
(2) Businesses can create values for stakeholders.
(3) Stakeholders can have various impacts on businesses.
(4) Ecosystems, non-human species, and future communities can no longer be neglected as stakeholders.

References

BBC. (2020, January 7). Ikea to pay $46m after child killed by drawers. *BBC News*. www.bbc.com/news/world-us-canada-51017438

Carroll, A., & Buchholtz, A.K. (2005). *Business and Society: Ethics and Stakeholder Management*. Thompson Nelson.

Carroll, A., Brown, J., & Buchholtz, A.K. (2017). *Business & Society: Ethics, Sustainability & Stakeholder Management* (10th ed.). South-Western College Pub.

Chryssides, G.D., & Kaler, J.H. (1993). *An Introduction to Business Ethics*. Chapman & Hall.

Clooney, G. (2020, June 1). George Clooney: America's greatest pandemic is anti-black racism. *The Daily Beast*. www.thedailybeast.com/george-clooney-on-the-murder-of-george-floyd-americas-greatest-pandemic-is-anti-black-racism

corporateethics. (2009, August 1). *What Are Stakeholders? – R. Edward Freeman*. www.youtube.com/watch?v=17hnaKFjDU8

Freeman, R. (1984). *Strategic Management: A Stakeholder Approach*. Pitman.

Freeman, R. (2004). *The Stakeholder Approach Revisited*. ResearchGate. http://dx.doi.org/10.5771/1439-880X-2004-3-228

Freeman, R., Harrison, J., & Wicks, A. (2007). *Managing for Stakeholders: Survival, Reputation, and Success*. Yale University Press.

Friedman, M. (1970, September 12). The social responsibility of business is to increase its profits. *New York Magazine*, 122–126.

Gössling, T., & Buiter, B. (2017) Socially responsible investment engagement. In R. Freeman, J. Kujala & S. Sachs (Eds), *Stakeholder Engagement: Clinical Research Cases*. Springer. https://doi.org/10.1007/978-3-319-62785-4_6

Hotten, R. (2015, December 10). Volkswagen: The scandal explained. *BBC News*. www.bbc.com/news/business-34324772

ISO. (2010). *26000: 2010 Guidance on Social Responsibility*. International Organization for Standardization. www.iso.org/cms/render/live/en/sites/isoorg/contents/data/standard/04/25/42546.html

Kanyal, J. (2019, December 11). Shah Rukh Khan meets acid survivors on Human Rights Day: If we keep trying, we shall overcome. *India Today*. www.indiatoday.in/movies/celebrities/story/shah-rukh-khan-meets-acid-survivors-on-human-rights-day-if-we-keep-trying-we-shall-overcome-1627376-2019-12-11

Khoury, D.S., Myerscough, M.R., & Barron, A.B. (2011). A quantitative model of honey bee colony population dynamics. *PLoS ONE*, *6*(4). https://doi.org/10.1371/journal.pone.0018491

Koehn, D. (1995). A role for virtue ethics in the analysis of business practice. *Business Ethics Quarterly*, *5*(3), 533–539. https://doi.org/10.2307/3857397

Online PM Courses – Mike Clayton. (2019, September 4). *Stakeholder Engagement Tips: 5 Tips For Project Managers*. www.youtube.com/watch?v=APc9S_8v7YY&feature=emb_rel_pause

Reuters. (2017, September 29). VW's Dieselgate bill hits $30 bln after another charge. www.reuters.com/article/legal-uk-volkswagen-emissions-idUSKCN1C4271

Savage, G., Nix, T., Whitehead, C., & Blair, J. (1991). *Strategies for Assessing and Managing Organizational Stakeholders*. Academy of Management Perspectives. https://doi.org/10.2307/4165008

Shammas, B., Bellware, K., & Dennis, B. (2020). Murder charges filed against all four officers in George Floyd's death as protests against biased policing continue. *Washington Post*. www.washingtonpost.com/nation/2020/06/03/george-floyd-police-officers-charges/

Shams, S.M.R., Vrontis, D., Weber, Y., Tsoukatos, E., & Galati, A. (2019). *Stakeholder Engagement and Sustainability* (1st ed.). Routledge.

Starik, M. (1995). Should trees have managerial standing? Toward stakeholder status for non-human nature. *Journal of Business Ethics*, *14*(3), 207–217. https://doi.org/10.1007/BF00881435

Starik, M., Clarkson, M., Chochan, P., & Thomas, M. (1994). The Toronto Conference: Reflections on stakeholder theory. *Business and Society*. https://doi.org/10.1177/000765039403300105

TEDx Talks. (2014, January 25). *Business is about purpose: R. Edward Freeman at TEDxCharlottesville 2013*. www.youtube.com/watch?list=PLsRNoUx8w3rOt0fc3G-lg2qL7er7no05k&time_continue=379&v=7dugfwJthBY&feature=emb_logo

Weiss, J.W. (2021). *Business Ethics: A Stakeholder and Issues Management Approach* (7th ed.). Berrett-Koehler Publishers.

6 Disruptive technologies and business ethics

Abstract

This chapter explores the increasing relevance of the connection between technology and business ethics. The ethics of data management and governance issues of big tech will be discussed. Data farming has become the pillar of private companies' business models while creating friction between human rights, privacy, and political autonomy. The chapter also discusses the negative impacts derived from unchecked technological advancements, and the arguments of technological determinism are explored. Sci-fi movies are used as vehicles of thought experiment to visualize the potential impacts of technology void of regulations and preventive actions. The chapter includes numerous case studies, such as the social credit system in China, Trump vs Twitter, GDPR, and UAVs.

Chapter keywords

(1) Data governance
(2) Technological determinism
(3) Businesses' technology responsibility

Study objectives

After studying this chapter readers will be able to:

(1) Understand the nature of technology, in particular its relation to business contexts.
(2) Gauge different technology's impacts on businesses and their stakeholders.
(3) Widen their horizons regarding how cutting-edge technologies such as artificial intelligence and genetic engineering will influence, impact on, or change everyday life, businesses activities, and personal and societal values.
(4) Differentiate between the empirical fact of "technological determinism" and the fact that "technology itself is not determinative".
(5) Understand the positive correlation between big data, power, and responsibility.

DOI: 10.4324/9781003127659-6

Case studies

6.1 The social credit system in China
6.2 Trump vs Twitter
6.3 GDPR
6.4 UAVs (drones)

Films

(1) *Ready Player One*
(2) *Gattaca*
(3) *The Matrix*
(4) *The Circle*
(5) *Citizenfour*
(6) *Snowden*

6.1 Technology, business, and ethics

Focusing on Information Technology (IT), but starting off with technology in general, this chapter presents the ethical challenges technologies such as Artificial Intelligence (AI), blockchain, big data analysis, fully autonomous driving, robotics, drones, and genetic engineering pose for businesses. The focus of this chapter lies on rapidly advancing technologies that will change individuals' and entire societies' lives at large. AI and fully autonomous robotics may create "classes" of useless people if educational systems are not pro-acting efficiently enough. Surveillance technology and computational big data analysis helping to minimize crime and terrorism, and preventing pandemics such as Covid-19, may at the same time make citizens transparent beyond personal privacy protection demands. The knowledge, information, or data gap between the individual person and an aggregated entity like Google, Facebook, Amazon, Microsoft, Tencent, and Alibaba is growing exponentially and can be tapped by whoever is getting access to the data. Data is not only the "oil of the future", but "also" the fuel of our present time. More general cases and some views into scenes of sci-fi films dealing with AI and genetic engineering help to imagine how technology will change the lives of humans in an unprecedentedly positive way, but at the same time may pose an existential threat to humanity.

6.1.1 Within the age of data governance

A common feature of books covering cutting-edge technologies such as AI, blockchain technology, fully autonomous robotics and driving, and genetic engineering is that parts of these books become outdated as soon as they are published. On the other hand, it is gross negligence to avoid, omit, or circumvent cutting-edge technologies in business ethics investigations that may pose serious challenges to the society and the business world. Besides these risks, such cutting-edge technologies imply as yet unimaginable opportunities for the business sector at large, and offer concretely and highly important possibilities for startups as well as for established corporations, which makes clear the ambivalence associated with such technologies.

One of the main takeaways of this chapter is probably that we will have to appreciate that, for the rest of our lives, we will have to repeatedly reinvent ourselves in order to excel in a technologically ever faster paced environment. The Covid-19 phase in 2020 for example paved the way for a more online business and educational infrastructure and a wider surveillance accepting culture.

Yuval Harari in his books *Sapiens* (Harari, 2015b), *Homo Deus* (Harari, 2015a), and *21 Lessons for the 21st Century* (Harari, 2018) describes three existential threats for humanity, future communities, and the planet at large. First, we are familiar with environmental external effects such as pollution and climate alterations resulting from consumption patterns and lifestyles in advanced and rapidly advancing economies (see Chapter 4). These external effects, on the one hand, pose human health hazards and, on the other hand, in the worst case, lead to eco-environmental collapse. The second existential challenge rests in the utilization of nuclear technology. Even in the twenties of the 21st century, nuclear war is still a not completely unthinkable scenario, and nuclear electricity generation, its accidents, and the final "disposal" or "storage" of nuclear waste greatly challenge human and environmental sustainability and the so far available nuclear waste storage technologies that are currently at our disposal. The third existential threat to future communities lies in rapid scientific technological advancements. Bio-engineering (Stasi & Meinhold, 2020), genetic design, AI, or superintelligence, and fully autonomous robotics may lead to scenarios we have seen, until now, only in sci-fi films.

Yuval Harari compares such rapidly advancing impactful technologies with tsunamis because of the unpredictability of their impact and aftermath. The most important question we have to ask ourselves in the light of these

Figure 6.1 Existential threats
Source: Based on Harari (2015a, 2015b, 2018)

Disruptive technologies 125

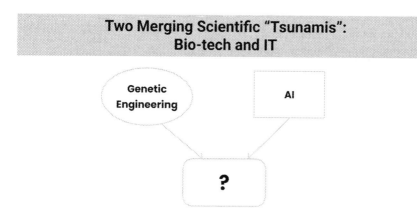

Figure 6.2 Bio-tech & AI

rapidly advancing scientific tsunamis, according to Harari (Harari, 2018), is what will happen if two specific cutting-edge technologies, namely "bio-tech" and "data-tech", are going to merge. What will happen if AI technology is fused with genetic engineering? We can hardly estimate answers to this question. However, futurists and sci-fi films predict scenarios that we are familiar with. Some of these scenarios are utopian and optimistic, others are dystopian, alarming, and pessimistic.

It is clear for Harari that future decisions will not be taken anymore by ourselves but by ICT systems, in particular by algorithms, because algorithms know more about us than we know about ourselves. Harari refers to this future scenario as "dataism", because individuals and societies will be governed by those who collect, process, compute, and apply data. The agricultural terminology "data harvesting" in "server farms", is quite interesting, because it sheds light on what happens to smaller IT firms and many startups. Like smaller farms in the US and elsewhere, promising innovative IT startups are often bought by larger IT companies. The results of large-scale farming are nowadays under intense scrutiny due to the questionable quality of the produce, resulting from intensive farming methods employing pesticides, antibiotics, fungicides, etc. The yield of big data, harvested and processed by Alphabet, Apple, Amazon, Alibaba, Tencent, Facebook, and Microsoft in their server farms, is yet to be seen, but the Facebook–Cambridge Analytica scandal shed a negative light on the practice of this large-scale data culture. There are also governments involved in this data governing process, the NSA in the US and the Chinese Government are intensively collecting and computing data, but, judging from the current perspective it seems more obvious that data handling, processing, storage, and governing in the future will rather be handled mainly by big high-tech corporations, implying that data, and its implicit power, is in the hands of large corporations.

6.1.2 Technology and business ethics

This chapter also refers to some sci-fi films in order to utilize their value and foresight concerning risk assessment and risk estimation. There are several ethical issues in the domains of technology, information and communication technology, and the media context. It is evident that technology – high-tech and low-tech – is produced by businesses, utilized in the business context, and sold by businesses to other businesses or consumers. In addition, sooner or later the hardware that is required for the use of the respective technologies in companies and private households has to be disposed of. An increasingly important challenge here is to extend the service life of the required hardware components despite the rapidly increasing technological progress in order to reduce the consumption of resources and to protect the environment.

Technology involves increasing productivity and service quality. Autonomous robots in the car manufacturing industry are an example. Technology reduces the amount of labor or makes labor easier. Mobile phone banking apps, for example, reduce the distances commuted to banks and the amount of paper used for transactions. Technology also leads to safer working and living conditions. Fully autonomous cars, at least in the long run, could reduce the number of accidents and road fatalities, and a high density of CCTV surveillance correlates with a lower crime rate (Tilley, 1993). The historical invention of toilets is an example of how technology also increases the quality and standard of living, including health and hygiene. Corona warning apps and comparable tracking systems on mobile phones can help in the fight against the Covid-19 pandemic.

Negative effects of technology are also multiple: the biggest fear in regard to AI and fully autonomous robotics is the potential high unemployment rate

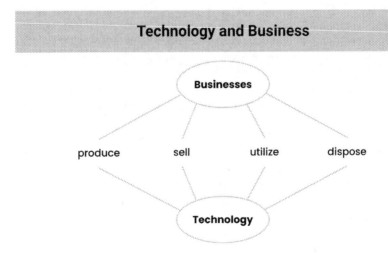

Figure 6.3 Businesses' utilization of technology

since jobs will be filled by autonomous robots and IT systems. Taxi drivers, assembly workers at conveyor belts, and cashiers are among those whose tasks will be more efficiently executed by technological devices. Yuval Harari fears a "class" or an "army" of useless persons (Harari, 2015a). The hardest hit will be persons at the lower end of the social and economic hierarchies and people in economically less developed regions in the world, where both the school and vocational education systems are weak. But there will also remain different, more or less satisfying, jobs due to increasing division and automatization, robotization, and digitalization of previously human labor. Certain cleaning jobs will still have to be accomplished by manual labor, as well as certain caring, counseling, and teaching jobs. If too many jobs are lost, and not as many jobs are created, some researchers and business experts propose governments should inaugurate an unconditional basic income, financed by taxes from the (high-)tech industry, that employs robots and AI (Standing, 2017).

Another problem that comes with the development of technology is natural resources depletion. For our mobile phones, tablets, computers, robots, servers, and electronics in general scarce metals and minerals as well as rare earths are needed to produce semiconductors and other essential parts. This leads to the depletion of non-renewable resources, environmental pollution, and human health hazards. The percentage of scarce and rare metals, minerals, and earths used will increase even further with the shift from combustion engine propelled transportation systems to electric transportation systems, due to the necessity of electric components in motors and the vehicles' computers, without which they will not drive, and the batteries needed to power electric vehicles.

Most pro-actionary handled technologies may carry some, more or less predictable, or even hitherto unknown risks. At this point, it is not yet easily predictable what kind of risks AI technology will pose. What is rather predictable is that the further collection, storage, computation, and utilization of big data will increase the encroachment on individual privacy. Search data consist of location and movement data, calling records, purchasing records, and website visits, just to name a few. Such data are useful for targeted marketing and political campaigning, but can at the same time be used for social profiling and social credit systems, as implemented in China. The invasiveness of current and future technologies, and the privacy encroachment that comes along with it, are topical ethical issues. While dictating this text via an Android app and driving (being driven) with the help of Google Maps, Alphabet, at the same time, is collecting more or less personalized data. After the Facebook–Cambridge Analytica scandal it became clear that big data companies are extensively collecting personal user data. When Mark Zuckerberg was questioned in a Congress hearing and mocked by a senator, who asked Zuckerberg if he would be comfortable sharing with the public who he recently texted and in which hotel he stayed last night, the Facebook CEO appeared puzzled, hesitated, smiled, and indicated that he preferred not to share such private data publicly in Congress (Washington Post, 2018).

The Congressman then replied, but this – the data sharing issue – is what this whole Facebook–Cambridge Analytica case is about. We want to have control over with whom and what kind of information we share. That Mark Zuckerberg does care about his own privacy became clear in a Facebook post in which he had posted a photo of himself with his laptop in the background. Users later commented on this post that "Zuck's" laptop camera and microphone were covered with stickers. In a very early leaked chat during Zuckerberg's time as a student at Harvard, on the messaging platform that would be later developed and named Facebook, Zuckerberg characterized the users of the early platform as "dumb", because they trusted him with their personal data (Wong, 2018).

6.1.3 Technological determinism vs technology is not determinative

There are multiple challenges when it comes to technology in general, not only in the domain of information and communication technology. One of these major challenges that are embedded in the nature of technology itself is *technological determinism* (Marx & Smith, 1994). Technological determinism means what can be technologically accomplished most likely will also be utilized, applied, and executed: "what can be done – will be done" (Grove, 2010). The very important connecting link between technology and business is that business opportunities are driving or motivating science, research, and development which, in turn, create ethical challenges, an ethical discourse, and finally kickstart the process of legislation.

6.1.4 Technology is not determinative

Yuval Harari points out that philosophy and ethics are even more important today than they were 2500 years ago. The reason for this is that while some of the ethical dilemmas had been theoretical until now, they have become real or will become real in the next several years. The eugenics discourse is at least as old as Plato, but only today we have the capabilities of genetic, genomic, and reproductive technologies that potentially will let us modify and design children who may be devoid of genetic diseases, have enhanced resistance capabilities, such as resistance to particular viral or bacterial diseases, or possess specific desired genetic phenotypical traits that follow certain beauty ideals.

The classic 1997 sci-fi film *Gattaca* presents a dystopian future society guided by human eugenics, bio-tracking, and bio-surveillance programs in which children are conceived through genetic selection. The title of the movie consists of the letters G, A, T, and C, standing for the four nucleobases of Deoxyribonucleic Acid (DNA): guanine, adenine, thymine, and cytosine. Persons conceived outside the eugenics program, the "invalids", face genetic discrimination because the best jobs are taken by the genetically optimized "valids". The movie raises questions regarding bio-tracking and bio-surveillance, and criticizes reproductive technologies facilitating eugenics.

The eugenics program in the film creates a divide in society that cannot be easily overcome.

On the other hand, who would not genetically switch off particular genetic traits that trigger diseases, such as Alzheimer's, cancer, Parkinson's, and other genetically potentially modifiable diseases, if not for oneself, but their children?

Film case study 6.1: *Gattaca*

Watch the film *Gattaca* and research the topic of eugenics.

(1) What are the entrepreneurial and medical opportunities of such a technology?
(2) What are the societal implications if such a technology would be:
   a. Available for every person on the planet?
   b. Initially highly expensive and only be available for very few individuals?
(3) What kind of ethical theories would help governments to regulate such technology?
(4) If companies that have the patents for such technologies were left to self-regulate, how should they deal with this technology?

A super intelligent entity having access to millions of people's personal data would have been named "God" thousands, or only hundreds of years ago. Today quantum computing and AI are in a position to analyze millions of people's personal data. Some futuristic scenarios that sounded like science fiction just a few years ago have become part of our everyday life. Examples would be an instant translation from one language into another and instant money transfer from one point of the globe to another, just with the help of mobile phone applications. However, ethics and legislation often lag behind the technological advancements developed and created by businesses. Business innovations trigger ethical discourse and more ethical discourse then encourages legislation.

Technological determinism means that technological innovation is realized sooner or later in consumer products. However, technology itself is not deterministic. Technology not being deterministic means that technology does not determine how we use it, with the exception of rare examples, such as non-discriminatory weapons. There is probably no meaningful ethical utilization of landmines, for example. According to just war theory, such weapons are considered *mala in se*, they are "evil in themselves", because they do not discriminate between "deserving targets" (e.g. an enemy sniper) and non-deserving targets (e.g. children). On the other hand, the first forms of gunpowder were intended for alchemistic-medicinal use, in search of a life-elixir. Gunpowder's usage for firearms only came at a later stage. This example shows that the invention of gunpowder does not determine what we are going to do with it. An old German saying reads "a knife can be used for preparing food or for killing". Technology can be life-maintaining, life-saving, or life-destroying. The first transformers for converting direct current (DC) into alternating current (AC) were developed in the 1880s and the first electrocution using AC with an electric chair occurred in 1890. Each and every technology can be weaponized. The most striking example must be nuclear technology. The technology can be used for efficient electricity production or as a weapon of mass destruction.

These examples demonstrate that technology itself is not deterministic. But technological determinism is almost a guarantee that once an invention sees the dawn of its applicability, it will be used, like in the cases of gunpowder, the knife, electricity, nuclear power, the internet, genetic engineering, and AI. AI and data-driven decision-making will seep more easily into our everyday life than a few decades ago, because information and communication technology has become an essential part of our culture and is more and more becoming second nature.

Technology, not only IT and high-tech, is often criticized for several reasons. Whether certain (digital) technologies are ultimately useful or necessary is not discussed here. What can be said is that, especially for private consumers and households, new digital technologies are constantly being developed in order to meet supposed customer needs and to keep pace with competition from other manufacturers, the benefits and innovative value of which must be at least partially questioned from an objective point of view. For example, many smart devices brought about by the so-called Internet of Things – networked refrigerators, washing machines or trash cans, beauty products and kitchen aids with Bluetooth functionality and the like – are only able to make people's everyday lives noticeably easier to a very limited extent. In addition, technology may too often promise quick fixes. Biomedical technology may promise to restore our health, instead of encouraging us to change our lifestyles, however a counter-example can be increased fitness due to the practice of exercising with the help of fitness-tracking devices. A high-tech environment may restore or replace natural environments. In many regards, some consumers expect technological wonders or miracles. This is just one example of how religion has been displaced also by technological paradigms. Despite all embracement of advancing technologies, we will still need to keep up with the fast-paced technological development.

The use of technological devices is also made responsible for distracting and wasting precious time. Easily observable examples are computer games or excessive photo and selfie shooting sessions. Does technology connect or disconnect people from each other? During the Covid-19 pandemic, it became clear that meetings can be accomplished safely via online technology. Such technology even made it possible for musicians to perform music without meeting in person at one geographical location. In contrast, we can often observe a group of people sitting around a table in a cafe, bar, or restaurant each of whom is immersed in an online activity via their mobile phones, and yet the people around the table hardly communicate with each other, at least not in person.

Another problem is the blurred distinction between reality and simulation when using ICT. An extreme example might be a drone pilot whose task is to "engage" (kill) insurgents via virtual reality technology, operating at a different location from where the drone is geographically located. Shooting characters in a video game and shooting real people in front of a screen via a drone does not look that much different on the computer screen in front of the person who is shooting. This distancing from reality via mediated reality and the resulting fusion or confusion of simulation and reality has been labeled as "hyper-reality" by the French sociologist and philosopher Jean Baudrillard (Baudrillard, 1994). A hyper-real world may look like that in the 2018 film *Ready Player One*. This film does not display a world of virtual reality, because reality and virtual reality become intertwined, and thus reality becomes "hyper-real". We are more familiar with the term "augmented reality", a technology that features, for example, as head-up displays (HUD) in automobiles and in smart glasses applications. In fact, using real-time traffic information via Google Maps when driving is already a form of augmented reality.

6.2 Sci-fi, AI, data, and business responsibilities

Elon Musk once stated, "If our intelligence is exceeded, it is unlikely that we remain in charge of the planet" (Harasim, 2017). The classic 1999 cyberpunk sci-fi film *The Matrix* predicts two extreme scenarios precautionary futurists are worried about: an almost complete environmental destruction of the planet and humanity, which has been enslaved by a totalitarian AI system so that humans can no longer destroy the planet, but instead serve as fuel rods of the AI system's electric power plant, supplying electricity and body heat. Although these predictions are harshly dystopic, they nevertheless point in a direction that is not completely implausible.

Such an extreme scenario is not and may not be the case in the near future. But already existing risks related to AI are that our thoughts, values, opinions, and behavior are manipulated by the consumer industry or a state entity, with the help of the data harvested from us. A prominent example are Chinese cities in which businesses and citizens are closely monitored with the help of CCTV, AI, and a comprehensive social credit system that assesses the social credibility and social, as well as economic, reputation of businesses and individual citizens. Citizens who display unfavorable behavior, such as violating traffic laws, no-show behavior despite a reservation, or incorrect waste disposal may be blacklisted or receive a low credit score and may be banned from public and private services such as air or high-speed rail tickets. People with high credit scores or whitelisted persons who have received points for donating blood or money to charity or who committed to voluntary unpaid social work may receive preferential treatment in governmental offices, hospitals, hotels, or entertainment venues in terms of reduced waiting time and discounts. The social credit system may even display the gathered personal data of individuals at public venues, such as bus or train stations, cinemas, and on the internet.

> ### Case study 6.1: The social credit system in China
>
> Research the social credit system in China.
>
> (1) How are businesses involved in the social credit system?
> (2) Research the history of the social credit system.
> (3) Create an ethical SWOT analysis of the social credit system.
> (4) Create an ethical stakeholder analysis of the social credit system.
> (5) What is your opinion of this system, given your personal cultural background and citizenship?

Electronic safety assisting technology will eventually guide and drive our cars, and the Internet of Things will assist us in many other aspects of our life. Both technological systems may be weaponized by criminals, hijacked by hackers and/or also manipulated by IT corporations in order to guide, manipulate, or change our opinions. A hack of critical infrastructure such as a city's transportation systems or an airplane's flight control system could facilitate large-scale terrorist attacks.

The terrorist attacks of September 9, 2011 (9/11) against part of the US critical infrastructure was also a symbolic attack targeting the World Trade Center Towers 1 and 2 (two iconic economic landmarks) and the Pentagon (as the most important US military landmark), and a further aircraft crashed before reaching its intended target, the US Capitol or the White House (the two most politically iconic landmarks in the US). The terrorists brought four aircrafts under their control with the help of box-cutters, multi-tools, knives, and pepper sprays, turning aircrafts and skyscrapers into weapons of mass destruction. This viciously creative and destructive combination of high-tech and low-tech is an example of how technology is non-determinative, but may be weaponized for non-discriminatory mass killings.

With these attacks in mind, it can be imagined that future technologies such as fully autonomous cars guided by a central traffic control system could be a critical target. Hackers could theoretically switch all the traffic lights of a city to green, accelerate all autonomous cars to maximum, and target further critical infrastructure, such as electric transformers, gas stations, bus or train stations, hospitals, and shopping malls. If such an attack were scaled, fatalities would likely be much higher than after 9/11.

Another prediction in the 1999 sci-fi film *The Matrix* is that reality and real-life events are replaced by computer simulations. Most likely something like this is not going to happen in the near future. However, there already exist simulated environments – think of the interior and exterior architecture of Las Vegas casinos and the simulated reality of virtual reality games; in these examples we are already confronted with various simulations of reality. So-called alternative facts and alternative truths communicated via Twitter, Facebook, and other social platforms, especially in the domain of populist politics, become "real" for followers of such populist politicians. These problems became especially evident after 2016 since one of the most powerful persons at that time, if not the most powerful person, in the world, the former US president Donald Trump, did not seriously care about the truth of what he communicated via Twitter, so that in 2020 Twitter for the first time tagged a message by @realDonaldTrump with linked tags like "Get the facts...", "Glorifying violence", and "Manipulated media". After Trump's supporters stormed the Capitol in January 2021, Facebook and Twitter blocked the outgoing US president's and his campaign's most important accounts. The reason given by Twitter was the risk of further incitement to violence.

> **Case study 6.2: Trump vs Twitter**
>
> Research fake news on social media platforms.
>
> (1) Perform an ethical SWOT analysis of a social media platform.
> (2) Perform an ethical stakeholder analysis of this social media platform.
> (3) Who is/should be responsible for fact checking? Why?
> (4) What is your opinion on Twitter's decision to permanently suspend Donald Trump's account?
> (5) Which of the ethical theories do you see reflected in your argumentation?

In the sci-fi film *The Matrix*, humans are used as renewable energy resources in the AI system's power plants. However, the current real risk is rather that IT users are tapped for data and information that is harvested from their IT accounts. If an application is free, the users pay with their personal data, corresponding with a loss of privacy. In turn, these data then can be used in order to guide or even manipulate users. Data that may be meaningless to us is valuable information that can be turned into knowledge for deeper understanding of trends and consumer patterns by data analysts.

The utilization of big data is becoming a more and more crucial issue due to the gap regarding data, information, and knowledge between an individual consumer and aggregated entities such as entire cultures, societies, networks, and businesses. The German philosopher and sociologist Georg

Simmel in his book *The Philosophy of Money* indicated this phenomena that an individual person's knowledge naturally increases over a period of time and in the history of humankind (Simmel, 1990). What an average person will know in 2030 is different from what an average person knew in 1930. Meaning, Simmel assumed, that knowledge always slightly increases for an average individual over the historical trajectory. However, the knowledge of a society or a network increases exponentially over the historical trajectory. This phenomenon results in an increasing gap between a single individual's knowledge and the data or knowledge of aggregated entities such as cultures, societies, and networks. This data and information or knowledge differential implies or manifests a power differential. Applying Amartya Sen's theory of power and responsibility to this context leads us to acknowledge that such an information and knowledge differential implies not only a corresponding power differential, but also a differential in regard to responsibilities that an aggregated entity has toward individuals from which they gathered the data.

The sci-fi film *The Circle* depicts and predicts an omnipotent data company harvesting all the data of each and every citizen on the planet (Ponsoldt, 2017). Such a data harvesting scenario could in fact be accomplished, if we fused data from the biggest IT companies into one database of big data. The Facebook–Cambridge Analytica scandal makes evident that the positive relation between data, power, and responsibility is not a hypothetical issue, but a highly relevant real-world business case.

On May 22, 2018, Facebook CEO and founder Mark Zuckerberg appeared before a hearing in the European Parliament to address questions regarding the Facebook–Cambridge Analytica data scandal, in which the data of almost 90 million users were collected in a massive data breach. These data sets could be downloaded because, before the scandal, Facebook allowed app developers not only to download Facebook users' data, but also the data of their friends.

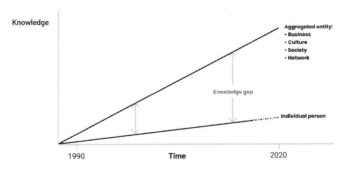

Figure 6.4 Knowledge and information gap

These data sets were finally utilized by Cambridge Analytica in the 2016 US presidential election campaign in order to manipulate voters to vote for Donald Trump. The campaign especially targeted so-called swing voters in order to manipulate their perception and opinion regarding the political opponent Hillary Clinton, so that potential voters would be more likely to vote, and for Donald Trump (Channel 4 News, 2020).

In the light of the impression that Facebook was not in a position to control its own data sets and to protect its users' data, Guy Verhofstadt, a former prime minister of Belgium, compared Mark Zuckerberg in the European Parliament hearing on the Facebook–Cambridge Analytica scandal with the protagonist in the aforementioned sci-fi film *The Circle*.

The similarity between Facebook, other big data companies in the real world, and *The Circle* in the sci-fi film is striking in many regards, especially in terms of the massive data handling, the huge number of users, and the potential to manipulate masses of people with the help of massive data sets.

Film case study 6.2: *The Circle*

Watch the film *The Circle* or read the book of the same title by Dave Eggers (Eggers, 2013).

(1) Who are the stakeholders of the IT company The Circle?
(2) The Circle developed sophisticated light portable cameras that can be stuck anywhere like a discarded chewing gum. These "SeeChange" cameras provide real-time, high-quality video footage with minimal effort accessible to anyone on the internet. Conduct an ethical SWOT analysis of the "SeeChange" technology.
(3) How can a company like The Circle, Facebook, or Alphabet find a balance between the protection of privacy and the need for transparency that can satisfy the preferences of the diverse stakeholders?

It became evident in these hearings, in front of the US Congress and in front of the European Parliament, at least from a political science perspective, that democracy itself is at stake, if elections can be manipulated and ultimately decided with the help of massive data sets. From a business ethical perspective, it becomes clear that businesses have to be much more responsible with the data they have been entrusted by their customers and users.

One of the ethical and legal questions that arises is who owns the data, who can use it and how it may be utilized. Guy Verhofstadt confronted Mark Zuckerberg in the European Parliament hearing and accused Facebook of not entirely complying with the General Data Protection Regulation (GDPR). The GDPR, which came into effect on May 25, 2018, is the European Union's (EU) privacy and security law. It is currently the world's strictest data law, due to strict data regulations and harsh fines, and imposes obligations onto organizations anywhere around the globe, so long as such a business, organization, or individual is targeting or collecting data of someone within the EU. Fines reach into tens of millions of euros (GDPR, 2018).

Businesses, organizations, or individuals are controllers and processors of personal data. "Data controller" is a "person who decides why and how personal data will be processed". A "data processor" "processes personal data on behalf of a data controller"; a "data subject" is the person from whom the data is "harvested" (GDPR, 2018). The seven Data Protection Principles of the GDPR state the following regarding persons and entities that offer, supply, and utilize data:

(1) Processing of data must be **lawful, fair, and transparent** to the data subject.
(2) Process data for **limited legitimate purposes** specified explicitly to the data subject.
(3) Collect and process as **minimal data** as necessary for the purposes specified.
(4) Personal data must be **accurate** and up to date.
(5) **Temporally limit storage** of personally identifiable data only for as long as necessary for the specified purpose.
(6) Data processing must ensure appropriate **security, integrity, and confidentiality** (e.g. by using encryption).
(7) Data controller is **responsible** for GDPR compliance with all of these principles.

Case study 6.3: GDPR

Research GDPR.

(1) Choose a business of your interest and try to find out if the company or the organization complies with the GDPR.
(2) According to your judgement, which of the GDPR regulations are too strict, too vague, or not strict enough? Why? Discuss.

A conundrum, a very complex issue, arises in the context of data and IT utilization in the light of the cases studied in this chapter: how do we meaningfully deal with the tradeoff between privacy, security, and convenience? Google Maps' location tracking makes navigation highly efficient and convenient, and due to real-time traffic rendering also more secure, because the application displays a traffic jam before the driver can see it actually on the road. This display of augmented reality on a screen gives the driver sufficient time to reduce speed, or change route, before arriving in the jammed area.

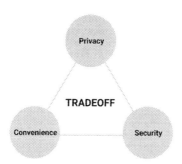

Figure 6.5 Privacy, security, convenience tradeoff

However, the location history is tracked, stored, processed, and maybe passed on or sold by Google. Hackers may force access to location data and pass it on to a malevolent person who may track, and predict a person's location data in order to stalk, rape, rob, or kill persons on their everyday movement paths and locations. CCTV surveillance in the city makes the city a safer place, but less anonymous. This will increase the safety for ordinary people, but sharply increases the risk for political dissidents in politically less democratic locations.

Film case study 6.3: *Snowden, Citizenfour*

Watch both the Hollywood thriller *Snowden* (Stone, 2016) and the documentary *Citizenfour* (Poitras, 2014). These films make it evident that there is a significant tradeoff between individual privacy and national security.

(1) In which way are businesses such as Microsoft, Alibaba, Google, Facebook, Apple, and others involved in the global surveillance?
(2) Is it ethically justifiable to clandestinely collect data on a large scale from users and organizations via IT businesses as the USA's NSA did?
(3) Which ethical theories would support this large-scale surveillance?
(4) Is it ethically justifiable that Edward Snowden shared classified secret service information with a journalist in order to inform the public who had no idea about the large-scale surveillance by the NSA?
(5) Which ethical theories would support Snowden's whistleblowing?

Case study 6.4: UAVs (drones)

Research the facts, issues, and laws regarding drones/Unmanned Aerial Vehicles (UAVs).

(1) Gather and comment on some of the technical and economic facts related to UAVs.
(2) Explain some business opportunities for UAVs.
(3) How are stakeholders affected by UAV business and UAV applications?
(4) Which ethical theories could be helpful for giving further recommendations regarding current and future UAV usage and safety?

Key takeaways

(1) We have to appreciate that, for the rest of our lives, we will have to repeatedly reinvent ourselves in order to excel in a technologically ever faster paced environment.
(2) Technological determinism means that what is invented is usually also utilized in one way or another.
(3) Technology is not determinative; it does not determine how it is utilized.

References

Baudrillard, J. (1994). *Simulacra and Simulation*. University of Michigan Press.
Channel 4 News. (2020, September 28). *Revealed: Trump Campaign Strategy to Deter Millions of Black Americans from Voting in 2016*. www.channel4.com/news/revealed-trump-campaign-strategy-to-deter-millions-of-black-americans-from-voting-in-2016
Eggers, D. (2013). *The Circle*. Knopf Doubleday Publishing Group.
GDPR EU. (2018, November 7). *What is GDPR, the EU's New Data Protection Law?* https://gdpr.eu/what-is-gdpr/
Grove, A.S. (2010). *Only the Paranoid Survive: How to Exploit the Crisis Points That Challenge Every Company*. Crown.
Harari, Y.N. (2015a). *Homo Deus: A Brief History of Tomorrow*. Signal.
Harari, Y.N. (2015b). *Sapiens: A Brief History of Humankind*. Vintage Books.
Harari, Y.N. (2018). *21 Lessons for the 21st Century*. Random House.
Harasim, L. (2017). *Learning Theory and Online Technologies*. Routledge.
Marx, L., & Smith, M.R. (1994). *Does Technology Drive History? The Dilemma of Technological Determinism*. MIT Press.
Poitras, L. (2014, October 31). *Citizenfour* [Documentary; Film]. Artificial Eye Film Co. Ltd.
Ponsoldt, J. (2017, April 27). *The Circle* [Film; Drama; Sci-Fi; Thriller]. 1978 Films, EuropaCorp, Imagenation Abu Dhabi FZ.
Simmel, G. (1990). *The Philosophy of Money*. Routledge.

Standing, G. (2017). *Basic Income: And How We Can Make It Happen*. Penguin UK.
Stasi, A., & Meinhold, R. (2020). When cows go oink, pigs go baaa, and sheep go moo: Development and regulatory challenges of intentional genomic alterations in animals. *Food and Drug Law Journal, 75*, 415.
Stone, O. (2016, September 15). *Snowden* [Film; Biography; Crime; Drama; Thriller]. KrautPack Entertainment, Vendian Entertainment, Endgame Entertainment.
Wong, J.C. (2018, April 17). *I was one of Facebook's first users: I shouldn't have trusted Mark Zuckerberg*. The Guardian. www.theguardian.com/technology/2018/apr/17/facebook-people-first-ever-mark-zuckerberg-harvard
Tilley, N. (1993). *Understanding Car Parks, Crime, and CCTV: Evaluation Lessons from Safer Cities*. Home Office Police Dept.
Washington Post. (2018, October 4). *Mark Zuckerberg testifies on Capitol Hill (full Senate hearing)*. www.youtube.com/watch?v=6ValJMOpt7s

7 Business ethics in media, marketing, advertising, and fashion

Abstract

The chapter dives into the definition and the purpose of media. Media controversies and their effects on society are explored. Marketing has shifted from addressing the consumer's needs to their wants, giving rise to meta-goods in advertisements. One of the industries that have pushed the boundaries has been the fashion industry, and this chapter analyzes fashion adverts using philosophical-anthropological implications. The rise of new forms of media channels has created social media influencers who have become one of the most effective marketing strategies. In recent times, we have also seen the risks of influencer marketing coming from influencers' actions reflecting on the associated brands. The chapter also discusses provocative and controversial marketing. The chapter includes numerous case studies, such as on the Darknet, Instagram poll triggered suicide, influencers, and controversial fashion marketing.

Chapter keywords

(1) Media
(2) Marketing and advertisements
(3) Deception
(4) Meta-goods
(5) Social media
(6) Fake news
(7) Influencers
(8) Fashion advertisements
(9) Controversial marketing and advertising

Study objectives

After studying this chapter readers will be able to:

(1) Understand the relevance of media for businesses.
(2) Evaluate advertising and marketing tools from an ethical perspective.

DOI: 10.4324/9781003127659-7

(3) Contribute in the creation of responsible advertising and marketing campaigns.

Case studies

7.1 The Darknet
7.2 Malaysian girl commits suicide over Instagram poll
7.3 Meta-goods in advertising
7.4 Influencers
7.5 Controversial fashion marketing

Films

(1) *The Cleaners*
(2) *The Century of the Self*

7.1 Introduction

This chapter elucidates how economies shifted from a "needs" to a "desires and wants" culture by highlighting the psychoanalytic, psychosocial, and philosophical-anthropological backgrounds of marketing and misleading and controversial advertising. The chapter will touch on some recent controversies of influencer marketing and place its main focus in particular on fashion marketing as an example of how marketing taps into human traits, desires, and wants. An additional focus will be media-communicated violence. Offensive and controversial cases about the marketing of luxury brands such as Saint Laurent, Calvin Klein, Gucci, and Dolce & Gabbana contrast creative controversial artistic elements with offensive, degrading, racist, and misogynic examples in fashion marketing. That digitally mediated violence may result in violence in the real world is demonstrated in a case where a young Malaysian woman with suicidal thoughts took a poll on Instagram to decide if she should commit suicide, which she ultimately did.

7.2 Media: Between salient, crucial information and "bullshit"

Media in general business and information and communication technology (ICT) contexts fulfill a number of tasks:

(1) Storing and accessing processes of one or more producers or users of information. Media serving for storing content can be a wall painting in a temple, a book, a CD, DVD, an electronic file, a blog on social media, or an entry on Wikipedia.
(2) Mediating between two or more communicators, for example with the help of symbols, letters, emails, phone calls, or application messages.

142 Media, marketing, fashion

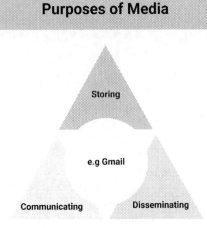

Figure 7.1 Purposes of media

(3) Mediating between sender and receiver, producer or disseminators and consumers. Examples are newspapers, radio or television programs, movies in cinemas, websites, and newsletters.

The media we use on our mobile phones and computers serve all three purposes: storing, communicating, and disseminating data and information. Google, Apple, and Facebook are services that do all three. In the business field we can see that the ICT companies of scale were eager to increase their market share by covering all three functions of mediation or media.

Apple Inc. from the beginning was offering well attuned hardware-software combinations and the iPhone became the first all-round mediating mass-consumer device, a kind of Swiss Army knife in the field of media. Software and internet giants Microsoft and Google both initially started with software and then expanded into hardware. Google launched the Nexus tablets and phones in 2010 and later the Chromebook in 2011 and Pixel laptops in 2013, Microsoft launched the Surface series in 2012, acquired Nokia's mobile business in 2014, and sold it in 2016 to HMD Global. Covering as many functions of media as possible usually increases the market share of companies. That this may lead to monopoly or oligopoly in extreme cases will be discussed in Chapter 9.

The technological term "media" represents various things and concepts; it is a very wide and inclusive term. Today's word "media" is derived from the Latin word *medium* and means being in the middle or mediating. Media are "mediating" (submitting, exchanging) content between persons and organizations and thus act as a means of communication, but also as storage. Ontologically (in terms of their "substance") media consist of hardware, such as mobile phones and computers, and software, for example apps and computer programs, including files such as text documents, pdf, presentation files, or spreadsheets. Data carriers are also considered media, such as Solid-State Drives (SSDs) and cloud storage, which again consist of software and hardware.

Classical media are, for example, television and newspapers, radio channels and hard-wired telephones, but also carrier pigeons, and snail-mail or express mail services. In a wider sense, a medium can also be a person that is storing information or communicating information from one person to another, or from one historical point in time to a later point in time, for example a messenger, a journalist, a historian, or a storyteller. In esoteric language, a medium is a person who communicates between living persons and spirits or ancestors.

In his book *Understanding Media: The Extensions of Man* (McLuhan, 2016), the Canadian philosopher, media, and communication theorist Marshall McLuhan coined the phrase "the Medium is the Message". What he means by this phrase becomes obvious when, for example, a report about a conference on the health impacts of sweets concludes that sweets are less unhealthy than generally assumed, especially if consumed in moderation. However, the journalist writing an article on the report had found out that the conference was sponsored by the sugar industry. In this case, the medium and how this message is conveyed must be scrutinized, not only the message. This can also be applied to messages from manipulative individuals' Twitter or other social media accounts which have been created for political propaganda or consumer manipulation. In this sense one of McLuhan's later book titles needs to be understood: *The Medium is the Massage* (McLuhan & Fiore, 2001). Media work on humans like a massage, pleasing, relieving, or shaping. McLuhan played with the word "message" and "massage", as "mess age" and "mass age". In times of mass production and mass consumption fostered by media a certain form of mess is also created. Scandals like the Facebook–Cambridge Analytica case are good examples in which media contributed to the creation of a "mess", challenging the function of democratic elections by using masses of data, taken from media, in this case harvested from Facebook, in order to "massage" and manipulate the US swing voters. From this perspective, it looks like McLuhan's puns are even more relevant today than they were during his lifetime.

7.2.1 Challenges and controversies in media contexts

Media and their utilization pose several ethical controversies which cannot be neglected in the business context because almost all media are either operated by businesses or are in one or the other way connected to or owned by businesses. Applications, and the devices on which they run, offer usefulness and convenience. Once location tracking for Google Maps on a mobile phone is enabled this reduces the user's privacy by making personal data accessible to third-party advertising and marketing businesses. Media such as social networks provide useful information and connect people around the globe, but at the same time flood users with useless and unsolicited information, sometimes referred to as information overflow, trash, spam (in email folders), or "bullshit". "Bullshit" is used here as a philosophical technical term, introduced by Princeton University Philosophy Professor Harry Frankfurt in 1986. "One of the most salient features of our culture is that there is so much bullshit" (Frankfurt, 2009). Bullshit is text or speech that intends to persuade without interest in furthering an actual truth. A bullshitter does not care about the accuracy of information mediated but concentrates rather on the effect of the mediated information. Frankfurt's claim about bullshitting is even more topical in today's social media reality in which politicians claim that there exist "alternative facts" and "alternative truths" (Hendricks & Vestergaard, 2019).

Information on social media platforms can also bias users by reproducing and reinforcing their preferences and manipulating users' decision-making processes when they make choices regarding purchases, or even voting, as we have learned from the first Donald Trump presidential election campaign. User data was collected and politically weaponized in what was later known as the Facebook–Cambridge Analytica scandal.

A significant problem is that the algorithms of the major search engines do not, or at least not sufficiently, differentiate according to whether certain messages are truthful or fictional. This has led to the spread of half-truths, conspiracy theories, hateful comments and tweets, fake news, and the like.

A related problem is that algorithm guided social media primarily displays its users' messages and information to fit their personal worldview. In this context, it should be noted that individuals generally tend to consume media content that corresponds to their personal views, interests, or political convictions. The algorithms of social networks are programmed in such a way that they take into account and reinforce such outlooks and human weaknesses. Anyone who has once "liked" a certain alternative news page on Facebook will see relevant or comparable messages displayed again and again. This in turn can lead to the user's worldview being narrowed ever further and becoming stuck in a kind of echo chamber. Against this background, it is particularly important that people find out about what is happening in the world via various news sources, including, in particular, classic neutral news sources like daily newspapers: "sapere aude!" (see Chapter 3).

Social media generate large amounts of profits via advertising but have, at the same time, been weaponized for propaganda purposes from entities such as political campaigners and terrorist organizations such as the Islamic State that posted video footage of beheadings on YouTube. At the same time, social media, such as YouTube, hosts highly meaningful and useful instructional and educational material, news, as well as high and low culture entertainment.

However, nowadays, social media platforms do not avoid criticism from their stakeholders anymore by claiming that they simply provide storage space and digital infrastructure for users. They have been made responsible for hosting materials such as pedophile content, bomb-building instructions, and footage of beheadings by terrorists. Social media platforms have been held legally and ethically responsible for the hosted content and subsequently have employed "cleaners" and detective algorithms to assess, flag, or delete inappropriate content. The 2018 documentary *The Cleaners* tells the story of contracted low-paid global content moderators for social media providers located in Manila, the Philippines (Nicholson, 2018).

Film case study 7.1: *The Cleaners*

Watch the 2018 documentary *The Cleaners*.

(1) Discuss which persons or entities are, or should be, responsible for content on social media.
(2) Which stakeholders should be responsible for censorship?
(3) What are the special risks that social media pose compared to traditional media (e.g. TV)?
(4) Which ethical theories and tools are helpful in determining how to discriminate between appropriate and inappropriate social media content?
(5) Do we have to re-think how we utilize social media, for example in terms of content or screen time?

In order to avoid mainstream social media, certain users move to what is called "The Darknet" or "dark web". The Darknet is an encrypted parallel network or overlay network of the internet which can be accessed via specific encrypting, anonymizing, rerouting, software tools such as the Tor Onion Router. While most of the "business" conducted within the Darknet is illegal, foremost drugs (Ilić & Spalević, 2017), some of the traffic is comprised of whistleblowing and communications by political dissidents. Thus, this technology is even recommended by civil liberty entities, such as the Electronic Frontier Foundation (EFF). Tor is also used by journalists from certain mainstream media, such as *The Guardian*, for communication with whistleblowers and political dissidents. What has been stated about the non-determinative nature of technology in the previous chapter, namely that it can be used for ethical and unethical purposes, can also be applied to tools like Tor. The software itself is open to use by hackers, drug dealers, pedophiles, political dissidents, or whistleblowers.

> **Case study 7.1: The Darknet**
>
> Research the Darknet, EFF, the "Tor Onion Router", and Chaos Computer Club.
>
> (1) Who are the stakeholders of the Darknet? How are businesses involved?
> (2) Create a SWOT analysis of the Darknet and its related ICT tools.
> (3) If ethically recommendable utilizations of the Darknet lie in providing platforms and means of communication for whistleblowers and political dissidents, why are so many users of Tor located in countries with developed economies?
> (4) Can and should the Darknet be regulated? If yes, how should it be regulated and by whom?

In investigative journalism cases, such as the NSA revelations by Edward Snowden, tools like the Tor Onion Router can protect whistleblowers and political dissidents by anonymizing or concealing their identity. Whistleblowers like Chelsea Manning, Julian Assange, and Edward Snowden have acted contrary to laws in the US; however, they defend their whistleblowing on the grounds that the general public needed to be made aware of the NSA's and other countries secret services' spying activities in order to make informed choices in elections.

There exists a right of information for nations' citizens, and media and journalism are crucial in providing, investigating, and editing this information. However, especially in regard to tabloid journalism, while also aiming to inform the general public, it often disrespects the privacy of individuals. The death of the widely popular Princess of Wales, Diana, a member of the British Royal Family, for example, has been blamed on intrusive journalists. Since some such journalists intrude into the privacy especially of prominent individuals by using drones and telephoto lenses, a number of celebrities have purchased entire islands, villages, or clusters of houses in order to be undisturbed and safe. Bill Gates (the founder of Microsoft) and Richard Branson (the founder of Virgin) are famous examples of business entrepreneurs who regained privacy by creating their private space with such adaptations.

How digitally mediated violence may result in violence in the real world is demonstrated by a case where a Malaysian young woman with suicidal thoughts took a poll on Instagram to decide if she should commit suicide, which she ultimately did: "A 16 year-old girl has reportedly killed herself in Malaysia, after posting a poll on her Instagram account asking followers if she should die or not, and 69% of responders voting that she should" (Fullerton, 2019).

> **Case study 7.2: Malaysian girl commits suicide over Instagram poll**
>
> Research the case of a Malaysian girl who committed suicide over an Instagram poll.
>
> (1) Mention important stakeholders of Instagram in this case and explain very briefly how each of these stakeholders could have an impact or influence on Instagram.
> (2) What dangers do social media like Instagram pose for (young) people with mental health problems? How could one counteract these dangers?
> (3) Explain very briefly the ethical issues of this case with the help of suitable ethical theories, presented earlier.
> (4) Imagine you were in charge of corporate social responsibility at Facebook and Instagram, how would you have reacted after this incident?
> (5) In this case, what would be ethically advisable to do if you were the Chief Information Officer at Instagram?

7.3 Marketing and advertising: Addressing needs, not wants

The 2002 BBC classic documentary *The Century of the Self* by Adam Curtis (Curtis, 2002) explains how marketing helped to shift mainstream consumer culture from a "needs culture" to a "desire culture" or "want culture". A famous example of this shift is how smoking was made desirable for and socially acceptable to women in the US, which by today's standards would be regarded as an ethically questionable marketing campaign. A nephew of Sigmund Freud (the founder of psychoanalysis), Edward Bernays, who is considered to be the father of public relations, attempted to break down the social taboo against women smoking in public. Bernays' clients included companies such as Procter & Gamble and American Tobacco. Bernays initially had helped advertise smoking to women to pursue the beauty ideal of a slim body. He was partially successful in increasing the number of female cigarette customers by advertising cigarettes as a substitute for sweets, snacks, and even food. However, most women who smoked did so privately, not in public, which limited the potential for them to smoke everywhere. The psychiatrist and psychoanalyst Abraham Arden Brill advised Bernays to refer to cigarettes advertised to women as "torches of freedom" because this would resonate with the first-wave feminist aspirations for emancipation from men and increased equality (see also Chapter 3).

Bernays decided to hire photographers for documentation and female models to walk and publicly light cigarettes during the 1929 New York Easter Sunday Parade, a cultural event which was also used by citizens to show off wealth and beauty. The documentation of this event, "torches of freedom", as symbols of emancipation and equality, was publicized in the media around the world. In the US, only 5% of cigarettes sold were purchased by women in 1923; in 1935 women constituted almost a quarter of cigarette customers. Subsequently, female buyers of cigarettes increased by a third in 1965 (O'Keefe & Pollay, 1996).

In *The Century of Self*, Adam Curtis simultaneously conflates and concludes several observations as claims. Consumption and other choices can be guided with psychoanalytic tools, devices, and tricks, so that the economy, within the 20th century, had been transferred from a "needs culture" into a "wants" or "desire culture". Because of this, businesses will eventually take over many hitherto governmental functions, because businesses can serve consumers desires more precisely and promptly than governments. This is observable in cases of privatization of healthcare, education, and transportation.

The Facebook–Cambridge Analytica scandal made it obvious that theory and practice of psychological and psychoanalytical consumer manipulation, which resulted in voter guidance and manipulation, are working even more impactfully at the beginning of the 21st century. Yuval Harari claims that consumption choices, which were guided by the consumers' personal decisions until the end of the 20th century, nowadays gradually give way to choices influenced by algorithms and artificial intelligence. Consumers increasingly delegate their choices and decision-making processes to algorithms and AI because humans simply process significantly less information than AI, thus making less well-informed choices. One straightforward example is the Google Maps application. Using a paper map, listening to traffic news, and then gauging the best possible route is a matter of concern for the past. Our route is no longer determined by our personal estimations anymore, but by algorithms, taking into consideration many variables, such as time, weather, road quality, traffic restrictions, real-time traffic feedback, and historical traffic patterns.

Consumer behavior is similarly guided by AI because the kinds of advertisements that appear on our IT devices' screens depends on the data previously harvested, by businesses such as Facebook, Google, and Amazon, from these devices. One example we want to focus on more closely is fashion advertising.

7.3.1 Meta-goods in marketing and advertising in the fashion industry

One claim that has been made in the context of marketing fashion and fashionable consumer goods is that advertising and marketing not only tap into psychoanalytically recognizable desires, or personality traits like those of the ocean model (Bay, 2018), but also into philosophical-anthropological features which are linked to what can be called "meta-goods" (Meinhold, 2014).

In the "torches of freedom" example given above, cigarette marketing tapped into the meta-goods of personal freedom, emancipation, and self-determination. The act of smoking cigarettes in public was symbolizing or signifying particular demands, desires, and values; to be more specific: meta-goods.

But what are meta-goods? Meta-goods are seemingly transferred into the consumer – when purchased or consumed. They metaphorically stand "behind" consumers' motivations and desires when they purchase a product or a service. In advertisements, meta-goods are often hidden behind or around the actual product. They are immaterial counterparts of products or services "charged" with values. Meta-goods are existential, intellectual, psychological, emotional, social, or spiritual desires, values, or symbols (Meinhold, 2007).

What is displayed or hinted at in advertisements is a product or service "infused" with meta-goods. The fashion industry and marketing approaches in general implicitly expand the concept of the human being, the person, or the individual beyond the body. Through the lens of marketing and advertising, a person is only a complete human being with appropriate consumer goods or utilized services. With this, marketing and advertising expand human nature, the body, and the soul. Marketing and advertising claim to improve the human body and nature. Like in agricultural processes, the soil can be improved or ameliorated by fertilization and fortification. The human body, the individual, or a person can be "ameliorated" with the help of consumer products and services according to the campaigns of advertising and marketing. The meta-good can also be compared to supplements in nutritional contexts, although it is controversial how well fortifying food supplements work. However, it can be assumed that some supplements, like B12, work very well to prevent malnutrition, while some others may not be that effective. Amelioration or fortification in the marketing context not only takes place by acquiring physical consumer products or services, e.g. a sneaker that lets you run faster or with better traction, but also, and sometimes mainly, with the help of meta-goods. We may *feel* more dynamic or energetic by wearing the same sneakers or sunglasses as a famous athlete, which is one of the reasons why some products bear the name of celebrities.

Marketing and advertising claim that we become smarter by purchasing smart cars, smartphones, or smart wearable tech. The consumer becomes more beautiful with beautiful clothes, handbags, or other well-designed objects.

7.3.2 Philosophical-anthropological implications of meta-goods in fashion adverts

With the employment of meta-goods, fashion marketing in particular, but marketing and advertising in general, communicates stories, myths, and even

150 *Media, marketing, fashion*

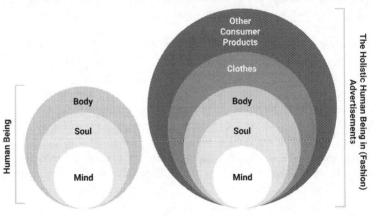

Figure 7.2 Fortification of humans in adverts

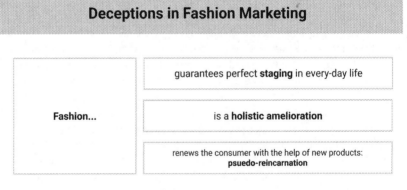

Figure 7.3 Deceptions in fashion marketing

blatant lies to consumers. While fashionable consumer products do indeed improve consumers' appearance in many ways, a prominent fiction communicated to consumers states that fashion improves human beings or individuals in three other dimensions in particular:

(1) Fashion guarantees the perfect presentation of ourselves in everyday life.
(2) Fashion is not only beautification of a person, but a holistic improvement.
(3) Fashion renews the consumer with the help of new products.

These three myths, stories, or promises can be based upon three assumptions regarding philosophical-anthropological traits of human nature:

(1) People want to be esteemed by others in their social context. This feature corresponds to Maslow's hierarchy of needs, in particular the need to be recognized by others.
(2) Humans live and think in a comparative mode. This simply means that we always compare ourselves with others, with friends, with neighbors, other family members, and many other individuals, including celebrities. This comparative mode of existence also implies a *competitive* mode of existence. We also compete with others and not only want to emulate others, but exceed them; in particular terms of appearance, consumption styles, and behavior in general. Sociologists speak of role models in the context of emulation.
(3) The third assumption is much more difficult to understand. It is concerned with metaphysical questions and transcendence. As a brief classification of the term metaphysics, it can be said that "metaphysics" focuses on the conceptual frameworks with which we generally deal with reality. "'Metaphysics' sheds light on the question of how the world works in general – whereas the various fields of science deal with the question of how the world works in detail" (Schramm, 2017). In its simplest terms, this assumption means that humans cannot really avoid thinking about what happens when they die or when they age, but also where they came from before they came into existence in this world. A major source marketing can tap into is that humans are usually afraid of dissolution and dying. This is why health and life insurances, as well as cosmetic companies, have convincingly powerful stories to tell when marketing their products. Moreover, businesses that promote fashionable products make use of this particular philosophical-anthropological feature, because fashionable products can create the impression of a younger appearance for its consumers.

Figure 7.4 Anthropological implications of fashion adverts

> **Case study 7.3: Meta-goods in advertising**
>
> Research your favorite products, brands, and adverts.
>
> (1) With what kind of meta-goods have these products, brands, and adverts been charged or infused?
> (2) What other kinds of values, psychological characteristics, or human features and character traits can you detect in the "narratives" or "stories" told by marketing and advertising strategies which you find more or less convincing, interesting, or aesthetically pleasing?

7.4 Influencers

The first and the second anthropological feature, our aims for recognition by our peers and our comparative mode of thinking and acting, are especially tapped into by Social Media Influencers (SMIs). Influencers can be viewed as third parties (neither consumer, nor producer), as stakeholders, or as part of the supply chain. SMIs are prominent individuals or teams, often playing the fictitious role of a potential consumer, who endorses a product, groups of products, or a brand, on social media. The advertising industry has experienced a significant increase of SMI utilization as a marketing device. Influencer marketing on social media is a very powerful and effective sales tool that is perceived as even more trustworthy by consumers than traditional celebrity marketing (Jin et al., 2019; Lou & Yuan, 2019; Taylor, 2020). SMIs legally need to disclose sponsorship compensation by labels as "sponsored content" which in turn may lead to depreciating or negative responses by viewers. SMIs who explain or justify their sponsorship compensation with a sentence like "sponsored content helps me to produce high quality content" reduce the number of negative responses (Stubb et al., 2019).

A number of SMIs also presented controversial or repulsive material on blogs or YouTube, such as the YouTuber PewDiePie's racist comments which lead to cancelled contracts with Walt Disney and YouTuber Logan Paul's video in Aokigahara, Japan, a forest at the base of Mount Fuji, also known as "Seas of Trees" or "Suicide Forest" which sparked controversy among YouTube viewers and other social and conventional media.

> **Case study 7.4: Influencers**
>
> Research: 1) undisclosed paid endorsements, 2) influencers' activities during the Covid-19 pandemic, 3) fake followers of influencers, and

4) ethically controversial postings such as Logan Paul's video in Japan's Suicide Forest.

(1) How did different stakeholders, such as followers, the general public, the media, and politicians receive influencers conspicuous travelling style during the Covid-19 pandemic?
(2) What kind of responsibilities do influencers have, especially towards young people? From a legal but also from an ethical perspective?
(3) What would you do differently in terms of your own presentation and the presentation of products if you were an influencer?

7.5 Controversial marketing and advertising

A very closely related topic of great importance is the dilemma between freedom of expression of opinion and creativity vs censorship and fears regarding the copycat effect. The copycat effect plays a significant role in literature, but also in the film and fashion industries, especially in the context of marketing and advertising. The copycat effect is a phenomenon in which individuals imitate the behaviors of other more prominent individuals, fictional characters, or celebrities; in particular, negatively connotated acts from an ethical viewpoint, and so-called copycat crimes. Famous movies which have been banned in several countries because of allegedly having triggered copycat crimes or having the potential to invite imitations of acts seen on screen are *Salò, or the 120 Days of Sodom*, *A Clockwork Orange*, *Natural Born Killers*, and the *Saw* franchise, just to name a few. But the phenomenon can also be found in literature. It is for example claimed that after the publication of *The Sorrows of Young Werther* by Johann Wolfgang von Goethe's, Germany's most famous poet, in 1774, a number of young men in Europe not only dressed up as Werther was described in the novel, but allegedly a few also committed suicide imitating the novel's protagonist. In psychology, this phenomenon has been called "the Werther Effect" or copycat suicide. However, suicides following the Werther publication have been dismissed as rumor by certain interpreters, but nonetheless, the novel was censored and the Werther clothing style was banned in a number of cities and countries.

When it comes to prominent examples in advertising, a number of fashion adverts have been banned because of depicting scenes such as gang rape, sexual violence, degradation of women, anorexic models, and racial discrimination. Alexander McQueen, Alexander Wang, American Apparel, Balenciaga, Benneton, Calvin Klein, Dolce & Gabbana, Gucci, Saint Laurent, Sisley, and Tom Ford are some of the fashion labels whose adverts were banned or censored due to salacious (obscene) or discriminatory content.

> **Case study 7.5: Controversial fashion marketing**
>
> Research controversial fashion marketing, degrading adverts, racial discrimination in marketing, and anorexic fashion models.
>
> (1) Is showing fashion models in provocative positions and scenes which look like gang rape or other scenes depicting models in inferior or vulnerable positions acceptable? How far can a fashion label go? Apply different ethical theories to address this question.
> (2) Or are such adverts creative media that are better (or additionally) situated in the realm of art and thus should underlie a different set of rules that is also applicable to works of art? If yes, why?
> (3) Usually, women's rights groups argue that controversial adverts may inspire or trigger copycat crimes. Others argue that such adverts are simply "bad taste". However, some feminists have argued that it is the model's choice to display herself as she wishes, and such adverts can also be taken as a sign of emancipation. Discuss the various positions.

Key takeaways

(1) Media are a crucial but ambivalent marketing tool for businesses.
(2) Utilizing media responsibly is pertinent for business sustainability.

References

Bay, M. (2018). The ethics of psychometrics in social media: A Rawlsian approach. *Hawaii International Conference on System Sciences 2018 (HICSS-51)*. https://aisel.aisnet.org/hicss-51/dsm/critical_and_ethical_studies/2
Curtis, A. (2002). *The Century of Self*. BBC.
Frankfurt, H. (2009). *On Bullshit*. Princeton University Press.
Fullerton. (2019, May 15). Teenage girl kills herself "after Instagram poll" in Malaysia. *The Guardian*. www.theguardian.com/world/2019/may/15/teenage-girl-kills-herself-after-instagram-poll-in-malaysia
Hendricks, V. & Vestergaard, M. (2019). *Reality Lost: Markets of Attention, Misinformation and Manipulation*. Springer.
Ilić, M., & Spalević, Ž. (2017). The use of dark web for the purpose of illegal activity spreading. *Društvo Ekonomista*, *1*, 73–82.
Jin, S.V., Muqaddam, A., & Ryu, E. (2019). Instafamous and social media influencer marketing. *Marketing Intelligence & Planning*, *37*(5), 567–579. https://doi.org/10.1108/MIP-09-2018-0375
Lou, C., & Yuan, S. (2019). Influencer marketing: How message value and credibility affect consumer trust of branded content on social media. *Journal of Interactive Advertising*, *19*(1), 58–73. https://doi.org/10.1080/15252019.2018.1533501

McLuhan, M. (2016). *Understanding Media: The Extensions of Man*. CreateSpace Independent Publishing Platform.
McLuhan, M., & Fiore, Q. (2001). *The Medium is the Massage: An Inventory of Effects*. Gingko Press.
Meinhold, R. (2007). Meta-goods in fashion-myths: Philosophic-anthropological implications of fashion advertisements. *Prajñā Vihāra*, *8*(2), Article 2. www.assumptionjournal.au.edu/index.php/PrajnaVihara/article/view/1242
Meinhold, R. (2014). *Fashion Myths: A Cultural Critique* (J. Irons, Trans.). Transcript-Verlag.
Nicholson, A. (2018, January 24). Sundance film review: *The Cleaners*. *Variety*. https://variety.com/2018/film/reviews/the-cleaners-review-1202673932/
O'Keefe, A. M., & Pollay, R. W. (1996). Deadly targeting of women in promoting cigarettes. *Journal of the American Medical Women's Association*, *51*(1–2), 67–69.
Schramm, M. (2017). How the (business) world really works: Business metaphysics & "creating shared value". In J. Wieland (Ed.), *Creating Shared Value – Concepts, Experience, Criticism* (pp. 81–117). Springer International Publishing. https://doi.org/10.1007/978-3-319-48802-8_6
Stubb, C., Nyström, A.-G., & Colliander, J. (2019). Influencer marketing: The impact of disclosing sponsorship compensation justification on sponsored content effectiveness. *Journal of Communication Management*, *23*(2), 109–122. https://doi.org/10.1108/JCOM-11-2018-0119
Taylor, C.R. (2020). The urgent need for more research on influencer marketing. *International Journal of Advertising*, *39*(7), 889–891. https://doi.org/10.1080/02650487.2020.1822104

8 Intercultural business ethics and sustainability

Abstract

As businesses continue to digitalize and become increasingly global and "borderless", ethical practices must be re-evaluated in order to encompass the differences in local norms. Attention to these ethical requirements has become crucial for the success of multinational business. The chapter introduces the concept of "merging cultural horizons", which can be used to understand cultural values and thus help to find compromises throughout business practices. To analyze cultural differences, Hofstede's cultural dimensions theory provides a framework to identify key values. The chapter includes case studies, e.g. on the employment of monkeys in business and on the Moral Machine experiment.

Chapter keywords

(1) Globalization and geopolitics
(2) "Blitz-scaling" and power asymmetry
(3) Cultural values, diversity, relativity vs cultural homogenization
(4) Ethical relativism
(5) Cultural dimensions
(6) Microsocial norms vs hypernorms
(7) "Merging of horizons" and "Über-setzen"
(8) Normative interculturality
(9) Hofstede's cultural dimensions

Study objectives

After studying this chapter, readers will be able to:

(1) Understand, explain, and manage intercultural encounters and transcultural social interactions, especially in business contexts.
(2) Compare differences in business culture using cultural dimension theory.
(3) Better navigate cross-cultural business environments.

DOI: 10.4324/9781003127659-8

Case studies

8.1 Rammstein: Amerika
8.2 Monkey business
8.3 Programming ethics into algorithms
8.4 Hofstede's cultural dimensions theory

8.1 Introduction: Intercultural issues in business ethics

Chapter 8 widens the book's perspective regarding challenges in transcultural business interactions, taking cross-cultural engagement approaches, and a few non-Western philosophical and ethical approaches into account. Specific cultural values such as correctness, punctuality, pragmatism, friendliness, saving face, and Ubuntu impact on services and products in the business domain, but at the same time also have an influence on the form of negotiations, including the (non-)conclusion of contracts. Challenges of cultural homogenization and hegemony through power asymmetries or "blitzscaling" elucidate multinationals' international dominance over SMEs, state actors (e.g. in the context of legislative processes), and NGO representatives. Diverse culturally relevant management and decision-making styles will be discussed (host, imperial, interconnecting, and global styles) as well as the relevance and reconciliation of hypernorms and culturally specific norms in globalized business contexts. Martin Heidegger's and Georg Gadamer's concepts of "Über-setzen" and "merging of horizons" will be introduced as bridging approaches between diverse cultural and national values. Geert Hofstede's cultural dimensions theory will be employed for elucidating the relationship between values and national cultures. Cases such as the one on animal labor demonstrate the dilemmas that companies operating across cultures are confronted with.

8.2 Globalized business

Despite the fact that all multinational corporations and many SMEs operate in diverse cultural domains, the topic of intercultural encounters and transcultural interactions in the business world is largely neglected in mainstream business ethics literature. Nevertheless, it is ultimately an undeniable fact that in our globalized business world, for decades, most mainstream products and services are brought about in processes which involve business activities in diverse countries and dissimilar cultures.

Mobile phones (e.g. from Samsung, Huawei, Xiaomi, Apple) are designed and engineered in South Korea, China, or the US, manufactured in China (sometimes, at least partially, under questionable working conditions concerning the treatment of local labor), and then sold worldwide. Rice grown and harvested in Thailand, India, and Vietnam is consumed worldwide.

158   *Intercultural business ethics*

Sodas and fast food (such as Coke, Pepsi, McDonald's, KFC, Dunkin' Donuts) are founded, headquartered, and based in the US, but produced and sold worldwide. Cars developed and constructed in Germany, Japan, the US, China, and India, are assembled and sold worldwide. Red Bull, headquartered in Austria, has its origins in Thailand, where it is still sold locally as Krating Daeng with a slightly different recipe. Sportswear (e.g. Adidas, Puma, Nike, ASICS) is designed in Germany, the US, or Japan, produced in Asia, and sold worldwide. The same applies to high-priced high-end fashion brands from France or Italy, some of which are also manufactured in Asia, India, or Turkey. Nike, founded as Blue-Ribbon Sports by Philip Knight, initially started with marketing Onitsuka Tiger (ASICS) shoes in the US. The design resemblance between Adidas' three stripes, Onitsuka Tiger's and ASICS' stripes, Puma's Formstrip, and Nike's Swoosh logo is interesting, if not striking.

Globalization, a process of international economic integration, is manifested in an intensified exchange of goods, services, financial flows, information, and people. The challenges identified by globalization critics include strongly intensified international competition, and the widening of social, economic, and technological differences, e.g. the digital divide between the "North" (US, Europe, China, Japan) and the "South" (South America, Africa, India, and developing economies in Southeast Asia). Simplistic and exaggerated provocations often accompany this criticism regarding Westernization, Americanization, McDonaldization, which lead, if – critically judged – not to an "intellectual proletarianization" of culture (e.g. in the form of "content-free" Hollywood mainstream movies and increased fast food consumption), at least to a polarization or "homogenization" of culture, e.g. a coffeehouse culture spearheaded by companies like Starbucks and other coffeehouse giants.

Case study 8.1: Rammstein: Amerika

Research the significance of the heavy metal band Rammstein's video, *Amerika*: www.youtube.com/watch?v=Rr8ljRgcJNM&ab_channel=RammsteinOfficial.

(1) Use this video to explain the context of the above provocation regarding Westernization, Americanization, and McDonaldization.
(2) Is the video exaggerating, simply stereotyping, or even promoting certain prejudices? Or can you find some facts that corroborate this kind of criticism regarding "Americanization"? Discuss different opinions and standpoints based on facts.

(3) What other culture is increasingly becoming dominant via consumer products and services in your local context? To what extent can an ethical ambivalence be seen in this circumstance?
(4) How does this influx of foreign mainstream cultural elements change your local culture and the business environment? In your opinion, are these changes positive or negative and why?
(5) What are the perceived and measurable advantages and disadvantages of foreign cultural influx via the business world into other areas of social life?

Globalization intensifies the need for a re-valuation of local values. Some of such values may be de-intensified, others may be re-intensified, leading often to a clash between nationalist and multicultural movements. This is becoming more and more evident, especially in everyday political life in many regions of the world. We can see such trends of specific local cultures becoming mainstream globally, especially in the culinary and popular culture domains. Italian pizza, American burgers, Swiss chocolate, and Hollywood movies have all gone mainstream and are available and in great demand almost everywhere around the globe. The business implications of these "products" are therefore huge. However, at the same time, we are experiencing nationalist slogans such as "America first", e.g. in the 2016 Trump election campaign, as well as an increase in neonationalism and terrorist acts which claim to counteract the hegemony of foreign cultures.

Nevertheless, it needs also to be observed that a conglomeration of nation-states within entities such as ASEAN (Association of Southeast Asian Nations) and the EU (European Union) has a tendency to foster more peaceful relationships between countries in these regions, initiated by economic, business, and social cooperation on various levels.

8.3 Business ethical issues in transcultural contexts

There exist multifaceted specific transcultural and intercultural business ethical issues transnational companies are facing: bribery, corruption, underpaid labor, forced labor and child labor, unethical working conditions, unethical treatment of animals, and environmental degradation are just a few typical examples of business cases in which companies from different industries are or have been involved. It is not possible to cover all of these examples in the context of this book. One recent example was the UK's ban on coconut products allegedly harvested by forced monkey labor in Thailand.

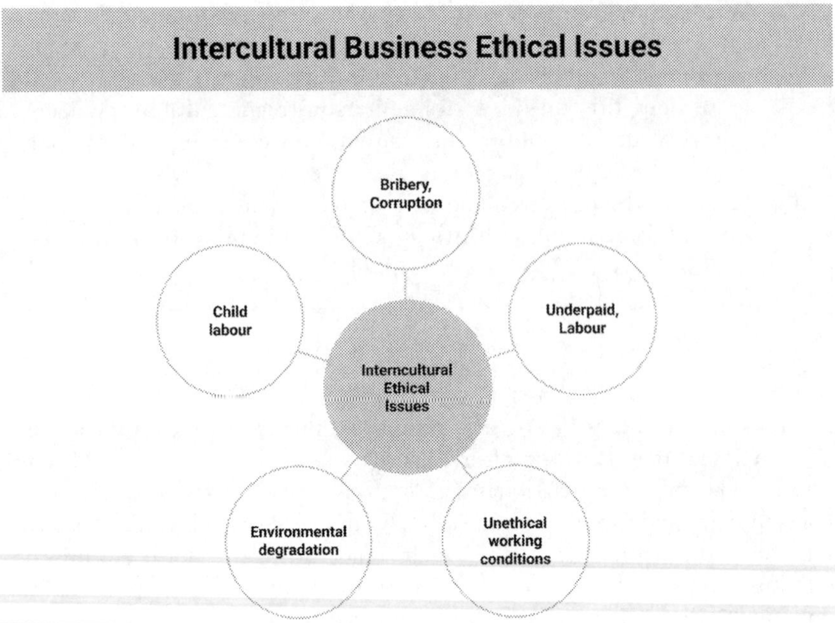

Intercultural Business Ethical Issues

- Bribery, Corruption
- Underpaid, Labour
- Unethical working conditions
- Environmental degradation
- Child labour
- Interncultural Ethical Issues

Figure 8.1 Intercultural business issues

Case study 8.2: Monkey business

Research the controversy regarding monkeys harvesting coconuts in Thailand.

(1) Discuss and analyze whether and to what extent it is justified that Western companies have banned coconut products from Thailand. Also try to include suitable normative ethical theories in your considerations, explained earlier in the book.
(2) How would you negotiate with Western coconut buyers who are targeted, e.g. by PETA, regarding animal rights and animal welfare if you were a Thai coconut farmer or a Thai coconut farmer representative?
(3) How would you negotiate with Thai farmers, who are following local customs and cultures, if you were a Western coconut buyer or a representative of a large Western retail company?
(4) Is there some kind of compromise that could lead to a win-win situation for all stakeholders involved or at least somehow meet the basic demands of all parties?

> (5) From a monkey's perspective, what would be the conditions under which you would be willing to harvest coconuts for the Thai farmer? Is such a question complete nonsense, or should these kinds of monkeys be considered as stakeholders? Is there even a need to extend the stakeholder approach to all sentient beings on our planet?

Local cultural values, such as the "Western" aggressive style of negotiation and discussion, African Ubuntu ethics, and the Thai etiquette of saving face are examples of local values that are not shared and equally well known everywhere around the globe. Not understanding these locally highly significant values may lead to huge misunderstandings between agents from culturally different contexts and, ultimately, even to the failure of business relationships.

Georges Enderle distinguished between four styles of international decision-making (Enderle, 2014), as follows. 1) The host country style is where the values of the country in which a company has set up its business away from home are adopted, e.g. in the form of accepting negative environmental impacts (such as discharging contaminated water into the sea, or allowing coconut harvesting by monkeys) that would not be acceptable in one's own country. 2) The imperial style is transferring one's domestic values to the host country, e.g. by applying the same strict environmental regulations or anti-corruption laws in the host country as in the country where the company is headquartered. In the example above, the harvesting of coconuts by monkeys or any comparable use of animals would be entirely unacceptable under all circumstances in the headquartered environment. 3) The interconnection style is a mediating management style, that seeks compromises between the host country's and headquartered cultural values, e.g. by trying to find a middle ground regarding environmental regulations. In the monkey business case, PETA and other animal rights groups could perhaps be convinced that "employing" monkeys for harvesting may lead to relatively high levels of physical and cognitive well-being among the monkey community. This is provided that the training of the monkeys is done gently and that the maintenance of them occurs under species-appropriate circumstances. In addition, this type of traditional harvesting could also serve as an example of how fair treatment of animals and preserving local culture may go hand-in-hand. 4) And finally, the global style, which is abstracting a cosmopolitan perspective, e.g. following a globally acceptable approach that is applicable in any country and culture, regardless of local circumstances. For the monkey business case, that would mean establishing a global universal guideline that may either not allow animal employment for harvesting or that comes up with guidelines for a harm-minimizing and fair treatment of animals when used in businesses, for whatever purposes.

Pragmatically, actors in business contexts need to closely follow the microsocial norms of specific host cultures, as long as they do not violate or contradict hypernorms (Velasquez, 2014). As already covered in Chapter 2 on integrated social contracts theory, an attempt must be made to reconcile norms and values that appear to be valid across geographical, cultural, and temporal boundaries. Those values or norms seem to differ and depend on historical or cultural contexts (Donaldson & Dunfee, 1995). Values and norms that are generally accepted by all societies, for example human rights, or at least some specifically human rights, are considered "hypernorms". Cross-cultural ethical variations, specific religious or cultural values and norms that are exclusively accepted in the context of specific religions, cultures, or societies, are called "microsocial" norms. Examples include the tradition of saving face in Thailand or respecting elderly people's advice as supreme in traditional African and some Asian contexts.

A highly interesting recent differentiation between microsocial norms and hypernorms delivers empirical research on the so-called Moral Machine experiment (Awad et al., 2018), a study that reveals a culturally based ethical relativity, but also cross-cultural overarching ethical values. The Moral Machine is an online thought experiment platform created by MIT Media Lab that explores potential ethical dilemmas in traffic situations faced by fully autonomous cars. Less complex thought experiments already existed in the literature such as the well-known "trolley problem" developed by Philippa Ruth Foot and Judith Jarvis Thomson in the 1970s (Thomson, 1976). The trolley problem had remained an exclusively philosophical and ethical-theoretical exercise until the advent of autonomous (driverless) vehicles.

In the so-called trolley thought experiment, a train wagon is speeding unstoppably and out of control down a railway track. Five people are tied to the tracks in front of the train and cannot move. The wagon thus will kill all five people on the tracks. Imagine you are standing next to a lever which can redirect the wagon onto a parallel track in order to rescue the five people. However, there is one person tied up on this parallel track. This is exactly why there is a dilemma or a tragic situation: one or more deaths will occur in this experiment under all circumstances. The key question now is: would you do nothing and let the five people die on the main track? Or would you pull the lever, diverting the wagon onto the parallel track, which on the one hand could save five lives, but at the same time would also kill the person on the parallel track?

What sounds like a scene from a horror movie used to be just an ethical thought experiment, carried out *only in our minds*, but not in the real world. However, once fully autonomous cars are on the road, ethically informed programmers will need to program ethical decision-making tools into the algorithms that navigate the traffic system on our roads in order to minimize fatalities in situations that soon could be real and lethal. It is, by the way, predicted that such traffic systems will minimize fatal accidents compared to non-autonomous driving in the long run (Wiseman, 2021).

The Moral Machine experiment tries to extract ethical decision-making and preferences from a large sample of people from different continents, connected to the internet, who were playing through this experiment (in total, the survey collected 40 million moral decisions in over 130 countries). The Moral Machine experiment results indicate that there are "hypernorms", e.g. in dilemma situations where the majority of users are more likely to save humans than animals, the younger, and larger groups of people rather than individuals. At least two of these moral principles, namely the protection of people instead of animals and the protection of larger numbers, could already be the first minimum requirements that autonomous vehicles, and the algorithms in such vehicles, should meet. Both are also principles that go hand-in-hand with utilitarian ethics to a certain extent, in particular with the principle of the greatest happiness for the greatest number or the maximization of average utility.

At the same time, however, there are "microsocial norms" that are specific to particular regions. For example, in the "French sub-cluster" the preference is to save women rather than men; in countries with higher levels of economic inequality, the majority opt for saving persons with a higher social status rather than those with lower social status. Again, these findings also reflect rule-based and negative utilitarian accounts. In order to come up with a cross-cultural solution, Rawls' tool of the veil of ignorance would help, combined with a concept that Hans-Georg Gadamer has termed the "merging of horizons". Otherwise, the fully autonomous car would have to change its "ethical mode" (such as changing the driving mode from "economical" to "sport mode") once it crosses the national border or the region, in a similar way as you would move to the other side of the road when crossing from a country where you drive on the left to one where you drive on the right. The future will show whether the algorithms of autonomous vehicles that are registered in different countries of the ASEAN region, Thailand, or Indonesia, for example, which have a predominantly Buddhist or Muslim population respectively, are programmed differently than those in the USA, Germany, or South Africa. Much, certainly, also depends on the legal requirements and laws in individual countries, which may differ greatly. In addition, it should also be noted, in this context, that we live in an increasingly globalized world in which different cultures increasingly overlap and mix. This potential fuzziness tends to make it difficult to incorporate cultural differences into the programming of such algorithms.

Case study 8.3: Programming ethics into algorithms

Imagine programming an algorithm that needs to be imbibed with ethical decision-making capabilities for fully autonomous cars used by car rental companies worldwide.

(1) Which ethical decision-making tools (e.g. normative ethical theories) would you include in your considerations?
(2) How would you deal with cultural, national, regional, and religious differences in your selection and application of ethical theories?

8.4 Merging of cultural horizons and "Über-setzen"

Buzzwords such as multinational corporations, global business, international business and transnational transactions make it evident that we need to have a deeper understanding of transcultural contexts and cross-cultural settings and that we should be able to navigate in these settings and contexts. One fundamental account of how to approach cross-cultural contexts can be derived from the German 20th-century philosopher Hans-Georg Gadamer, who reached an age of 102 years (1900–2002). He was a student of the controversial philosopher Martin Heidegger. Gadamer's major book, *Truth and Method* (Gadamer, 2013), contains some remarkable sections that deal with the concept of "horizon", which offers itself as an easily understandable and applicable tool for appreciating and engaging in cross-cultural contexts and challenges. "Merging of horizons" is a very useful process to engage in and manage issues in intercultural business contexts.

Ethical toolbox 8.1: Merging of horizons

A horizon is not a rigid boundary but something that moves with one and invites one to advance further. ... The horizon is the range of vision that includes everything that can be seen from a particular vantage point. Applying this to the thinking mind, we speak of narrowness of horizon, of the possible expansion of horizon, of the opening up of new horizons, and so forth. A person who has no horizon does not see far enough and hence over-values what is nearest to him. On the other hand, "to have a horizon" means not being limited to what is nearby but being able to see beyond it. A person who has a horizon knows the relative significance of everything within this horizon. In a conversation, when we have discovered the other person's standpoint and horizon, his ideas become intelligible without our necessarily having to agree with him. The horizon is ... something into which we move and that moves with us. Horizons change for a person who is moving. Transposing ourselves consists neither in the empathy of one individual for another nor in subordinating another person to our own standards; rather, it always involves rising to a higher universality that overcomes not only our own particularity but also that of the other. The concept of "horizon" suggests itself because it expresses the superior breadth of vision that the person who is trying to understand must have. To acquire a horizon means that one learns to look beyond what is close at hand. ... understanding is always the fusion of these horizons supposedly existing by themselves. We are familiar with the power of this kind of fusion ... this process of fusion is continually going on. In the process of understanding, a real fusing of horizons occurs. (Gadamer, 2013)

Intercultural business ethics 165

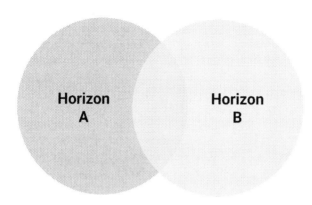

Figure 8.2 Merging of horizons

Besides moving our horizon, e.g. when travelling across cultural boundaries, and merging (or fusing) our horizon with someone else's horizon, for example by sharing protocols in different business cultures (saving face vs tackling issues straight forwardly), we can also expand our horizons through learning and studying. In cross-cultural business contexts, as in many other real-life situations, moving, expanding, and merging of horizons is absolutely essential in order to navigate and cooperate successfully in such a context.

> **Study questions 8.1: Merging of horizons**
>
> (1) What is a "horizon"?
> (2) What is meant by the "narrowness" of a horizon? Give examples. Do you personally know people who have a "wide" horizon? In what form does this wide horizon appear? How did this person's wide horizon come about?
> (3) What role do horizons play in global business interactions? Give examples of horizons in global business contexts.
> (4) Give examples of merging/fusion of horizons in business contexts.
> (5) Give examples of how the fusion of horizons can take place successfully in a global business context. Which problems could arise if businesses ignore issues related to different cultural horizons?
> (6) Which influencing factors could favor or hinder the merging/fusion of horizons in business contexts?

Martin Heidegger, teacher of Hans-Georg Gadamer, used the German term for translating, "Über-setzen", to indicate that it is important not only to understand the language of another culture, but to project oneself (to transit) into the other culture. The English word "transit" comes from Latin language, "trans ire", meaning "go beyond" – in German "Über-setzen". Before we translate, we already should have transitioned into the other culture (Heidegger, 2010). This is easily understandable, because students learn better when they study in the cultural context in which the language they want to learn is spoken. The German word *Übersetzen* means to translate or the act of translation, for example from language A to language B or vice versa; *Übersetzung* means translation. However, understood more literally, the word means to transition and aims at the transition itself. The idea is that if we really want to understand another cultural context, we cannot simply remain in our cultural context and look at the other culture from our own cultural context's perspective. Instead, we have to leave our comfort zone and temporarily break out of the patterns of our own cultural context. In short, we need to transition into the other culture, we transgress or transition. Über-setzen literally means to go beyond, to transition to the other side.

This quite philosophical, in particular hermeneutical, approach can be easily understood when imagining that one stands on one side of a river or canyon and judges what is seen and what exists on the other side of the river or canyon simply by viewing it from the other side. That is completely inappropriate according to this understanding of Über-setzen, because in order to really attempt to understand what is on the other side, we need to transition to the other side, "Über-setzen". Only then we can see and understand what the place looks like in reality. The vegetation, fauna, microclimate, and geological conditions as well as the behavior patterns and habits of people may be different on the other side. But we can only *understand* that if we "stand" there physically and experience the other side up close, so we can see, feel, and smell it, personally.

What happens here in natural contexts is not very different to cultural circumstances. As we misjudge the appearance of the other side from our own side, we may easily misjudge cultural circumstances and contexts in business situations from our own, possibly parochial, perspective. The merging or fusion of horizons inevitably requires the act of Über-setzen.

Über-setzen and merging of horizons can be seen descriptively, meaning that transcultural interactions take place in the business world as well as in other domains in a more or less synergetic, constructive, and fruitful way, or normatively, as normative interculturality or transculturality, meaning that guidelines and rules need to be established so that transcultural interactions not only take place in a peaceful manner, but also benefit the well-being of all involved stakeholders, no matter the cultural background. While this sounds overly idealistic, normative interculturality or transculturality is essential in business contexts in which our own culture needs to be transcended and seen also from the perspective of the host culture with whom we want to engage

Intercultural business ethics 167

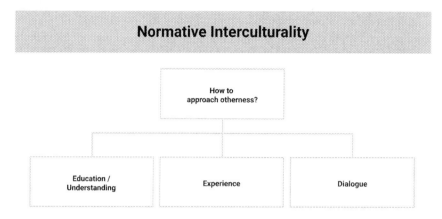

Figure 8.3 Normative interculturality

in a collaboration. A simple example would be respecting religious or cultural holidays of the host country in the context of one's own business. In order to successfully manage interculturality normatively, understanding, experience, and dialogue are needed for Über-setzen into the other culture, so that the horizons at stake can be merged.

Maybe it is necessary, expanding on the example of cultural or religious holidays above, to have some minimum business presence in a host country's office due to a high volume of business activities in the home country; therefore both sides need to negotiate a minimum availability of staff in the host country's office despite the holiday. In practical terms, this could potentially be achieved on a rotation basis, so that every year someone else needs to take the shift on that holiday.

8.5 Hofstede's cultural dimensions theory

Geert Hofstede, a Dutch social psychologist, who had worked for IBM and conducted research on international management and organizational anthropology at Maastricht University, introduced the six cultural dimensions theory that still serves to manage and deal with cross-cultural issues in business contexts today. The tool he developed can be tried out here: hofstede-insights. com/country-comparison. The six cultural dimensions represent preferences of one value over another that differentiate countries, cultures, and organizations from each other. The following six dimensions are summarized from Hofstede Insights (2021).

(1) Power distance
    Power distance expresses the intensity according to which members of a culture accept, but also expect, that there exist high power differentials

between individuals or groups. This indicates how inequalities are managed in a particular cultural context. In the business context, power distance plays an important role, especially in the context of dealing with internal corporate hierarchy levels or in the course of centralizing corporate management.

(2) Individualism vs collectivism or "I vs we"
Individualism is a preference for contexts in which individuals mainly take care of themselves, including friends and family members, whereas in collectivist contexts members of a society or culture expect care and loyalty in a wider context, but especially among members of an ingroup or relatives. Collectivistically oriented countries tend to be characterized by a high power distance. In contrast, in strongly individualistic countries there is usually a less pronounced power distance.

(3) Femininity vs masculinity or "tender vs tough"
Cultures differ according to what extent they adhere to traditional roles between men and women and to what extent traditionally masculine or feminine values control the behavior of their members. The term femininity, in this context, represents values such as quality of life, care, modesty, cooperation, and consensus orientation, while masculinity refers to values such as assertiveness, competitiveness, achievement, performance, and reward orientation. This in turn can have far-reaching consequences for (international) human resource management. For example, there is less competitive thinking in "feminine cultures" and more emphasis is placed on a friendly working atmosphere, a fair distribution of roles between men and women and the like. In masculine-dominated cultures, on the other hand, men and women more often occupy different hierarchical positions in companies. In addition, questions of recognition, career advancement, payment and other prestige and status factors are more relevant.

(4) Uncertainty avoidance
Uncertainty avoidance measures how significantly members of a culture feel uncomfortable with ambiguity and uncertainty. Cultures with a strong focus on uncertainty avoidance prefer fixed codes (rules) of behavior, laws, and safety regulations and also have rigid belief systems in order to have the future under control. Such cultures are also usually not very tolerant toward unorthodox ideas and behaviors compared to cultures with weaker uncertainty avoidance which may endorse unorthodox ideas and behaviors. While the level of avoidance of uncertainty is rather low in individualistic cultures, cultures shaped by collectivism tend to be more inclined to avoid uncertainty.

(5) Long-term vs short-term orientation
Societies, depending on their culture, either tend more to maintain and cultivate particular traditions or encourage efforts for innovative change, which is here referred to as a long-term vs short-term orientation, especially in business contexts. Every country, society, culture, subculture, and social milieu maintains particular links with its own past, while

more or less encouraging engagement with current and future challenges and opportunities. While respect for tradition or the cultivation of virtues that are related to the past and present is more likely to be attributed to a short-term orientation, long-term orientation rather stands for cultivating virtues with regard to future success, but also for perseverance and a higher savings rate and investment activity.

(6) Indulgence vs restraint

This dimension, which Hofstede added in 2010, aims to determine the extent to which personal needs can be met within a culture or society. Indulgence means that a culture allows relatively free gratification of human drives or urges in terms of life enjoyment and entertainment, while restraint represents the suppression of such drives and needs by regulation via strict social norms. Indulgence-oriented cultures usually have a more optimistic view of the future, whereas in restraint cultures a more pessimistic mood prevails and more emphasis is placed on control and seriousness.

While Geert Hofstede's approach could be criticized for stereotyping and promoting prejudices, its value lies in its potential to provide a quick initial approach to engage in and manage situations in intercultural business contexts. The German term for prejudice is "Vorurteil" ("prejudgment"), which has been fruitfully used by some German philosophers as "Vor-urteil" (Sommer, 2009), meaning pre-judgement. A primary judgment is only acceptable temporarily as a first approach and needs to be revised as soon as more detailed information becomes available. Such types of pre-judgments may be helpful in unfamiliar or indistinct contexts. In a high crime context, for example in countries with high rates of lawbreaking, such as South Africa, where home break-ins, car theft, hijacking, and armed robbery are relatively common, it is usually advisable not to approach one's own parked car if a group of people is standing close by. While it is a prejudice that people seemingly aimlessly loitering around in South African city centers "are all criminals", it is a wise pre-judgment to assume that the group of people standing around one's own car could potentially be criminals. Therefore, it may be wise, for the time being, to pretend that this is not one's car by walking past and not presenting car keys or any sign that could reveal that one is the owner of the car.

Case study 8.4: Hofstede's cultural dimensions theory

Check out the hofstede-insights.com/country-comparison.

(1) Choose four of your favorite countries or countries to which you have travelled or to which you would like to travel and test how these countries compare according to these six dimensions.

(2) Do the results represent your experiences or expectations? Or do they reflect stereotypes and prejudices?
(3) What is the relevance of this cultural experiment for concrete business situations? Discuss.
(4) Which of Hofstede's cultural dimensions do you think can be particularly critical for the success of business transactions and why?

Key takeaways

(1) Companies need to implement organizational changes for more inclusive and cross-cultural business environments.
(2) Differences in culture can be compared, understood, appreciated, and utilized with the help of Hofstede's cultural dimensions approach.
(3) Cultural values can be represented and understood with the help of "horizons".
(4) Cultural horizons can be merged to increase compatibility between business cultures.

References

Awad, E., Dsouza, S., Kim, R., Schulz, J., Henrich, J., Shariff, A., Bonnefon, J.-F., & Rahwan, I. (2018). The Moral Machine experiment. *Nature, 563*(7729), 59–64. https://doi.org/10.1038/s41586-018-0637-6

Donaldson, T., & Dunfee, T.W. (1995). Integrative social contracts theory: A communitarian conception of economic ethics. *Economics & Philosophy, 11*(1), 85–112. https://doi.org/10.1017/S0266267100003230

Enderle, G. (2014). Exploring and conceptualizing international business ethics. *Journal of Business Ethics, 127.* https://doi.org/10.1007/s10551-014-2182-z

Gadamer, H.-G. (2013). *Truth and Method* (Reprint ed.). Bloomsbury Academic.

Heidegger, M. (2010). *Der Spruch des Anaximander.* Klostermann Vittorio GmbH.

Hofstede Insights (2021). *National Culture.* https://hi.hofstede-insights.com/national-culture

Sommer, U. (2009). Vor-Urteil. In *Strafverteidigung im Rechtsstaat* (pp. 846–862). Nomos Verlagsgesellschaft mbH & Co. https://doi.org/10.5771/9783845216942-846

Thomson, J.J. (1976). Killing, letting die, and the trolley problem. *The Monist, 59*(2), 204–217. https://doi.org/10.5840/monist197659224

Velasquez, M. (2014). *Business Ethics Concepts and Cases* (7th ed.). Pearson Education Limited.

Wiseman, Y. (2021). *Encyclopedia of Information Science and Technology* (5th ed.). IGI Global. http://services.igi-global.com/resolvedoi/resolve.aspx?doi=10.4018/978-1-7998-3479-3

9 Systemic issues

Abstract

This chapter locates business ethics in geopolitical and economic contexts. It briefly explains business ethical implications embedded in economic philosophies in the Western context. Beyond that, alternative economic systems and their philosophies will be pointed out. Such alternative concepts are "sufficiency economy philosophy", which is based on Thai Buddhist economics, Sikkim state's organic approach, ecological economics, which focuses on the ontological dependency of the economy on the eco-environment, circular economy which emphasizes new resource input reduction, waste minimization, and output recycling, and social-ecological market economy, a system that moderates between competitive free markets, social support for the less privileged, and environmentalism. Finally, the chapter introduces the World Happiness Report that has increasingly become prominent also for measuring some of the above-mentioned economic systems' success. The chapter includes case studies, e.g. on Facebook's quasi-monopoly status and on Sikkim organic state.

Chapter keywords

(1) Sufficiency economy philosophy
(2) Ecological economics
(3) Circular economy
(4) Socio-ecological market economy
(5) World Happiness Report

Study objectives

After studying this chapter, readers will be able to:

(1) Understand ethical and sustainability implications of economic systems.
(2) Appreciate ethical and sustainability potentials of alternative economic systems.
(3) Recognize the World Happiness Report as one indicator of economic systems' success.

DOI: 10.4324/9781003127659-9

Case studies

9.1 Facebook quasi-monopoly
9.2 Sikkim organic state
9.3 Circular economy
9.4 World Happiness Report

9.1 Introduction

The academic discipline of business ethics and ethical or unethical business conduct can be found on the micro, meso, or macro level. Interestingly, the German language has two different notions as a translation for business ethics, namely "Unternehmensethik" and "Wirtschaftsethik". "Unternehmensethik" could be translated as business ethics, corporate ethics, or even entrepreneurial ethics, which covers the micro-level of business ethics. The focus of business ethics from this standard perspective's vantage point is on the company's ethical transactions in market competition. "Wirtschaftsethik", on the other hand, refers rather to the macro level and can be translated with business ethics in a wider sense, the ethics of economic systems, or even as the ethical dimension of the philosophy of economics. This bird's eye perspective on business ethics does not focus on individual transactions of the company, or, in other words, on the moves within "the game". Still, it aims to ethically analyze, understand, and optimize the rules of the game (public policy, regulations, and laws) that apply in market competition, be it with or without businesses' involvement. The meso-level deals with both sides as the interconnecting level between corporate dimensions or individual issues of business ethics on the one hand, and the systemic issues of the philosophy of economics dimension on the other.

This last chapter situates business ethics challenges in the context of geopolitics and economic systems, also considering non-Western theories and practices. It briefly elucidates the economic, sociological, and philosophical foundations of economic systems and economic models. It complements the discourse by non-Western and alternative concepts such as Buddhist economics, Thailand's approach to Sufficiency Economy Philosophy (SEP), circular economy, Germany's social-ecological market economy, and the perspective of the Indian state Sikkim, the first organic state in the world. This chapter closes the circle of topics connecting the overarching concept of well-being back to the first three chapters on philosophical foundations, which have also dealt with concepts of well-being.

When studying business ethics cases or issues, we can detect one of three variants of cases or a combination thereof: individual, corporate, and systemic issues (Velasquez, 2014). Typical cases reported by the press are usually corporate cases, such as the Volkswagen Dieselgate affair, the Wirecard scandal, and the Boeing 737 MAX crashes, just to name a few prominent recent negative cases. Corporate issues may at the same time be cases of particular individual stakeholders, such as a case of fraud (e.g. corruption) or an incident of sexual harassment in which two employees are involved. However, if such fraud or harassment cases are not singular incidences, but rather issues where a company is not addressing them sufficiently, the situation may become a much broader corporate case. In extreme cases, such issues can endanger the company's very existence. Examples of corporate cases are sexual harassment cases of Uber drivers, e.g. in India and the US (Newcomer & Chapman, 2019). If such cases occur even throughout an entire industry, they can be called systemic cases. While the Harvey Weinstein scandal is a corporate case that became known through individual cases, this scandal is just one manifestation, reflection, or instance of a systemic issue, involving the sexual harassment of actors, and not only female actors, in the film industry worldwide. Other systemic issues include the dishonesty and greed in some banking industry sectors, exemplified by cases such as the Greensill Bank collapse, the Wirecard scandal, the Panama Papers, and the 2008 financial crisis, caused in part by unregulated investment banking activity.

These systemic issues and scandals are influenced by certain specific national economic systems or are (more or less) only made possible by them. China was less hit, or at least in a different way, by the global financial crisis in 2008 due to its (systemic) distance from Western economies. Economic systems determine and regulate the production and distribution of services and products as well as the financial and information flow. They regulate who produces, how much, what will be produced, who will get what and how much in an economy (Velasquez, 2014).

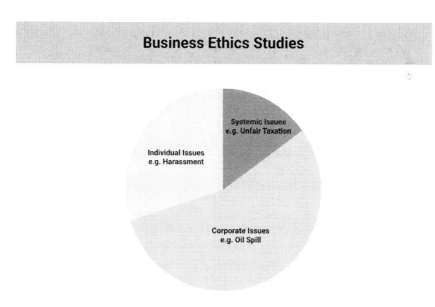

Figure 9.1 Issues in business ethics studies

9.2 Economic systems, economies, and well-being

Economic systems, while determining the production and distribution of products, services, information, and financial transactions, from an ethical and philosophical standpoint, should shape economies that serve the overall well-being of the largest possible amount of people within the respective economy's national boundary. Economies are also construed beyond national vantage points, such as the ASEAN economy, the economy of the European Union, or even the world economy. Depending on how and to what extent these economies serve their citizens who, in turn, may have a different risk aversion depending on their cultural affiliation, these different economic forms also involve various ethical implications.

Businesses situated, headquartered, or operating in different economies have to adjust their operations depending on the economic systems and legal frameworks. That means that a large part of the corporate culture is also shaped by the economic system, unless a corporation is so large that it may shape not only the economy, but the entire economic system, which can be done indirectly through political lobbying. For example, it is well known that in terms of revenue or market capitalization ("market cap") the largest companies are comparable to smaller nation-states, which indicates the overreaching power of such companies. Market cap is determined by the number of shares multiplied by the market value of the shares.

In the Western context, Plato (427–347 BCE) in the *Republic* and the *Laws*, and Aristotle (382–322 BCE) in the *Politics*, addressed questions regarding ideal economic systems and their contribution to the overall well-being of citizens. The English philosopher, political theorist and physician John Locke (1632–1704), like Immanuel Kant, an Enlightenment thinker, is often referred to as the "father of liberalism". Locke claimed that we have rights that we are born with. Such so-called natural rights are the right to our own life, our own liberty, and our own property, all of which are essential prerequisites for well-being. According to Locke, we acquire property by involving our labor with some natural resource (Locke, 2020). Property acquisition and a (rudimentary) economic system predate forms of government. Locke does not propose any limitation upon amassing non-perishable property and he does not sufficiently address inequality implied in the liberal approach he suggests. However, many scholars trace the phrase "Life, Liberty and the pursuit of Happiness" in the American Declaration of Independence back to Locke. It is seen in his natural rights defense of "life, health, liberty, or possessions" (Locke, 2020) in his *Second Treatise of Government* (1690), which stands in the tradition of social contract theory. Locke's ideas on property have again become significant in the current context of intellectual property, such as the property of digital assets, shared data, and genetically modified organisms, as all of these acts involve the "mixing of labour" with "natural resources" (Locke, 2015).

In *The Wealth of Nations* (1776), the Scottish economist and philosopher Adam Smith (1723–1790), often referred to as the father of modern economics, coined the notion of the "invisible hand" (Smith, 2019). The invisible hand, more frequently cited than well understood, basically means that market competition automatically (invisibly) promotes public welfare, not through benevolence, but via the self-interest of individuals, which results in mutual benefits via market competition. The shortcoming of Smith's approach is that often market forces alone do not prevent phenomena such as monopolization, external side effects, and the so-called "race to the bottom". Hyper-competition drives production to locations with the lowest wages, the fewest rights for workers, and the least environmental protections.

As a reply to Smith's theory, and being aware of these aforementioned issues, the British economist John Maynard Keynes (1883–1946) in his book *The General Theory of Employment, Interest and Money* (1936) opted for the possibility of state intervention in any economic system in order to remedy the shortcomings of economic liberalism. According to Keynes, free markets alone do not coordinate societies' resources most efficiently and therefore government intervention will help in cases of unemployment, inequality, and other external effects (Keynes, 2019). Keynes' challenges concerning the liberal neoclassic economic systems led to a revolution in economic scholarship and thinking. In terms of public policies, Keynesianism became popular during the Great Depression, which was a severe worldwide economic downturn in the 1930s, but was discredited in the last quarter of the 20th century, which subsequently provoked a widespread deregulation of the economic sector. However, Keynesianism significantly resurged again after the global financial crisis in 2007 and 2008. The incentives governments provide their citizens for using and purchasing sustainable energy and technology – such as renewable energy, solar panels, and electric vehicles, just to name a few of the abundant examples – reflect Keynesian approaches. Other current examples include stimulations by governments intended to foster innovative start-ups or rescue businesses, e.g. during the Covid-19 pandemic.

A tradition of thinking that would not endorse such stimulating interventions is social Darwinism, which is, in a nutshell, Charles Darwin's (1809–1882) natural selection theory found in his book *On the Origin of Species* (1859) applied to societal and economic contexts. Like a deadly virus that weeds out persons with weaker immune systems, and thus indirectly promoting the fittest with stronger immune systems, the economic repercussions of a virus pandemic similarly diminish the survival chances of less profitable businesses. However, as we can see from what has been happening around the world during the Covid-19 pandemic, governments embraced neither neoliberalism nor social Darwinism, but administered state interventionalist Keynesianism with all of its positive and negative consequences for businesses, including small one-off payments to independent artists and cultural entrepreneurs in countries like Germany, plus billion-dollar rescue schemes for national airlines around the world.

Herbert Spencer (1820–1903), in a similar fashion to liberal and neoliberal economists, believed that free competition ensures that only the most capable individuals and businesses survive and rise to the top. "Inconvenience, suffering, and death are the penalties attached by Nature to ignorance as well as to incompetence" (Spencer, 1860). While Spencer's observations are descriptively correct in many circumstances, normatively such approaches seem not to foster an environment which reflects the reality in which the majority of people would like to live nowadays.

Other problems apart from combating pandemics are failures of deregulated competitive free markets, such as the 2008 global financial crisis, and lateral effects, and the tendencies of such markets to provide an economic environment that may allow monopolies or oligopolies to fixedly establish themselves. But even in our current economies, most of which are regulated in one way or another, the establishment of quasi-monopolies is possible. Examples are Facebook, as the major social networking site, Alphabet's Google as the major search engine, and Microsoft's Word as the major word processing program. Alphabet's Android mobile operating system and Apple's IOS operating system can be cited as examples of oligopolies or duopolies.

Case study 9.1: Facebook quasi-monopoly

Guy Verhofstadt, a former Belgian Prime Minister who also held several leading positions in the European Parliament, accused Mark Zuckerberg of wielding a monopoly at the European Parliament hearing on the Facebook–Cambridge Analytica scandal.

Research concerning accusations regarding Facebook's monopoly status in relation to other Facebook products, such as Instagram and WhatsApp.

(1) Are companies like Facebook, Apple, Amazon, Google, and Microsoft too large for regulation? Discuss.
(2) Can you name alternatives to Facebook, Google, and Microsoft Office that you would use on a day-to-day basis, including in a professional context?
(3) Many of these companies have been "blitz-scaling", meaning growing large very fast and buying up competitors. What exactly does "blitz-scaling" mean and what does this strategy look like in the real business world?
(4) What are the advantages and disadvantages of monopolies?

The world's most frequently used software is produced in the US, a large global market share of computer hardware produced is in Asia, and other specific products are produced in other parts of the world, therefore we can speak of a globally distributed division of labor. David Ricardo (1772–1823), held that free trade and the division of labor, distributed amongst several countries, maximizes utility. Any country may have an absolute advantage in one or the other service or product, and can produce a commodity cheaper than another country. According to Ricardo, countries should specialize in goods where they have a comparative advantage, meaning opportunity costs of producing a commodity are lower for that country than for another. Opportunity costs are the costs of what has been given up, representing the best alternative forgone. While Ricardo's arguments can be proven mathematically, the major argument lies in Ricardo's support for international trade and globalization for the benefit and well-being of any country involved. There are opponents of globalization who criticize its tendency to destroy indigenous small businesses and smaller economies, and other ecologically minded critics who oppose globalization for its environmental impacts due to the high costs and wasted energy for transportation of goods around the globe.

9.3 Alternative systemic approaches

9.3.1 Sufficiency economy philosophy

In Thailand, SEP has been promoted by the government and by a number of economists and philosophers, especially after the 2008 global financial crisis, which also hit the ASEAN region. Moderation is one of the major features of SEP, which can also be applied in regard to emphasizing the use of local products and services that do not require long-distance transportation around the globe. SEP is an ethical public policy directive derived from Thailand's King Rama IX, Bhumibol Adulyadej's speeches in which he addressed students at Kasetsart and Khon Kaen University in 1974. SEP intends to meet the preferences of many stakeholders, and in that regard SEP can be interpreted as a preference utilitarian account, while focusing not on short-term profitability but rather on long-term results (Mongsawad & Thongpakde, 2016), which, in turn, can be seen as promoting an economically sustainable future.

From a traditional Buddhist economics perspective mainstream economics is motivated by greed, while Buddhist economics by preference intends to maximize utility for all actors involved within an economic system. With the help of this approach, suffering through poverty will be minimized. Interpreted from this harm-minimizing perspective, Buddhist economics is negative utilitarian in its approach. "Moderation serves as a tool to filter out greed and consumerist behavior" (Mongsawad & Thongpakde, 2016). A main feature of SEP is reflected in the key notion of sufficiency. "Sufficiency means moderation, reasonableness, and the need of resilience for protection from the impacts of internal and external changes" (Mongsawad & Thongpakde, 2016). Moderation implies consumption patterns and lifestyles which follow a middle path, and thus avoid extremes. You will note that this is exactly the key feature in the Aristotelian ethical account of virtues covered in Chapter 3 (Aristotle, 2018). Aristotle promotes ethical virtue as being well thought out through insisting on moderation between deficiency and excess.

While SEP is currently of limited interest among younger Thai citizens, due to the current political situation in Thailand, it fits well with trends such as "think global – act local". SEP accords well with the current Fridays for Future activists, advocating for adjusting consumption styles compatible with scientific findings on ecological emergencies and the climate crisis.

9.3.2 Ecological economics

Ecological economists, environmental ethicists, and many tribal philosophies, plus most religions, assume that humans ultimately need to comprehend not only our dependence on natural resources, but also our connectedness with nature, and our non-optional embeddedness in natural ecosystems. From this fact of reality, ecological economists derive the ontological, dependency, or integrated model of ecology, society, and economy, in which businesses and society depend for survival on the natural ecosystem. A number of businesses have integrated the ontological sustainability understanding into their business philosophy; Patagonia, Freitag, and Ecosia are examples of such businesses, as previously explained in Chapter 4. Ecological economists (Daly & Farley, 2004) urge policymakers to review and alter their economic systems along a set of recommendations, many of which find reflections in the businesses mentioned above, but in particular – for example – in the organic state of Sikkim (see below).

Non-renewable resources must be used extremely carefully, unless technology can guarantee that future communities will get comparable benefits from the reduced non-renewables we have left behind. Alternatively, we have to find substitute materials, e.g. renewable alternatives, to replace these non-renewables. Renewable resources need to be utilized in such a way that they can regenerate. One might think here, for example, of sustainable forestry, and moderated fishing that avoids overfishing beyond the renewal rate. Biodiversity should not decrease any further, especially if it comes to threatening endangered species. In addition, according to many ecological economists, further human population growth should also be limited. Emissions due to transport traffic, for example, or from factory waste, need to be limited in such a way that the regeneration of ecosystems can be safeguarded. Prices have to reflect the "ecological truth" and, thus, external effects need to be internalized by monetization of externalities. This, in turn, will comparatively increase the price and will make environmentally polluting products more expensive. Environmentally friendly products will then turn out to be comparably less expensive. In either case, innovations should be compatible with eco-systemic sustainability.

In the Western context, this ecosystemic compatibility of human life, technology, and innovations, the "aspiration to live in balance with nature" can already be found in Zeno of Citium's stoic philosophy, since human nature is a subset of cosmic nature (Laertius, 1925). A similar more recent concept is "homoeotechnology", "*imitatio naturae*" (Sloterdijk & Heinrichs, 2001). The German philosopher, Peter Sloterdijk, contrasts homoeotechnology (*homeo*, Ancient Greek ὅμοιος, "similar" or "alike") (van der Hout, 2014) with "allotechnology" or "heterotechnology" (*allo*, from Ancient Greek ἄλλος, "other"). While traditional technology is "based on principles that are different from, and often disturb or interfere with, nature's own dynamics and processes", homoeotechnology is (more) compatible with eco-systemic sustainability (van der Hout, 2014). An example of allotechnology would be "hard engineering" by building a concrete sea wall to prevent soil erosion in a coastal area, whereas a homoeotechnological approach in the same context would be "soft engineering" by (re)planting mangrove trees to prevent soil erosion.

9.3.3 Sikkim organic state

Sikkim, India's smallest state by area, has succeeded in producing all agricultural products entirely organically since 2016, and, with that, it became the world's first 100% organic state, a process that Sikkim state started in 2003 by adopting sustainable development practices (Gill, 2018).

> **Case study 9.2: Sikkim organic state**
>
> Research Sikkim in India and its status as a "100% organic state".
>
> (1) Why was it decided to make a transition to organic agriculture?
> (2) What were the obstacles in this transition?
> (3) How is this organic approach integrated into the state's overall economy?
> (4) How much of the experience gained in this organic transition is transferable to larger states, entire countries, economies, and particular businesses? Which aspects of the situation testify against such transferability?

9.3.4 Circular economy

Linear economies follow a standard and hitherto mainstream "linear" process of harvesting or extracting resources, production, sales, purchase, utilization, and finally disposal. The idea and practice of circular economic systems not only minimizes new resource inputs, but also minimizes waste and emissions by emphasizing recycling, reuse, sharing, refurbishing, and re-manufacturing. For this reason, used electric car batteries, for example, are being discussed as a topical example of a circular economy, since these batteries can be reused as household batteries after slight modifications in the control unit and outer casing. The idea of circular economies (or closed economies) was first conceptualized in Kenneth Boulding's essay "The economics of the coming spaceship earth" (Boulding, 1966), by contrasting it with linear economies (or open economies). The idea goes back to the spaceship earth thought experiment by Boulding mentioned in Chapter 4. The concept of a circular economy, or a closed economy, is also reflected in Earnest Callenbach's ecotopian "steady state economy" (Meinhold, 2014).

> **Case study 9.3: Circular economy**
>
> Research the circular economy.
>
> (1) Which companies follow, or claim to follow, this kind of approach? What can be learned from their approaches that could be transferred to other business models?
> (2) In which business domains (besides the aforementioned electromobility) do future applications of the idea of a circular economy lie?
> (3) If you were an entrepreneur, would you consider the idea of circular economy for your business formation? How would you imagine such a circular economic startup?

9.3.5 Socio-ecological market economy

The social-ecological market economy is an economic system that is prevalent in Europe, especially Germany and other northern European countries. This system combines limited social system support and reduced state interference to promote social equilibration in concert with the above-mentioned ecological considerations, plus utilizing the dynamics, agility, and strengths of a free market economy. The term "social market economy" was coined in 1946 by Alfred Müller-Armack (1901–1978), a German politician and professor of economics at the Universities of Münster and Cologne. In a social-ecological market economy, ecological sustainability considerations, the ideal of a socially fair state and the market system are all combined with the aim of merging economic freedom with environmental protection and social justice. A social market economy is based on a capitalist system (i.e. there still exist considerable income differences), but at the same time there is also a certain redistribution from high-performing to lower-performing society members in order to maintain a social security system for less privileged individuals or groups in society.

A social-ecological market economy, in a way, intends to form a fusion of three economic systems: ecological, social, and capitalist economy. This is an interesting reflection on the macro-level of what is known on the micro-level as the "triple bottom line", as we have already covered in Chapter 4. Toms' "caring capitalism" and Brunello Cucinelli's "humanistic capitalism" reflect social market economy as concrete business examples on the corporate micro-level.

In a purely socialist economy, ideally, there should be an equal distribution of income amongst all society members. But this has problematic effects on work and performance incentives, since high-performing members of society would be confronted with the fact that a large portion of their income is taxed away and redistributed to less privileged members of society who have contributed comparatively little. As a result, such high performers would be encouraged to reduce their work efforts, or seek opportunities elsewhere. Due to that possibility, the Gross National Product (GDP) of this society would be much lower than in a comparable capitalist society. Under socialist conditions, everyone has an income, but only a small one that is just sufficient to live on. Everyone receives equally little in an entirely socialist system, with the lowest total benefit and the lowest average benefit.

In reality, purely socialist societies are also characterized by low prosperity; however, since everyone gets the same amount, the situation of disadvantaged persons or groups would be less problematic here than under capitalism, e.g. no one lived below the poverty line in the former German Democratic Republic.

In an entirely capitalist system, wages and working conditions are determined by private sector decisions only, rather than by the government. As a consequence, there are very large income disparities. Among the members of such a society, there are economic "losers" who have (almost) no income at all (e.g. a physically disabled person who is unable to work), but there are also economic "winners" with an extremely high income.

In a social-ecological market economy, in contrast, differences in income are allowed and appreciated, since a social market economy is enshrined within a capitalist system. But, at the same time, there are also certain public policies regarding redistribution in favor of the less privileged members of the society, so that the *average* benefit is somewhat lower than in the exclusively capitalist system. This solution would be preferred by Rawls (see Chapter 3). On the one hand, Rawls would support income differences, because the aim of the veil of ignorance is not to weaken the willingness to work of productive members of society, but at the same time Rawls would also agree to redistribution in favor of the less privileged, because in the original position, behind the veil of ignorance, nobody would know in which societal position they would end up (Wagner, 2019).

The social-ecological market economy occupies a "moderating" middle ground between capitalism and socialism, and adds an environmental sustainability component. On the one hand, the social-ecological market economy is a market-based capitalist system because – unlike in socialism – income differences between people are allowed and appreciated. This is also important, otherwise the performance incentives for the high-performing members of society would decrease sharply and a lower standard of living would result for everyone. On the other hand, and in contrast to the purely capitalist system, there exists also a social security system that offers social security for less privileged members of a society (e.g. unemployment benefits for those who lose their jobs; a health insurance system, and so on). This means that redistribution from the high-performing members of society to the under-performing members of society exists as well as eco-taxes and eco-incentives. Therefore, taxes in countries with such an economic system are comparatively higher. The social-ecological market economy also reflects cultural factors (i.e. risk aversion, which is relatively high in Germany) and a cultural shift toward a more environmentally beneficial lifestyle. Seen from another vantage point, German society can also be regarded as an individualistic one, which is why a capitalist system is generally preferred. However, since Germany is less individualistic than the US, more value is placed on the societal component, this being also reflected in individual employment relationships. For example, great importance is attached to protection against unfair dismissal, which is one way in which unions have a lot of power.

9.3.6 World Happiness Report

The World Happiness Report relates the topic of economic systems with the ethical theories that focus on happiness, eudaimonia, and well-being. The 2021 report features countries with social-ecological market economies in all top ten spots, meaning social market economies that have stringent environmental policies in place (Helliwell et al., 2021).

Case study 9.4: World Happiness Report

Research the current World Happiness Report.

(1) At what position in this report does the country in which you were born, or educated, stand right now? How can this be explained empirically?
(2) How do these countries compare to other countries you have travelled in, or in which you would like to study, work, or reside?
(3) Do the empirical results of the World Happiness Report reflect your own personal experiences?
(4) How should businesses, with a strong concern for stakeholders, react to these reports?

Key takeaways

(1) Globalization of the economy has increased the need to understand local values.
(2) Economic systems that emerged in the Western context have evolved in various geolocations.
(3) In terms of well-being, successful economic systems merge environmentalism, social support, and relatively competitive free markets.
(4) The World Happiness Report also indicates the success of these economic systems.

References

Aristotle. (2018). *Nicomachean Ethics*. The Internet Classics Archive. http://classics.mit.edu/Aristotle/nicomachaen.1.i.html

Boulding, K. (1966). *The Economics of the Coming Spaceship Earth*. http://dieoff.org/page160.htm

Gill, P. (2018). *The World Has Its First Fully Organic State: And It's in India*. Business Insider. www.businessinsider.in/the-world-has-its-first-fully-organic-state-and-its-in-india/articleshow/66260408.cms

Daly, H., & Farley, J. (2004) *Ecological Economics: Principles And Applications*. Island Press.

Diogenes Laertius (1925) *Lives of Eminent Philosophers*, Vol. 2, Books 6–10. Harvard University Press.

Newcomer, E., & Chapman, L. (2019). *Uber reports 3,000 sexual assault claims last year in its safety review*. Economic Times. https://economictimes.indiatimes.com/small-biz/startups/newsbuzz/uber-reports-3000-sexual-assault-claims-last-year-in-its-safety-review/articleshow/72393813.cms

Helliwell, J.F., Layard, R., Sachs, J., & De Neve, J.-E. (2021). *World Happiness Report 2021*. Sustainable Development Solutions Network. https://worldhappiness.report/ed/2021/

van der Hout, S. (2014). The homeotechnological turn: Sloterdijk's response to the ecological crisis. *Environmental Values*, *23*(4), 423–442. https://doi.org/10.3197/096327114X13947900182030

Keynes, J.M. (2019). *The General Theory of Employment, Interest, and Money*. General Press.

Locke, J. (2015). *The Second Treatise of Civil Government*. Broadview Press.

Locke, J. (2020). *Second Treatise of Government*. Strelbytskyy Multimedia Publishing.

Meinhold, R. (2014). Reflections on Sustainable and Holistic Lifestyles in "Ecotopia" as Perspectives for Well-Being in the ASEAN Context. In *Ecological, Social & Economic Sustainability—Perspectives for Thailand and ASEAN*. Assumption University. Konrad-Adenauer-Foundation. Bangkok.

Mongsawad, P., & Thongpakde, N. (2016). Sufficiency economy philosophy: A holistic approach to economic development and mainstream economic thought. *Asian Social Science*, *12*(7), 136. https://doi.org/10.5539/ass.v12n7p136

Sloterdijk, P., & Heinrichs, H.-J. (2001). *Die Sonne und der Tod: Dialogische Untersuchungen*. Suhrkamp

Smith, A. (2019). *The Wealth of Nations*. BookRix.

Spencer, H. (1860). The social organism. *Westminster Review*, 73, 51–68. Velasquez, M. (2014). *Business Ethics Concepts and Cases* (7th ed.). Pearson Education Limited.

Wagner, C. (2019). *Managementethik und Arbeitsplätze: Eine metaphysische und moralökonomische Analyse*. Springer-Verlag.

10 Conclusion

Abstract

This chapter sums up the main issues and findings of this book. There is a need for a wider business ethics perspective because current challenges such as disruptive technologies, eco-environmental disasters, and also transcultural business interactions require professionally informed ethical decision-making competencies and well-balanced decisions. Entirely "ethics free zones", or "business ethics free zones" do not exist in the real world, not at the present time and most likely not in the future. Future communities, ecosystems, and non-human species need to be taken into account when ethical decision-making wants to make a contribution to well-being now, as well as towards a sustainable future. Therefore multidimensional value perspectives as well as multidimensional sustainability concepts have to be taken more seriously into account. In the corporate context, sustainability should at least include the ethical, economic, and ecological dimensions, but may also include less frequently employed dimensions such as digital, cultural, and spiritual sustainability.

Chapter keywords

(1) No "business ethics free zones"
(2) Disruptive technologies
(3) Transcultural interactions
(4) Future communities
(5) Ecosystems
(6) Non-human species
(7) Multidimensional value perspective
(8) Multidimensional sustainability concepts
(9) Wider business ethics perspective

Study objectives

After studying this chapter readers will have a wider horizon and a deeper perspective regarding the relevance of business ethical cases, issues, theories, and concepts.

DOI: 10.4324/9781003127659-10

10.1 Ethical business is not a contradiction but an opportunity

By the end of this book it should have become evident that there is no such thing as "an ethics-free zone", neither in the business world nor in any other domain of our life. As one of the most important philosophical subdomains, ethics is increasingly important nowadays due to multifaceted challenges in the business world. Disruptive technologies such as artificial intelligence and algorithms need to be imbued with ethical decision-making competences. The increasing volume of transcultural interactions and international business activities require professional cross-cultural ethical decision-making skills and competencies. Moreover, the looming climate disaster and eco-environmental crises need to be managed in a sustainable way. Considerations for future communities, non-human species, and natural ecosystems can no longer be excluded from real-world business decisions.

Acting according to the law is often not sufficient and also does not automatically imply ethical conduct. Major scandals in the business world, not only recent ones, have been ethical scandals, such as the Facebook–Cambridge Analytica scandal, the Boeing 737 MAX crashes, the Harvey Weinstein sexual harassment scandal, the global financial crisis in 2008, the Volkswagen "Dieselgate" affair, the Wirecard accounting scandal, and the collapse of Greensill Capital, just to name a few current ones.

Therefore, ethically guided and sustainability-oriented business examples from the real business world, referred to in this book as "positive cases", have been particularly emphasized and elucidated throughout. Examples highlighted and focused on are the tree planting search engine Ecosia, environmentally responsible outdoor company Patagonia, Brunello Cucinelli, the "philosopher-designer" who demonstrates that capitalism can be "humanistic", and the Freitag brothers, who conduct business in a cyclic and sustainable way. With such examples it can be observed that ethical and sustainability-oriented business is gradually moving out from a niche phenomenon into a more widely accepted field in the real business world, even up to that point where organic and Fair Trade become mainstream, as it is the case for most Starbucks coffee products.

The "unavoidability" of ethics means that basically any decision-making process implies ethics – not only in the business context. Ignoring ethical implications and neglecting potential and *de facto* stakeholders has resulted in some of the scandals stated above. Therefore, decision-makers at all levels in organizations need to be familiar with basic ethical theories. Corporate social responsibility and applications of business ethics have been embedded in management and underline the causality running between ethically responsible business and economic success. Businesses need to focus on a multidimensional perspective of value in order to be able to create values for diverse stakeholders. In the light of sustainability frameworks, business stakeholder relationships need to include stakeholders beyond the mainstream

10.2 Ethical theories, sustainability, and the expansion of the stakeholder concept

As we have pointed out, major normative ethical theories relevant in the business context include virtue ethics, deontological ethics, utilitarianism, care ethics, and environmental ethics. Virtue ethics aims to develop human character and well-being. The Western approach to virtue ethics is largely informed by Aristotle's theory of eudaimonia. Immanuel Kant's duty ethics renders our actions ethically correct if they can be formulated according to the so-called categorical imperative, a universal moral law. However, Kant also emphasizes that laws, regulations, and rules need to be reassessed constantly, critically, and constructively: "dare to know", dare to research, and dare to reconsider must be the motto of an open-minded ethical decision-maker, always expanding their horizon and sharing perspectives respectfully, sensitive of the cultural context. Utilitarianism, a form of consequentialism, was popularized by Jeremy Bentham and further developed by John Stuart Mill. This theory measures morality by the amount of utility, pleasure, or happiness for the greatest number of people, and if possible, for all sentient beings. Care ethics takes interpersonal relationships, compassion, and care as foundational, whereas John Rawls's theory of justice aims at fairness by removing biases through the "veil of ignorance" in the "original position". Amartya Sen emphasizes that power positively implies responsibility and environmental ethics expands our responsibility towards the natural environment and future communities, taking sustainability most seriously into account.

Because of today's intercultural situation, there is a serious need not to be exclusively Western-oriented, but to supply the decision-makers with a wider international outlook. Several chapters therefore have also referred to non-Western concepts such as the African "Ubuntu" ethics, the Thai "sufficiency economy philosophy", the Asian ideal of "saving face", and the Japanese concept of "Ikigai".

Like ecological economics and environmental ethics, serious corporate environmental responsibility campaigns and environmentally oriented business ethics strategies have understood the ontological natural embeddedness of businesses plus the pragmatic dependence of organizations on natural ecosystems. This is reflected in strategies like internalization of external effects, cyclical production and consumption methods, and the embedding of preactionary technologies with forward pushing approaches into precautionary decision-making strategies.

Environmental business ethics and sustainability expand the classical understanding of stakeholders in order to include future communities, ecosystems, and non-human species which are increasingly becoming key factors in business considerations. The consideration of these stakeholders in addition to the mainstream stakeholder discourse arises from increasing demands of environmentally conscious investors, consumers, and the general public, but it also considers and highlights the often-neglected impact that these stakeholders have on businesses. Therefore, the concepts of sustainability and the effects of environmental impacts on future generations need to be elucidated and well understood.

Understanding the complex relationships between businesses and stakeholders is highly pertinent in ethical decision-making. Neglecting stakeholders, potential stakeholders, and values pertinent to them, has often resulted in scandals that impact on the reputation of a company for a long period of time. Volkswagen's "Dieselgate" affair made it evident that the company had neglected the values and potential power of customers, specific investors, particular environmental and governmental organizations, and the general public. The Facebook–Cambridge Analytica scandal made it evident that the two companies neglected their responsibility toward users' data privacy, but also the general public's moral and legal rights for unmanipulated democratic elections and voting mechanisms. The Boeing 737 MAX crashes and many other safety issues at Boeing revealed that the value of safety was not treated as an absolute and first priority. In particular, the media, the public eye, and certain stakeholders directly affected, such as passengers, pilots, and other crew members, may no longer be willing to accept such a safety de-prioritization. A business whose key value should be safety cannot be sustainable in the long run by de-prioritizing it, because safety still remains a key value for those stakeholders who utilize the business's product, particularly in the Boeing 737 MAX case, with its passengers, flight attendants, and pilots.

However, analyzing positive cases reveals that companies are increasingly taking non-traditional stakeholders' values more seriously into account. Companies like Fjällraven, Patagonia, Brunello Cucinelli, Freitag, and Ecosia consider eco-environments and future generations as stakeholders, at least to a certain extent, and take into consideration relevant values accordingly. This is rewarded by consumers and investors alike, since otherwise these companies would not be that successful, neither financially nor in terms of their cultural and societal impact.

10.3 Disruptive technologies and controversies in media, advertising, and fashion

The increasing relevance of disruptive technologies such as artificial intelligence, machine learning, data farming, algorithm utilization, and genetic design has placed the need for ethical decision-making support urgently on the agenda. Dystopian sci-fi movies visualize the potential impacts of technology without any regulations or precautions. Technology is deterministic in the regard that once a technology is developed it can hardly be stopped anymore from implementation due to its versatile utility. However, technology is not determinative – there is no technology inherent moral indication of what to do with it. Ethically guided decision-making will help to develop, utilize, and manage disruptive technologies for the benefit of various stakeholders.

New media and the technologies behind them, such as algorithms and blockchain, are examples of such controversial disruptive technologies which will not be stopped from further development. But how we fruitfully utilize them for the benefit of stakeholders will largely be decided by businesses and consumers.

Already, around a century ago, marketing had gradually shifted from addressing consumers' needs to focusing more on their wants. In particular, the fashion industry has pushed the boundaries employing meta-goods in advertisements by utilizing philosophical-anthropological implications. Provocative and controversial marketing in the fashion industry and elsewhere needs ethical guidance in order to meaningfully take the diverse stakeholders' values into account. New forms of media encouraged social media influencers who have become one of the most effective marketing approaches, bringing new and emerging ethical challenges.

10.4 A need for a wider perspective in business ethics

Businesses continue to digitalize, become increasingly global and quasi-"borderless". Moral decision-making processes in business contexts need to be re-evaluated in order to incorporate the diversities in local norms, which again is crucial for the success of transcultural business activities. The concept of "merging cultural horizons" can be utilized to comprehend cultural values and to find compromises when cultural conflicts arise. In order to empirically analyze such cultural differences, Hofstede's cultural dimensions theory provides a meaningful framework for identifying the key values of the stakeholders involved.

Business is always located in macro-economic and geopolitical contexts. New technological challenges and opportunities, the climate emergency and eco-environmental disasters require serious consideration of alternative economic systems as additional guidelines in micro and macro contexts. Such alternative concepts, blueprints, and models are for example the sufficiency economy philosophy, based on Thai Buddhist economics; the Sikkim real-world example of an organic state; ecological economics, which locates the economy ontologically within the eco-environment; circular economy, which emphasizes new resource input reduction; waste minimization and output recycling; and social-ecological market economy, which moderates between environmentalism, social support for less privileged stakeholders, and competitive free markets. The World Happiness Report has introduced and combined new parameters and measurements for businesses and the success of the above-mentioned economic systems.

Key takeaways

(1) There is no such thing as an "ethics-free zone", neither in business nor anywhere else – not at the present time, and most likely not in the future.
(2) Disruptive technologies require constantly updated ethical decision-making competencies.
(3) Transcultural interactions require culturally sensitive ethical decision-making competencies.
(4) Future communities need to be considered as stakeholders.
(5) Ecosystems need to be considered as stakeholders.
(6) Non-human species need to be considered as stakeholders.
(7) Decision-makers should obtain a multidimensional value perspective.
(8) Decision-makers need to be aware of multidimensional sustainability concepts.
(9) There is a need for a wider business ethics perspective.

Index

accidents 36, 58, 99, 124, 126, 162
advertising 140–1, 144, 147–9, 152–3, 187
AI 122, 148, 185
Airbus 14, 39, 106, 119
algorithms 125, 144–5, 148, 157, 162–3, 185, 188
Alibaba 60, 108–9, 123, 125
Alphabet 37, 68, 125, 127, 176
Amazon 49, 88, 123, 125, 148, 176
animals 7, 34, 39, 54, 68, 75, 82, 96–7, 139, 159, 161
anthropocentrism 77, 95
Apple 31, 67–8, 125, 142, 157, 176
Aristotle: eudaimonia 28, 33, 35, 38–41, 43, 53, 182, 186; virtue ethics 23, 28, 29, 186; well-being 1, 4, 10, 24, 28–30, 32–3, 35–41, 44–5, 48, 53–5, 57–8, 71–2, 91, 107–8, 161, 166, 172, 174, 177, 182, 184, 186
ASEAN 7, 101, 159, 163, 174, 177, 183
Assange, Julian 16, 146
AtKisson, Alan 10, 90
autonomous driving 25, 99, 100, 105, 123, 162

Bayer 75, 103
B corporations 1, 3, 84
Ben & Jerry's 3
Bentham, Jeremy 24, 28, 30, 53–4, 58, 186
Bhumibol Adulyadej 177
Bill & Melinda Gates Foundation 57
biodiversity 37, 86
biomedical 25
Boeing 13, 14, 27, 39, 106–7, 112–13, 117–18, 172, 185, 187
Boston Consulting Group 2, 4
Brin, Sergey 68, 73
Brunello Cucinelli 3, 13, 14, 24, 30, 38, 49, 60, 117, 181, 185, 187

Buddhist 40, 51, 53, 163, 172, 177, 188
bullshit 141, 144, 154
Burtynsky, Edward 80, 97

Calvin Klein 141, 153
Cambridge Analytica 28–9, 31, 127–8, 134–5, 143–4, 148, 176, 185, 187
care ethics 22, 24, 28–30, 59, 60, 71, 186
CCTV 126, 131, 137, 139
child labor 5, 159
China 7, 15, 68, 122–3, 127, 157–8, 173
circular economy 171–2, 180, 188
climate 12, 15, 55, 75–6, 88, 91, 9–5, 111, 124, 178, 185, 188
CO_2 emissions 94
cognitive health 36
collectivism 168
compassion 28, 59, 60–1, 71, 186
connectedness to a community 36
consequentialism 23, 29, 54–5, 76
contamination 82, 85
Corporate Social Responsibility 2, 22, 107
corruption 19, 159, 161, 173
Covid-19 5, 6, 12, 16, 19, 20, 22, 25, 37, 38, 40, 53, 92, 113, 123–4, 126, 130, 153, 175
cryptocurrencies 25
Cucinelli, Brunello 3, 13, 14, 24, 30, 38, 49, 60, 117, 181, 185, 187
cultural dimensions 156
cultural relativism 19
culture 11, 18, 24, 38, 51, 66, 84, 95, 124–5, 130, 141, 144, 147–8, 156, 15–19, 161, 166–70, 174

Darknet 140, 145–6
Darwin, Charles 175
Darwinism 175

Index

data 51, 60, 68, 121–3, 125, 127–37, 142–4, 148, 174, 187
deontology 13, 23–4, 28–30, 47, 57, 59, 78, 99, 186
DesJardins, Joseph 75, 77–8
Dieselgate 46, 63, 104–6, 113, 117, 121, 172, 185, 187
discounting 94
Dolce & Gabbana 141, 153

ecological economics 31, 74, 97, 171, 186, 188
ecological footprint 84, 86
ecological rucksack 86
ecological truth 98, 178
economic systems: neoliberal-oriented 19; social-ecological market 19, 172, 180–2, 188
Ecosia 3, 85, 89, 178, 185
ecosystem 34, 39, 91–2, 97, 178
Ecotopia 97, 101–2
Enderle, Georges 161, 170
engineering 10, 15, 25, 43, 46, 99, 117, 122–5, 130, 179
entrepreneur 24, 30, 43
environmental ethics 23, 25, 28–9, 55, 62, 78, 97, 186
Environmental Protection Agency 106, 113
environmental quality 36
Epicure 40, 53, 57
Epicurean 40, 53, 57
ethical theories: care ethics 23–4, 28–31, 60–1, 64, 76, 78, 186; consequentialist 23, 29, 54–5, 76; deontological 13, 23–4, 28–30, 47, 57, 59, 78, 99, 186; environmental ethics 23, 25, 28–9, 55, 62, 78, 97, 186; utilitarianism 22–4, 28–31, 40, 53–5, 57–9, 71, 78, 163, 186; virtue ethics 23, 28, 29, 186
ethical toolbox 51, 66, 68, 164
ethics: normative ethics 1, 6, 13, 17, 22–3, 27, 76, 78; prescriptive ethics 6
external effects 74, 76, 98–100, 124, 175, 178, 186

Facebook 28–9, 31, 68, 73, 123, 125, 127–8, 133–5, 139, 142–4, 148, 171, 176, 185, 187
fairness 10, 28, 29, 30, 62, 64, 86, 94, 108, 186
fake news 47, 51, 144
fashion 140–1, 143, 145, 147–51, 153, 155, 158, 175, 187, 188

feminism 28, 61–2
Fjällräven 90, 101, 104–5
food 5, 16, 33, 46, 53, 75, 82, 85–6, 130, 147, 149, 158
forced labor 159
Ford Pinto 29, 31
Foxconn 49, 68
freedom 36–8, 50, 56, 63, 147–9, 153, 180
Freeman, Edward 105, 107–8, 115, 120–1
Freitag 1–3, 24, 38, 83, 97, 178, 185, 187
Fridays for Future 24, 39, 76, 86, 94, 111, 178
Friedman, Milton 7, 115
future communities 71, 74, 76, 78, 84, 94, 100, 105, 111–12, 116, 120, 124, 178, 185, 186
future generations 13, 39, 61–2, 74–5, 84, 86, 89, 90–2, 94, 98, 104–5, 187

Gadamer, Hans-Georg 163–4, 166
GDP PPP 68
GDPR 122–3, 135–6, 138
geopolitics 156
global warming 15, 81, 92
globalization 158, 177
Glyphosate 75
Golden Rule 24, 48
Google 37, 68, 123, 127, 131, 136–7, 142, 144, 148, 176
government 22, 109, 111, 174–5, 177, 181
Greenpeace 113
Gucci 141, 153

Harari, Yuval 124, 127–8, 148
health 5, 19, 35–6, 38, 42, 46, 53, 64–5, 75–9, 81–2, 85, 86, 91, 98, 100, 105, 107, 124, 126–7, 130, 143, 151, 174, 182
Heidegger, Martin 157, 164, 166
horizons 157, 163, 164, 166–7, 170, 188
human resources 49, 50, 68
hyper-reality 131

Ikigai 29, 44, 186
influencer 140, 152, 153
Instagram 140–1, 146, 154, 176
instrumental value 32–5, 45, 49, 50, 96
integrative dependency model 74, 77
intercultural 16, 25, 156, 157, 159, 164, 169, 186
intergenerational justice 65, 76, 79, 86, 88–9, 94, 104

Internet of Things 86, 100, 105, 130, 132
intra-generational justice 65, 87
intrinsic value 32–5, 40, 45, 49, 95, 96

Jainism 57
Jarvis Thomson, Judith 162
Jobs, Steve 78
justice 10, 18, 30, 33, 55, 62–5, 69, 76, 86, 87, 88, 91, 94, 180; compensatory 63; distributive 63; intergenerational 65, 76, 79, 86, 88–9, 94, 104; intra-generational 65, 87; retributive 63

Kant, Immanuel 24, 28, 30, 47–9, 51, 52, 54, 63, 66, 71, 76, 116, 174, 186; categorical imperative 24, 28, 30, 48, 49, 54, 71, 186; sapere aude 47, 51, 52, 144
Keynes, John Maynard 175

last person argument 75, 95
law and ethics 13, 15, 16
luxury 141

Ma, Jack 60, 108, 109
management 1, 7, 34, 57, 59, 65, 88, 104–9, 112, 114–16, 122, 157, 161, 167–8, 185
marketing 2, 3, 63, 84, 118, 140–1, 143, 144–5, 147–55, 158, 188; influencer 140, 152, 153
The Matrix 31, 73, 92, 123, 131, 133
Mbiti, John 61
Meinhold, Roman 73, 92, 93, 97, 102, 124, 139, 149, 155, 180, 183
mental health 36
Merck 69
meta-ethics 13, 17, 20; altruism 20; egoism 20; emotion 20; integrated social contacts theory 13; nature 20; reason 20; social cultural 20
meta-goods 149, 188
microplastic 82, 85, 94
Microsoft 123, 125, 142, 146, 176
Mill, John Stuart 24, 28, 30, 54–5, 57, 63, 186
Monsanto 75
Müller-Armack Alfred 180
Musk, Elon 98, 131

nanoplastics 82, 85
Nestlé 79–81
NGO 25, 157

non-human species 75–6, 78, 95–6, 104–5, 111, 112, 120, 184–6
non-renewable resources 79, 86–7, 92
norms: hyper-norm 19, 24, 30, 49; micro-social 19

original position 64–6, 94, 181, 186
overconsumption 86
overpopulation 86

Patagonia 3, 24, 38, 74–5, 83–5, 97, 113, 178, 185, 187
PETA 160–1
philanthropic 2, 117
physical health 36
Plato 40, 45, 63, 73, 128, 174
politician 180
pollution 82, 85–6, 94, 98–9, 102, 124, 127
power asymmetry 68, 156
pre-actionary 74–5, 99, 100
precautionary 65, 74–5, 77, 99, 100, 131, 186
privacy 16, 27, 122–3, 127–8, 133, 135–6, 144, 146, 187
purpose of life 36

quality and quantity of relationships 36

Rawls, John 28, 30, 62–4, 66, 94, 108, 186; original position 64–6, 94, 181, 186; theory of justice 28, 62, 67, 71, 186; veil of ignorance 28, 64–6, 108, 163, 181, 186
recycling: down-cycling 83; upcycling 2, 83
regulations 51, 58, 64, 95, 122, 136, 161, 168, 172, 186, 187
renewable resources 78, 86, 87, 90, 92, 94, 98, 127, 178
responsibility 3, 7, 8, 10, 12, 14, 19, 22, 25, 28, 29, 31, 39, 52, 62, 65–9, 71, 74, 75, 77–8, 84, 91, 94, 97, 100, 104–5, 107, 112, 117, 120, 122, 134, 185, 186, 187
Rubber Killer 74–5, 83
Ruth Foot, Philippa 162

safety 36, 39, 57, 72, 106–7, 112, 113, 117, 132, 137, 168, 183, 187
security 36, 39, 106
Saint Laurent 141, 153
Sartre, Jean-Paul 6
Schopenhauer, Arthur 59–61

Schwab, Klaus 68
science fiction 129
Sen, Amartya 28, 31, 62, 67–8, 94, 134, 186; power and responsibility 28, 62, 71, 134
shareholders 13, 109, 112, 113, 114, 115
Smith, Adam 63, 174
Snowden, Edward 16, 51, 146
social contract 63, 174
social credit systems 127
social-ecological market economy 19, 172, 180–2, 188
social market economy 19, 172, 180–2, 188
social networks 144
social profiling 127
spaceship earth 180
SpaceX 98
Spencer, Herbert 175–6, 183
stakeholder 13, 25, 27, 74, 78, 84, 100, 104–9, 111–17, 119, 121, 185, 186, 187; communities 38, 78–9, 84, 90–1, 94, 109, 111; customers 13, 63, 65, 69, 78, 84, 90, 94, 98, 99, 106, 108–9, 111, 113, 135, 187; employees 13, 49, 67, 68, 78, 94, 109, 111, 114, 173; financiers 78, 109, 111, 113; suppliers 13, 89, 109, 111, 113
Starbucks 38, 65, 98, 158, 185
startup 124
surveillance 16, 124, 126, 128, 137
sustainability 3, 25, 38, 74–9, 88, 90–2, 95, 97–8, 100–2, 106, 107, 154, 156, 178, 180–1, 184–7; intergenerational justice 65, 76, 79, 86, 88–9, 94, 104; intra-generational justice 65, 87; spaceship earth 180; Sustainable Development Goals 74, 77, 91, 103
sustainability compass 10
SWOT analysis 104–5, 118

technological determinism 128, 130
technology 5, 10, 15, 27, 37, 73, 86, 95, 98–100, 113, 122–4, 126–32, 139, 141, 145, 175, 179, 187; artificial intelligence 122, 148, 185; Bio-tech 125; engineering 10, 15, 25, 43, 46, 99, 117, 122–5, 130, 179
Tencent 123, 125
Tesla 98
The Big Short 11
thought experiment 28, 33, 42, 64, 66, 77, 91, 95, 96, 122, 162

Toms 3, 61, 181
Total Shareholder Return 8, 76
Total Societal Impact 1, 2, 4, 8, 12, 75
transcultural 159, 164, 166, 184–5, 188
Trees 88–9, 152
triple bottom line 77, 90, 181
trolley problem 162, 170
Trump, Donald J. 133–5, 144
T-shaped education 4
Twitter 122–3, 133, 143
Tycoon Music 50

UAV 122
Über-setzen 157, 166–7
Ubuntu 29, 59, 61, 71, 157, 161, 186
uncertainty avoidance 168
underpaid labor 159
user 65, 127, 144
utilitarianism: act 11, 16, 17, 19, 20–1, 31, 35, 43, 48–9, 51, 55, 57–8, 60–1, 116, 143, 149, 166, 178; pleasure 24, 30, 35, 40, 45–7, 53–7, 186; preference 32, 5–8, 93, 94, 108, 168, 177; rule 57; utility 24, 30, 31, 54–5, 57–8, 163, 177, 186–7

vaccine 45
values 2, 9–11, 17–9, 25, 32–5, 38–40, 49, 53, 69, 92–3, 104, 106–9, 112, 117, 122, 131, 149, 157, 159, 161–2, 164, 168, 170, 183, 185, 187–8; aesthetic 9–10, 15; competence 9–10; creativity 9, 92, 153; functional 9; instrumental 32–5, 45, 49, 50, 96; intrinsic 32–5, 40, 45, 49, 95, 96; legal 2, 9, 51, 67, 77, 117, 135, 163, 174, 187; monetary 9, 34, 63, 107; negative 1, 2, 5, 8, 15, 25, 32–5, 38, 50, 57–9, 79, 93, 108, 113, 119, 125, 152, 161, 163, 172, 175; neutral 32, 34, 66, 144; reputation 9, 14, 39, 57, 80, 131, 187
veil of ignorance 28, 64–6, 108, 163, 181, 186
virtue ethics 23, 28, 29, 186
virtues 10, 23, 24, 29, 30, 32, 35, 39–43, 46, 69, 169, 178; deficiency 42, 43, 46–7, 178; excess 42–3, 46, 47, 178
Volkswagen 46, 49, 63, 68, 104–7, 113–14, 117, 118, 172, 185, 187

Wagner, Christoph 22, 27, 65, 93, 181, 183
Walt Disney 152
Walzer, Michael 22

water 37, 75, 78–82, 85, 87–92, 97, 99, 161
weapons 94, 129, 132
Weinstein, Harvey 28, 50, 173, 185
well-being 1, 4, 10, 24, 28–30, 32–3, 35–41, 44–5, 48, 53–5, 57–8, 71–2, 91, 107–8, 161, 166, 172, 174, 177, 182, 184, 186
whistleblowing 16, 37, 51, 145, 146

World Economic Forum 60, 68
World Happiness Report 36, 182, 183, 188

YouTube 144, 152

Zimbardo Philip 21
Žižek, Slavoj 21
Zuckerberg, Mark 127–8, 134–5, 139

Printed in the United States
by Baker & Taylor Publisher Services